ANYTHING BUT A WASTED LIFE

Sita Kaylin was born in San Francisco in 1970. After dropping out of high school, she graduated Pre-law from San Francisco State University. She started stripping in college – law school never happened. She's a veteran sex worker who currently calls Los Angeles her home. She divides her time between writing, seeing private clients, taking photos of half-naked women, hanging with her tipsy friends and bugging her Maine Coon cat, Monkey.

This is for those who love me for who I am, and those who love me for who they think I am.

I

IT'S A TYPICAL night in the dressing room – girls drinking, talking shit, one dancer inserting a tampon, another on her cell phone. Two of the girls at the mirror are speaking uncomfortably loudly while a line-up of women spray themselves with sickeningly sweet body spray. And then there's me, leaning over the counter applying my ho-bag make-up. Two plastic Vitamin Water bottles sit next to my Mac brushes, one containing apple-infused vodka and the other, actual Vitamin Water. I swig one, then the other – total shit. I hate vodka, but the apple flavor leaves my breath smelling less like a barroom floor, plus, it's cheap. I apply shiny powder to my cheeks and over the thin lines around my eyes to mask my years of experience. I'm a thirty-seven-year-old stripper and trying not to look it.

I started stripping in college, more than fifteen years ago. One of my roommates worked at the Lusty Lady in San Francisco, a female-owned and operated peep show, while another acquaintance worked at the Mitchell Brothers O'Farrell Theatre, the city's premier strip club. Their lives were full of glitz and financial freedom, while I was broke, working three jobs and struggling to find the time and energy for homework. I was enrolled in a pre-law program at San Francisco State University; my goal was to redesign the prison system. Desperate to find a way to balance everything and tired of not having enough money, I decided to give stripping a try. Suffice to say, law school never happened. Within a year, I was making more money than the judges in the San Francisco court system. The prison system would have to wait.

I'd never had so much money. I was raised by a single parent and had been on my own since I was sixteen. Most girls – myself included – start dancing with the intention of doing it for less than two years. I sincerely believed I would dance through law school and then quit. Nearly every girl stays between two and seven years. Only a few of us continue for as long as I have.

When I started, stripping was incredible. It was a special underground world, a unique adventure for the wealthy. But times have changed. I make an eighth of what I used to, and there's a strip club on practically every corner. It's harder work now and the money isn't as good.

I suppose I'm a bit spoiled. I wake up when I want, work when I want and get paid in cash. It's not a bad life and I'm good at what I do. Sometimes I think it's a curse to be skilled at making men feel good. The funny thing is, most of them want to make *me* feel good. That's the secret. Their wives don't come anymore (at least not with them), so they want to make me climax. It makes them feel like a man, I suppose. So I fake it – all night. I've found that the trick is to make it seem like I shouldn't, that I'm shy. I hide my face in their necks while I grind my pussy on their leg and breathe softly in their ear. I build up the breathing in a believable way, then back off a little and say, 'Wow, I think I could come.'

'Are you serious?' he asks, big puppy eyes and wagging tail. 'That would be incredible!'

'No, I really shouldn't,' I say, coyly.

'Why not?'

'Because it's my job to make *you* feel good,' I say with a smile. Then I'll drape my half-naked body against his and start the slow movement with my hips again while I put my mouth by his ear. Sometimes, if we're close to the end of our dance and I know he won't be paying for another, I'll go right into the act. Or I'll drag it out so he'll want to continue and pay for more. After I'm 'finished', I'll act all demure and hide my face in his shoulder.

'I can't believe I just did that,' I say.

'That was awesome' is the typical response.

'How much do I owe you?' I ask with a wink and a smile as I get up and start to get dressed. This usually gets a laugh and distracts the guy from the fact that he just paid good money for me to have an orgasm, or so he thinks. One more satisfied and delusional customer; he'll be back.

There was a time when I actually *did* climax during lap dances. In fact, the first time I ever made myself come was in front of a customer. I didn't even mean to. It was at the Lusty Lady, the peep show and jack-off joint. Customers stood or sat in small, Plexiglas-windowed private booths and put money in a machine. A window opened for a limited time through which they watched naked girls on the other side. A real-life scene played out like in Madonna's '*Open Your Heart*' video (a concept stemming from such clubs, no doubt). In addition to the live girls, similar coin-operated booths that showed adult videos were available. We got paid an hourly rate. The only place we could earn tips was in a separate, single booth called the Private Pleasures, which was down the narrow hall from the main stage. Dancers had to request to work in this room. If our requests were approved, we worked the main room for two hours and then the Private Pleasures for two hours.

One night, I was in the Private Pleasures when a club regular solicited a private show. I had heard about this guy, but hadn't had the pleasure of meeting him yet. His thing was to have the girl turn off the lights, lie back and massage her clit while he rattled off some ridiculous sex fantasy. Pretty generic shit, like sex on a plane with a stranger, et cetera. So there I was, lying back on a bunch of pillows like a genie in a bottle, fingers on my clitoris, trying to block him out. And suddenly, I came. I couldn't believe it. I was shocked because although I'd been having orgasms with my lovers for years, I had never done so on my own. Apparently, it wasn't convincing enough for him.

'You just faked that,' he said, annoyed.

'Actually, I didn't.'

'Yeah you did. I can tell.'

Not really giving a shit whether he believed me or not, I told him to piss off. I was twenty-three and it was my first self-induced orgasm. I had tried a couple times when I was younger, but I had felt embarrassed and given up. My self-esteem was messed up when I was young, and making yourself come is a rather loving thing to do. But all of a sudden and completely out of nowhere, it had happened.

From that night on, whenever I worked the Private Pleasures room, I'd close the curtain and make myself come instead of going to the dressing room during my ten-minute break; it was my little secret. I could hear people milling around outside my booth, people who essentially paid us to fake orgasms, and there I was doing it in private, for free. Unwittingly, that guy had opened up a whole new world for me.

A year later, I got hired at Mitchell Brothers. The owner was a complete prick and was always threatening to fire us. For a few years in the mid-1990s, he actually did fire about twenty girls a month for no reason other than to assert control and make sure we never forgot who was really in charge. Most strippers are independent contractors, but club owners never want you to forget that it's their club and their rules. It was unnecessary bullshit, but he knew he was sitting on a gold mine and he had us by the G-string. Women were flying in from all over the country, and outside the U.S., in the hope of getting hired at Mitchell Brothers. This guy was ruthless and cut-throat. He shot his brother dead and only did three years in San Quentin for it.

During this period of unrest, I moonlighted at other clubs in the city. The money wasn't even close to what I could make at Mitchell Brothers, but I needed the job security. I had just purchased my first home and was terrified of being fired while I had a mortgage to cover. One of those other clubs was the Crazy Horse on Market Street, which was sort of a sleazy joint, but you could say that about most of the clubs in the city at the time. It opened as a movie theater in 1909 and suffered a lowbrow conversion into a strip club in 1995. The club had an eerie feel to it that I can't quite put into words. We lap-danced in the original theater seats facing a carpeted, T-shaped stage. Carpet has no business on a strip club stage: it absorbs all the junk from the bottom of our heels, as well as lotion, oil, sweat and our womanly secretions from moves like splits, for example.

This main room was huge: long and narrow with impossibly high ceilings. There were two other rooms where we could give slightly more private dances for a higher price. One of these areas was a room within a room in the huge theater, closed off by walls that didn't quite reach the ceiling.

One night, I was giving a guy a lap dance in the room within a room on one of the long pleather benches. We wore bikinis during lap dances and I could straddle the customers – something we weren't allowed to do at Mitchell Brothers. This guy was really nasty. His breath smelled like puke and he kept rubbing his finger in the top crevice of my ass, not something I normally let guys do. But there I was, straddling him, rubbing my clit on his crotch and allowing him to molest my butt crack. The more disgusting he got, the closer I came to climaxing, don't ask me why. And then I came.

I didn't tell him. I did it quietly, and our song was over moments after. I had mixed feelings about it. The orgasm felt good, but it wasn't like me to come with someone I didn't know, and, in fact, I was slightly appalled by it. I rarely came with anyone until I felt comfortable and had built up some trust. This was different. I didn't give two shits about what he thought of me. I wasn't worried about how I smelled, what my body looked like in the light, or how long it was taking. It was liberating.

The next time it happened was with a young Asian kid. He wasn't gross like the other guy. He was nice, but I was hot and bothered and wanted to come. In fact, I wouldn't let him leave until I did. We had surpassed the time limit he'd paid for, but I didn't get off his lap. To be honest, he seemed a tad freaked out, but I kept him pinned down until I came. The poor thing. When I was finished, I stood up and walked away without a word. It was shameless and fun, not in a vindictive way, but in a thanks-for-being-my-human-vibrator kind of way.

All of that was early in my career. Now, more than fifteen years later, I don't try to come on the customers anymore. There's no taboo about it. I suppose I could if I really wanted to, but fuck it, why bother? These days, my priorities are different; it's a matter of keeping my sanity and the smile on my face intact. Speaking of my sanity, I just got a text from a regular customer letting me know that he just walked in. Time to turn on the charm.

2

ONE OF MY favorite and most surreal things about being a stripper is the 180 we perform all night, over and over again. One minute, I'll be in the VIP, sexin' it up with a customer, my eyes closed in faux ecstasy, sweat forming in the small of my back. We (he) are having the time of our (his) life, but the moment he pays and I walk away, my body relaxes and my facial expression changes completely. Then, I either go to another guy – and slip back into the sparkling version of myself with come-hither eyes – or to the dressing room where I can truly be myself. It's not so much that I'm not myself with the customers, it's just that I wouldn't be there if they weren't paying me. So, with them, I'm a compartmentalized version of myself. It's one of the reasons why we use stage names; we do it not only to protect our identities but also to help us with the roles we're playing. Choosing a stage name is an interesting thing. It becomes your other identity, so it has to be something that will resonate with you and roll off your tongue. If someone yells either of my names in a public place, I'll turn. That's how integrated we become with our stage names. Men are constantly asking if our stage names are our real names, so it helps if your stage name sounds like a real name; it's why I chose Shannon when I moved to Los Angeles. But girls don't always get the name they want. Most clubs have a roster of between one hundred and four hundred dancers, and no two girls can have the same stage name. That's how some girls end up going by Hazel instead of Ginger. For nine years at Mitchell Brothers, I was Rochelle Hayes – the only club I've known where the dancers had fake last names as well – but I never really felt like I looked like a Rochelle. Shannon is feminine and more fitting to my work persona, and it's who I've been ever since. Some clubs will let you change your stage name after you've started – Mitchell Brothers was not one of them – but it's difficult once you're well known with the clientele, not to mention it breaks the fourth wall we are trying to create.

I just 'love' the customer who's totally into it, but as the lap dance starts and I tell him the rules, he has a fit. Once, a high-maintenance man I had just danced for actually started acting like he was going to leave when he heard my rules. I had to backpedal with serious stride.

'Sweetie, please relax,' I said, calming him. 'We're going to have fun, I promise.' I continued, 'Tips are only appreciated, they aren't mandatory.'

I've been starting my private dances in the same way for my entire career. The song starts, I straddle the guy and whisper into his ear, 'As long as you tip well, you can touch my breasts, not between my legs, there's no kissing anywhere on my body, and you have to have fun.' I found that it's better to be clear about the rules and get them out of the way up front. It's also best to end on a happy, upbeat note because men are simple creatures. It usually works, but this guy bitched, 'You'd think in this economy, you'd be happy to get a dance at all.'

I ignored his comment, as I knew that no good would come from getting into a debate about the financial plight of our country.

'I *am* happy, sweetie,' I said. 'Now let me make *you* happy. Sit back.' I got him to relax, which was no small feat. By the end of the dance, he was smiling and hugging me. I like happy customers. We went to the bar to pay for the VIP, and he gave me a one-dollar tip. I suppose he felt he had to make his point that I should be kissing his feet in gratitude for paying for a lap dance at all.

The relationship between customer and stripper is a strange one, whether it's a first meeting or after many years of knowing each other. I use the word 'knowing' in the loosest sense. Customers 'know' us as insulated interpretations of ourselves. Strippers use the term 'regular' for a customer who comes in on a regular basis to see a specific girl. Sometimes, a few girls share a regular, but these men mostly latch on to an individual dancer. There are also club regulars who may or may not spend much money on the girls, but provide a type of family feel. Like the rest of this floating island of make-believe, they have their place. Each and every one of us makes an unspoken deal when we come through the doors of the club: what is said and done inside the club is anonymous, and we're all playing a part. This unspoken agreement straddles a fine line. The men know why we're here and we know why they're here – although their reasons vary. It's our job to fulfil their needs. If a dancer is really good at her job, the men will feel as if we're there for reasons other than money.

Don't get me wrong, working at a strip club has its perks. The women are amazing and fun, we can drink and act a fool, the music is electric, and watching women on stage is entertaining as fuck. It's a party. Even so, the job is a difficult one, especially when you don't feel like flirting (the alcohol helps), or being naked, or sexy, or when you plain don't have the energy to cater to or deal with a bunch of lonely, needy men.

Strippers do a lot more than pole tricks. This job isn't for everyone. Most days, we're more therapist than porn star. Stripping is an acting job with a side of grinding. The psychoanalysis is even more common with regular customers because we hear about their weekly highs and lows, their job troubles, wife troubles, dick troubles. You name it, strippers hear it all – every single one of us. Everyone from the girls who worked for six months to lifers like myself, we've all heard the same stories. It comes with the territory. Regulars tend to be soul-suckers; they require a lot of personal attention and there's often an emotional element to the relationship because of the attachment they form to us.

My customers take a lot out of me, but when it's slow, it's always nice to know you have one, two or three men coming in to spend a reliable, guaranteed amount of money. Regulars are most dancers' bread and butter. But the relationship isn't for everyone. I know strippers who loathe the idea of a regular. They prefer their work to be anonymous and to end when the song is over. Admittedly, that would be easier and more rational. Although one could argue that having regular customers is a wise fiscal decision. Every stripper has a unique style and approach. I've known girls who were downright cold to the men. They dance, they get their money, they're gorgeous and sexy, but they don't talk and they don't engage. And then there are dancers like myself who don't know how to shut it off. It's just not in my nature.

3

I WASN'T HIRED the first time I auditioned at Mitchell Brothers. I hadn't been dancing long and I made all the classic novice mistakes during the audition. My hair was short back then, so I bought a three-quarter wig. The fake hair started just behind my bangs; it looked pretty real, but it was wild and unstyled. I chose a Monday night to audition – the club held a weekly amateur contest on Monday nights – and selected a song from the *Cool World* soundtrack. I was a nervous wreck. Auditions at Mitchell Brothers were notorious for being hell on Earth, and I did everything wrong. Besides the bad wig and the bad song, I'd worn a black patent leather outfit with matching thigh-high boots.

There's nothing inherently wrong with black patent leather, but on an olive-skinned, dark brunette, it looked a little too dominatrix-y. On top of all this, I was something of a tomboy growing up, so I wasn't very skilled at walking in heels. The stage at Mitchell Brothers is beautiful, but it's made of slippery wood, and it's rather large for a strip club stage.

So there I was, with zero experience and a zillion nerves. It was both the shortest and the longest four minutes of my life. It's a miracle I'd remembered to take my clothes off! I did, however, manage to swing myself around the pole, my patent leather boot sticking to it and making an awful screeching noise. I put the A in amateur that night. It was no big surprise that I wasn't placed in the top three and they didn't hire me.

I stayed at the Lusty for about eight months. I desperately wanted to get to Mitchell Brothers – that's where the real money was – but I needed to hone my stripping skills and the Lusty wasn't going to cut it. So I started working at a bikini bar in San Mateo. That's where I learned how to be a *real* stripper. We didn't lap dance and weren't allowed to show our private areas (because of the alcohol sales), but we stripped down to the smallest bikinis imaginable and worked solely for tips. This meant I had to learn how to flirt and master the art of seduction. My hair was finally long enough to ditch the wig and I was strapped with a suntan and glow-in-the-dark outfits from Las Vegas – one of the only cities at the time where a stripper could buy clothing made especially for the job. After four months of unravelling a billion one-dollar bills in San Mateo, I was ready to give the O'Farrell Theatre another try.

This time I danced to Sade, my make-up was more expertly done, and I wore white heels and a Day-Glo green, rhinestone-studded mini dress. I was nervous as hell, but I smiled, was sultry, and won first place. I finally got hired.

4

WHEN I FIRST started dancing at Mitchell Brothers in 1993, the city had a fairly uptight mayor and police chief, and the rules at the club reflected as much. The sex industry was different back then. It wasn't in every television show, music video and movie like it is today. Today, women wear outfits to nightclubs that I'd wear on stage! There are bars and dance clubs now with stripper poles, for fuck's sake. Why go to a strip club when you can see drunk girls making out and wearing next to nothing who might go home with you at the end of the night? If you're lucky, one of them might attempt an uncoordinated pole trick and flash you her coochie.

Many factors have contributed to the demise of the strip club. Economy and competition are major reasons, but the more widely accepted stripping became – with women signed up by the thousands – the more the sparkle dulled. Our money was hit hard. Life and money were better when these things were left to the professionals.

Mitchell Brothers is on the corner of Polk and O'Farrell in San Francisco. There are huge murals on the outside walls. One depicted a rainforest (an artist was recently commissioned to repaint the main wall), and the other has an underwater scene featuring life-size whales and dolphins. When I was a kid, I remember thinking the building was a zoo or an aquarium and that Tommy's Joynt – a city landmark that had murals depicting busty saloon girls in the seventies – was a brothel. That I came up with the idea of a brothel at nine years of age is a little strange. Maybe it was a foreshadowing?

The O'Farrell Theatre is a sizable club: there are three themed rooms, a movie theater and a gorgeous continuous live stage show called New York Live. It's a unique strip club that's worlds apart from any other club I've seen. At its inception, the club was a porn theater. Jim and Artie Mitchell were young film-makers, known for their psychedelic pornos, the most famous of which was *Behind the Green Door*, which was shot inside the club. By 1980, the club became a major player in popularizing close-contact lap dancing. For a short time in the 1990s, the writer Hunter S. Thompson served as one of the club managers. He watched me perform on stage once. When I went upstairs to grab my CDs from the DJ, he told me I was very sexy. Although I was excited by his presence, I wanted to maintain a modicum of composure, so I said, 'You should have joined me.' He flashed a devilish grin. This was during a period when he and Johnny Depp were hanging out; Johnny was preparing to play Thompson in *Fear and Loathing in Las Vegas*. They came into the club often to play cards in the upstairs offices and, of course, to watch the girls. If those office walls could talk.

Unlike most strip clubs, which generally consist of a main room and a VIP area, Mitchell Brothers is made up of five sections, four of which feature unique live shows.

The Kopenhagen Room: two girls would do four shows a night. We'd wear matching costumes (sexy cops, schoolgirls, nurses) and choose two songs to go with the theme ('*Dr. Feelgood*' for the nurse outfits, et cetera). The guys were given flashlights with orange cones on the end, like the ones used by the people who direct planes at airports. The techs announced the shows throughout the club and then they'd wrangle up patrons, give them the lowdown and announce us. We'd turn the lights off from backstage and do a two-song tease ending with some light girl-girl action on the carpeted floor. The only illumination came from the flashlights. After some wild clapping, we'd sell either individual nude lap dances (Mitchell Brothers was the first club where that was allowed) or a girl-girl show.

The Green Door: six girls did four shows a night. The room was large and open, the stage in the corner initially cut off by a dark velvet curtain. Something about it being in the corner always reminded me of the Chuck E. Cheese's stage with the animatronic players. There were four large, round, padded tables on the floor with fixed stools and four booths with dividers along the wall. A tech would introduce the show over the microphone. The first song would come on, the lights would go down, and the curtain would lift, revealing six naked girls on stage. Water would pour down on us, making our tanned skin glisten. Eventually, the club had to get rid of the water element because of the rot it caused on the stage.

We'd start with a daisy chain, each of us simulating (or not) going down on the next. We'd do two or three versions of the daisy chain during the first song, moving in sync, always smiling, giggling and acting turned on. We had detachable showerheads to play with. For a short time, they gave us pink mousse soap in a can, which was super fun. I'd write 'slut' on my partner's ass and then slap it, spraying pink suds into the audience.

For the second song, each pair of girls – these partnerships had been planned a month in advance – would walk to the round, padded tables where the men were sitting. Wet and naked, we'd put down colorful towels, climb on the table and play with each other, our legs often thrown over the men's shoulders, with our tits, ass and pussy in their faces. The men were not allowed to touch us. Surprisingly, they kept their hands to themselves. Truthfully, the experience was so unlike anything most men had seen that they were dumbstruck. I rarely worried about someone touching me in a private place. It just didn't happen. When it did, those guys usually got hit hard by the girls and thrown out of the club. After paying forty dollars at the door – and enormous amounts for the shows – no one wanted to get kicked out. At the end of the second song, we would sell a girl-girl show involving a double-headed dildo, other fun toys, a strap-on, et cetera.

New York Live was a continuous live performance in a gorgeous room with one of the best stages I've ever seen. It was a large, expansive wooden stage with two brass poles at each end. The room had high ceilings and a large mirror ball. Long, gold sheer curtains near the back of the stage opened and closed for each dancer. We were lucky to have some of the best performers in the country. The DJ sat in a booth upstairs and commandeered a spotlight as well as the music, curtain and narration.

The Ultra Room was a large, oval-shaped spaceship tucked-in behind the men's bathroom. When I first started at the club, this room had a sheet of one-way glass separating us from the men and a slit where they could slip in cash through. The glass was eventually removed, and we could climb into the narrow standing-only booths with the men. Each booth had vibrating floors; don't ask me why. Like the Kopenhagen, the Ultra Room also featured two girls doing four shows a night with themed outfits and songs.

Before Private Booths were put in the hallway, there was the Private Show. It was a single room with two doors. One entrance was for the girl. It opened onto a Formica island surrounded by water; the other entrance was for the customer. A four-foot high Plexiglas wall separated the dancer (and the water) from the customer. There was a security measure in place in the form of an invisible laser beam above the Plexiglas that, if crossed, would set off an earsplitting alarm. It wasn't the greatest system, particularly because we had to collect cash from the customer before each show and the only way to do that was to reach over the Plexiglas. Even though we'd tell the guys to hold the money up high, they'd set the alarm off more often than not. After the price was negotiated, I'd start my music and strip down while the guy jacked off. At the time, the Private Show room was the only spot a guy could get off in the club.

Lastly, we had the Cine Stage, which was a large movie theater showing adult films. Dancers working New York Live could lap dance in the seats around the stage, as well as in the seats in the Cine Stage. We also used the Cine Stage for large-scale plays that the girls produced a few times a year.

In 1996, San Francisco elected a new mayor, Willie Brown. Mayor Brown was all party and he even patronized the club a time or two. Jim and Artie Mitchell were long-time staples in San Francisco and if you were a city official, you knew the brothers. By the time I started at the club, Jim had already killed Artie (Emilio Estevez and Charlie Sheen made a movie about it called

Rated X), but the brothers were notorious in the city. And Willie Brown was a fan of the industry. In fact, his law firm was known for its efforts to legalize prostitution. Bless his heart; it ought to be legal. Two consenting adults should have the freedom to do what they please as long as they aren't hurting anyone. It's absurd that I have to worry about being busted when dancers and prostitutes outnumber garbage workers two to one. Don't quote me on that, I just made it up, but trust me, there's a buttload of us. Add to that the fact that it's the oldest profession and it will always exist. Shouldn't it be legal, insured and recognized like every other profession? Willie Brown thought so.

Life at the club changed dramatically while Mayor Brown was in office. It started with little things like sheer outfits in the audience and men touching our butt-cheeks. It's easier to entice a guy to pay for a dance if he can see your nipples. Doesn't this sound so innocent now? It goes to show just how much the industry has changed in the past twenty years.

Recently, I was talking to a friend about 'extras' and I jokingly said, 'Time plus comfort equals handjobs.' In the industry, we use the term 'extras' to denote any act performed during a dance that is forbidden by the club. However, I only offered them at Mitchell Brothers during my last few years there. It took years for me to get to that point because of both my comfort level and local politics; under Mayor Brown, strip clubs, and strippers, could get away with a lot more. The next step in the evolution of the club was private dances.

The club built eleven stand-up, padded, semicircular booths with thick velvet curtains called Cabanas. With just enough room for two, they were the first place we could give a private contact dance. They were a big hit. The privacy allowed for the possibility of letting a customer touch you in places they couldn't out in the open, if you permitted it. I remember the first time I let a customer touch my breasts. It felt extremely personal. It seemed like a violation and it actually made me a little nauseous. I had been dancing for a few years with nothing more than the occasional hand on my thigh and having a stranger squeeze my breast and play with my nipple broke through a sexual barrier in my mind. It was a barrier I hadn't even been aware of until it was broken. I was surprised by how negatively the intimate fondling affected me, but allowing customers access to my breasts increased my income substantially. Eventually I got used to it. For my entire career, I've maintained my rule to allow customers access to my breasts only. My vagina was – and is – the only region strip club customers cannot touch.

There were only a couple of clubs in the country at the time that offered full-contact private dances. I know that some of my fellow dancers, past and present, might have been annoyed by these changes, and while I sympathized, the reward was too great to ignore. Sadly, the loosening of the rules eventually led to the demise of the striptease. My justification was – and still is – that I always brokered extra money for the privilege of private dances. I wasn't undercutting the girls who wanted to stick to the original format.

The club tore down the Private Show and put in three Private Booths. For the duration of my time at the club, these became my favorite rooms. Each room was approximately five by eight feet with mirrored walls and a red, cushy loveseat. Next to the loveseat was a small side table with a drawer and a little lamp with a red light bulb. A small garbage can was wedged in between the couch and the table. Each room had a thick, heavy, red velvet curtain on a ceiling track, which wrapped three quarters around the room. Immediately outside, red velvet ropes separated the rooms from the hallway. The last thing we needed was a patron stumbling in during a private show. There was a tape recorder on the side table as well (tape recorder!). I had a cassette with the classic soul hit '*I Want'a Do Something Freaky to You*' by Leon Haywood that I would play and rewind all night long. The track is about five and a half minutes long, which is how long the show lasted. It sounds short, but trust me, it seemed much longer.

Not knowing how these new rooms would work or how the customers would react, girls were a little afraid to sign up for them, but a fellow dancer and I jumped at the opportunity. We had the rooms to ourselves for a solid month and we made a killing. I charged two hundred dollars for five minutes. This got you a naked lap dance and a handjob if you wanted one; they all said yes. That was the first time I ever did 'extras' in the club. I had been hearing about girls doing naughty things in the other rooms, but I was always fearful of being seen or arrested; undercover cops came in all the time. But in the Private Booth, I felt more comfortable. It wasn't my morals that had kept me from breaking the rules until that point – I had already received money for sex outside the club by the time these rooms were built – I was afraid of getting busted. I had been dancing long enough to know the signs of an agent. Generally, they asked too many specific questions about how much certain things cost and exactly what they would get for their money. But during those last couple of years at the club, I was pretty brazen, especially since the mayor was on our side. I never told any of my co-workers what I was doing; we didn't discuss these things. I knew some of the other dancers wouldn't be happy if they knew. However, I certainly wasn't the only girl providing 'extras' by that point. We didn't talk about what we did or how much we made. We'd say that we'd had a good night or a bad night, but we never talked numbers. Not discussing how much you've made in a night is common strip club etiquette that most dancers adhere to.

During the dance in these new Private Booths, I'd tell the guy to sit in the middle of the love seat, he'd hand me the money, and I would push play on the tape recorder. I'd do a thirty-second tease standing up, squeezing my boobs and showing him my ass. Then I'd climb on top, straddling him, and whisper my rules in his ear.

After a minute of lap dancing and squeezing his hard cock through his pants, I'd say, 'Okay, sweetie, you can unzip and bring him out.' As he did this, I'd reach into the drawer of the side table, grab a condom (the club had personalized gold-wrapped condoms), tear it open with my teeth (so posh), hand him the rubber and say, 'Here, baby, roll this on,' with a big, warm smile.

Some guys would put up a fuss and ask me to do it, but I'd explain that under no circumstances would I be touching their bare penis and that if they wanted to get off, they'd man up and roll the fucker on. Sometimes they had difficulty putting the condom on. A few even said they'd never done it before. Eventually, with my coaching, they'd figure it out. I always found it amazing that the guy would still have a hard-on after all this fussing, but they almost always did. Once the condom was on, I'd take over.

At three minutes in, I knew I had two and a half minutes left to make him come. I'd straddle the guy again and place my exposed pussy just above his cock. My left arm would be on the back of the couch to support me as I held my body against him and my tits would be in his face while I stroked him with my right hand. Maybe it was the hope that I'd lower myself the inch or so down onto his member. Maybe it was fear of letting me down, or my bouncy boobs. Or maybe it was the fact that an unfamiliar, nude girl was jerking him off. Perhaps it was the vanilla body spray. Who knows? But they always came. Of course, I never told them that they had two and a half minutes until the end of the song in which to get off; no one likes pressure. But after watching our girl-girl shows and the talent on the main stage, these guys were primed for a release. The whole thing took under five and a half minutes from start to finish. Hell, even I came a time or two in the Private Booth. It was pretty hot having my pussy hovering just above a stranger's stiff cock. I like the forbidden, too. Sex with a customer in the Private Booth has served as great masturbation material for me for a long time. Some of the best fantasies are the ones that stay fantasies.

In my time doing 'extras' at the club, only a handful of guys didn't climax. That was a tricky situation. I'd say something like, 'It happens, sweetie, don't worry. You can pay me extra to stay longer if you want.' Most guys find it difficult to stand their ground when dealing with a naked woman and a soft cock.

After my happy customers ejaculated, it was a different but similarly abrupt ending. 'Thank you, baby,' I'd say, smushing my bare breasts in their face while making a kissing noise. I'd climb off them and rewind my song, saying, 'Zip up and take the condom off in the men's bathroom.' I never let them take it off in the Private Room; the smell would have been nauseating. Also, it was too risky as their come might leak out of the condom. I once jerked a guy off while standing up in a Cabana and didn't realize he was removing the condom until a dollop of hot jizz landed between my toes and on my heels.

Some guys would protest and whine at the zipping up bit, but most seemed a little weirded out and couldn't wait to get out of there. They were happy, but I'd venture a guess that a handful had a case of 'I-can't-believe-I-just-paid-for-that' syndrome.

These extras always involved me doing things to the customers; they weren't allowed to do anything to me. It was a crucial distinction. It's a lot easier to compartmentalize a condom-covered handjob than a stranger's dirty fingers inside my body. None of the other clubs I've worked at have had completely private rooms, so when I stopped working at the O'Farrell, my handjob money went out the window. There's no way in hell I'm going to risk getting caught by a co-worker who can see the lap dance through a sheer curtain. It's unfortunate, because I made a lot more money when I could make men come in under five minutes.

I live and work in Los Angeles now. A couple of dancers I knew from San Francisco had moved to LA and were still stripping, so I reached out to them before my move to find a good club. That's how I ended up at the Bare Elegance. The Bare is uber tame compared to Mitchell Brothers, but it's a good place to work. I continued to work at Mitchell Brothers for the first few months after my move to Hollywood, but the drive got old and to be honest, things were getting a little out of hand at the club. Most strip clubs charge the dancers a stage fee – the rest of the money earned is ours to keep – while others forgo the stage fee but take half of the dance price. The stage fee at Mitchell Brothers had increased to more than three hundred dollars by the time I left – it was seventeen when I first started. This meant that we were in the red until we crossed the three hundred mark, which is nuts, but what I'm really talking about is what was happening in the club. I was no angel, but they were hiring nineteen-year-old girls who had pimps and were doing 'extras' for pennies on the dollar. It also got real tiring being asked for blowjobs and intercourse all night. I was sad to end my time in San Francisco, and I was sad to say goodbye to my friends, but nine years was a good run at the O'Farrell Theatre.

Interesting to note: Within my first few months at the Bare Elegance, I learned that the owner had killed his partner and was serving time in prison. I guess it says something about the business that two of my home clubs had the same tragic story.

5

I DROPPED BY the liquor store near the club on my way in. This has become part of my routine. To my pleasant surprise, the clerk remembered me and knew my poison: blackberry-flavored vodka. I had been drinking tequila for a bit, but I started to worry that I smelled too strongly of alcohol so I switched it up. I didn't drink for the first half of my career, but when I started, I drank Goldschläger. I figured cinnamon was good for my breath, but Goldschläger is disgusting and I quickly moved on to other libations.

As I walked into the club, I caught the eye of one of my regulars, a guy I refer to as Cargo Pants as he almost exclusively wears Abercrombie & Fitch-type cargo pants. I wasn't expecting him to be at the club that early. I usually like to get a good buzz going before dealing with any of the customers, especially a regular. Plus, I like a little time to ease into stripper mode.

I waved to him, checked in with the DJ, went to pee, then walked over to his table to say hello and tell him that I'd be out in a little bit. I needed to put make-up on, chug some vodka and spray myself with something that smells like a gumball.

'Hi baby, so happy to see you,' I chimed as I sat down. We caught up on the latest in his life and whatever silliness I could pull out of my ass. I was getting goosebumps because of the way he was touching my legs. I blamed it on being cold, but it was him. I hate having goosebumps. My skin isn't smooth and soft if I have goosebumps. Why do men think that goosebumps are good? I suppose sometimes they're a sign that you're excited. Once in a while, I get them when a person is going down on me, just before I come, but mostly it means my skin is annoyed (or cold). Cargo Pants is often too hands-y on the floor, out in the open. If you want to molest my legs, get me in the VIP! The difference, of course, is money. That's probably why I didn't like it; I knew he was trying to get something for free. I used the excuse that I was cold and put on his long coat to cover my legs and keep them hidden away from his paws. He told me that we could go to the VIP when the next two-for-one was called. I told him that I was going to run to the dressing room super quick. I needed one more swig and a moment away from him. While I enjoy his company just fine, up until the moment I'm making money from him, I often like to take tiny breaks in the dressing room in order to maintain the overly positive attitude he likes so much about me.

Now I'm ready to dance for him.

As I'm walking back over to him, a two-for-one is called; great timing! I'm still wearing his big jacket. We walk to the VIP area, which is separated from the main room. The VIP Lounge has nine semiprivate chairs separated by walls. It costs a hundred dollars for three songs.

Cargo Pants has long, thick, curly hair. I'm not a fan of long, thick, curly hair on men, but he doesn't know this. He thinks I like it; I play with it during our dances. For all I know, he's kept his long hair all these years because he thinks I like it. I've known Cargo Pants for at least three years, maybe more. I recently learned that he used to be another girl's regular, but since we met, he's been exclusively mine. He comes in at least twice a week to see me.

Halfway through the first song, I take his shirt off. He thinks this is something I do only with him. He thinks it's *our* thing. While it's true that he was the first one I did this trick with, I've since used it on other financially worthy men. It's an easy scheme to make them feel special. A stripper's breasts against a customer's bare chest in a strip club is atypical, but it makes my job easier. I don't have to do as much. If I just hold them like this, they're pretty happy. Most of my fellow dancers would be grossed out by this move, but a naked chest is probably a lot cleaner than the stage floor. Just sayin'.

Cargo Pants and I usually start standing up with his back against the wall, another semi-unique move. I hold on to the brass bars with a leg up or I turn around and bend over, pushing my butt into his crotch. He tries to kiss me. I giggle and dodge, giggle and dodge. This is my life. For our second move, he sits on the chair and I stand with my back to him. He rubs his chin hairs on the small of my back. I pretend to be turned on by this. I pull his hair, I touch his nipples, I do anything and everything to make our dance pleasurable. The best gift I can give him is to make him think I'm feeling good in return.

After three VIP sets – approximately forty-five minutes – we're done. Thank god. Although we have fun together, and I genuinely like lap dancing, I exert a lot more energy with Cargo Pants than with some of the other customers.

We walk to the bar to pay. After he pays for the dance and I get my cut, he gives me a hundred-dollar tip. I'm always grateful for this extra money; it makes a huge difference, especially when the house takes sixty percent!

I give him a big hug and we go sit down. I assume a few more minutes of my time will suffice, but no, he starts telling me a long, drawn-out story about a book he's reading. All I can think about is the vodka in my locker and how I'm losing money sitting here talking to him. I've made all the dough I can from him tonight, and I've already spent more time with him than I would with a non-regular. I think he's aware that if he stops speaking, even for a second, I'll disappear. He knows the score. He finally wraps it up and we hug one last time. I walk to the dressing room, sip some much-needed booze and water and reapply my make-up.

In most strip clubs, the dressing room is basically a bar. I would say at least half of us are slugging a little hooch. Flirting is our job, and booze is the catalyst. The constant make-up retouching is because I'm so physical during lap dances that I have to reapply my eyeshadow and foundation twenty times a night. My eyes are red from the booze, body spray and glitter – no amount of Visine will help that, it's a lost cause.

I shoot the breeze with my friends, spritz myself with more gumball goodness and take the stage. The next guy remembers me from a couple of years ago. I wish I could say the same. He recalls things about me that even *I* don't remember. We dance and I notice that his face smells like the beach. He works on boats and uses Coppertone. His name is Captain something. I forget as soon as he tells me. When we're done, we go pay. I notice that one of my other guys has come in and is waiting for me. Fuck, no time for vodka.

We go to the VIP and he tells me I'm sexy. I suck on his thumb, which is gross, given the environment, but I've known him long enough to know he's an avid hand-washer. He says I'm going to make him come doing that. We never do more than one set, so there's no need to make it last. I whisper in his ear and describe how I would suck him off. He ejaculates in his pants, which means the dance is over one song early.

I flirt with the DJ and the cute cocktail waitress. We are all totally inappropriate with each other. My whole job is inappropriate. How many other careers exist where it's totally acceptable for your co-workers and bosses to slap you on the ass and fondle your boobs?

Our ex-general manager walks in. He comes in to get dances from time to time, which is strange, but nothing's by the book here. John is a good guy. We used to flirt heavily when he worked here. In fact, a few years ago, when he was just a manager, I gave him a blowjob in the office after closing time. I was high, happy and horny and he was the lucky beneficiary. Being hypersexual all night can either make you extremely tired or extremely turned on. Usually, it's a little of both.

We walk into the VIP area. John picks the booth. He tells me it's the only one without a camera. Why didn't I know that? I make a mental note to remember that for later.

The dance starts. We always have a good time together. John knows the business of stripping isn't a serious one, and our dances usually reflect this. We swap shirts. John is bulging with muscles, so my little white fishnet top looks ridiculous on him. His wife-beater looks like a dress on me. We bite each other's necks, we wrestle, we laugh. He unzips his pants when I'm not looking. He's never done that before, so I give him shit and he puts it away.

The third song ends and we're done. My neck is all red. John hands me my tip and says we should keep each other's shirts on as we go to pay for the dance. I'm game! We walk to the bar, catching curious stares from my co-workers. Allison, the bartender, laughs at us. John hands her the dough. A couple of girls are sitting at the bar, and we giggle at the ridiculousness of it all. These are the times when I really love my job. John and I swap shirts again, hug a final time, and I walk to the dressing room. The club will be closing soon, so I get dressed and go upstairs to the office to pay out. Randy, my current manager, talks my ear off. I'm beyond exhausted, but he won't stop talking. He's on a tear. Half an hour goes by and all I want to do is start the long drive home, but I don't have the heart to interrupt him. What a life.

6

THE GIRLS IN the dressing room are talking about their first loves. My first real boyfriend – and the first person I ever said 'I love you' to – was a boy named Jimmy. We were together for just under two years. I was eleven when we first started going steady. Jimmy was one year older. He was kind and came from a good family. He looked like Ricky Schroder.

My mother and I had finally moved out of the communal house we had been sharing with two other single parents and their children, and into our own home in a neighboring town about a mile away. Jimmy lived down the road from the new house. We still visited the communal house so that my mother could do drugs, and I could hang with my sisters, but I hated being there. Consequently, I spent a lot of time at Jimmy's house. His world was so normal; I craved non-crazy as if it were oxygen. I craved non-hippie food, sitcoms and loving parents. I loved Jimmy's mom and younger sister as if they were my own flesh and blood. This turned into a pattern: I've adopted almost all of my significant others' families. I never felt very safe in the one I grew up with, but I knew I deserved love and tenderness and that I had a lot to give in return. I'm a firm believer in love and partnership, and over the years, I've been welcomed with open arms by many endearing families. Some of them are still in my life today.

Jimmy was my first and only truly innocent, adolescent love. He used to leave sweet notes on my windowsill every morning. I remember the first time he cupped my Jordache jean-covered butt. We were at a coed sleepover at a friend's house in Point Reyes. After playing the Ouija board, all the kids took a walk in the cool night air. That was when Jimmy's hand slowly slid from my waist to my tiny cheek. My every nerve ending blazed. I loved it. I wanted more. Jimmy and I kissed endlessly and held hands constantly. My fingers would go numb when we watched TV. Every time I see the first *Creepshow* film, I'm transported to the back row of the theater in San Rafael, eating Hot Tamales and making out with Jimmy.

Jimmy and I often spent the night at each other's houses, more so at his, since I was desperate to escape my world. Our mothers never questioned this. We weren't having sex – we were barely taking our clothes off. I suppose our parents assumed this, but who knows? I do know that my period started once while I was at his house, and I asked his mom if she had a tampon. After that, she put the kibosh on sleepovers in his room. Before that, when we slept in the same bed, it was the kind of cuteness that only happens during your early love life. We slept on our stomachs with our arms around each other because that's what we thought adults did even though it was uncomfortable.

Jimmy always kept his corduroy pants on. He was very shy, whereas I was quite the opposite. I developed early, and in eighth grade, I was already a C cup. I was also sexually charged and curious. I wanted to try stuff beyond just making out.

One night, while Jimmy was at my house and on my waterbed, I took my shirt off, and he sheepishly asked me to put it back on. The poor guy, I was more than he could handle. I was a burgeoning bad girl. Before Jimmy, I was the one getting caught making out with boys behind the school. It was a sweet relationship, but I finally broke it off. I needed to find a dirty-minded, kindred spirit.

7

'YOU'RE TOO SMART to be working here.'

Do you know how many fucking times I've heard that? I just rubbed my naked body all over a man who smelled like piss and I have a small cut on my inner thigh that could be turning into a staph infection this very moment. How smart can I be? Would I have been happier if I had gone to law school? Would I have been happier dealing with prison inmates as I had planned? Or working at Kinko's? What does that comment even mean? It's one of those backhanded compliments. Would you say the same thing to a cab driver or a bartender? You think I'm foxy, you gather that I'm not a total ditz, and you want to get in my pants. If you think the way to do it is by 'complimenting' my intelligence, you're wrong, pal. Try offering me a suitcase full of cash, that'll warm me up. I have a good life; I think that's pretty smart.

A friend of a friend made a negative crack about strippers the other night. I should have asked what the fuck he was doing with his life that was so important or earth-shattering; at least I make people laugh and feel good. I should have asked why I have to be either a brain surgeon or a 'stupid' stripper – who made these idiotic rules? But I didn't. Some people just cannot understand that there are intelligent women who choose to take their clothes off for money.

Having said that, my night began with me putting on a leather collar with a tiny bell that a regular had bought for me – it was totally ridiculous. I call this guy The Choker because he likes to choke me. He doesn't do it too much and sometimes I like this during sex so it's no big deal. But he does this one thing that drives me crazy: he rubs my inner thigh with his thumb and I *hate* it. Rub, rub, rub, in the same spot. It makes my skin crawl, not to mention causes a raw spot on my thigh. I would say something, but men are sensitive and we're supposed to love everything they do.

❦

A girl is dancing to '*Hotel California*' by the Eagles. This song transports me to a coke-riddled Passover the adults attempted to observe once when I was around twelve. These were liberal Jews. Seventies Jews. Coke-y Jews. I think the holiday is in April – I have no fucking idea, I'm the worst Jew. Six or seven adults and maybe five kids gathered at my best friend's house. We had the salty parsley, meant to represent tears, and an egg (don't ask me why), as well as some other meaningful shit. Everyone got a Bible. Wait, Bible? That can't be right. Torah? I wasn't raised knowing. Anyway, we each had this book and were supposed to take turns reading passages from it, but in between readings, the adults took turns scampering off to the bathroom to hork lines of blow. I remember thinking how ludicrous it was. Not the physical aspect of what was happening – I was used to the drugs – but the idea that they were trying to celebrate an old spiritual tradition. I will say one thing about celebrating Passover with a drug dealer: I got a twenty-dollar bill for finding the matzah! Twenty bucks was a lot of money to a kid in the seventies.

❧

An unfortunate thing just happened to me. Unplanned things happen on stage when you're a nude entertainer; the most common is visible tampon strings. Contrary to popular belief, we are human, after all. We try to check ourselves before going on stage, but there's not always enough time. And let's be honest, I get lazy sometimes.

So, I'm up on stage, doing my thing and feeling first-rate – the audience is lively and tipping well – when I catch a glimpse of something glowing from my snatch. I'm on stage and it's packed, so it's not like I can sit down, spread my legs and take a good look. But after one of my legs-around-the-pole moves, I definitely see light coming from my bathing suit area. It's a bit of toilet paper stuck to my business. Motherfucker. Just my luck that all the black lights had recently been replaced, so it looks like toilet paper on steroids, glowing brightly. I try to peel it off casually with my finger, pretending that I'm playing with myself. No go. The fucking thing won't come off! Now I'm acutely uncomfortable and I know there's at least two and a half minutes left of the song, an eternity in this situation. I give up on removing the paper. It's super thin and apparently glued to my skin, so I try to hide my muffin from everyone. Not an easy task when you're in the buff, dancing on a small, circular, elevated stage only three feet from people, but I do my best. The song finally ends and the torture is over. I practically run offstage. I swiftly gather my clothes and collect my money, a surprising amount, considering. Pity tips. As I walk to the dressing room on the other side of the large, crowded club – completely mortified – I pass a guy sitting in the very back of the room. He hands me money and informs me that I have something stuck to my vagina.

Thanks, dude.

8

I'M WORKING IN the San Fernando Valley tonight. Ah, the Valley. I like the change of scenery from time to time. The Valley Ball – the club here – is a sister club to the Bare, but not as bourgeois. The Valley Ball has some excellent features. For example, they have tiny, single, personal dressing rooms for a six-dollar rental fee. I love this. It's a four-by-four foot room with a mirror on the wall and a drummer's stool. The stool is an odd choice, maybe there was a bulk sale at Guitar Center or they fell off a truck. I love these rooms because I can do whatever I want in here with no one bugging me. I can drink in peace. I can write without my manager giving me the stink eye. It's my own world, and I get to lock it up.

My assigned personal closet for this evening reeks of vanilla. Vanilla is a stripper's secret weapon and an endless source of personal nausea. Any scent I wear at work eventually makes me ill. I never wear my outside perfumes at work. I will, on occasion, wear a work scent when I'm not at the club, but never vanilla, as I've burnt myself out on the scent. I can tell if someone is wearing vanilla by Body Fantasies a mile away. My friend recently said that vanilla body spray on a stripper is like chum in the ocean. It's true; it's a moneymaker, no doubt.

My birthday is coming up. In the grand scheme of things, I'm young, but in the dancing world, I'm straight out of the Mesozoic era. I might start lying about my age. On second thought, I don't have the energy. Time to hit the floor.

After a round on the floor with no luck, I head back to my locker for a swig. Tonight I'm drinking a homemade whiskey sour in an Arrowhead water bottle. No ice, lukewarm. Pure class. The girl next door to me is on her cell phone with a customer.

She's being overly cute and pleading for him to come in. She just said, 'Thirty is the new twenty-one.' Can forty be the new fifteen? I'm not there yet, but I'm knockin' at its door. You wouldn't know it if you closed your eyes, though. I smell like dime-store cotton candy tonight. It's the olfactory equivalent of our customers feeling like kids in a candy store.

I would have killed for cotton candy when I was a kid but I wasn't allowed to eat sugar. Fuckin' hippies. My childhood had the late sixties, early seventies scent of rebellion. My parents – both baby boomers – were rebelling against how they'd been raised. I was born in 1970 at the French Hospital on Geary Street in San Francisco and raised in Marin. I spent my first thirteen years in San Geronimo Valley, which consists of four very small towns. The total population is currently around 3,500, but I believe there were even fewer of us back when I was there. Janis Joplin and the Grateful Dead lived in 'the Valley' in the sixties. Marin County was a great place to be during that period of time; it was open-minded to the nth degree. A ton of famous bands and artists came out of Marin.

My parents were a happy, young couple. Both raised in Los Angeles, they met in their last year of high school. My father went to Cal Berkeley while my mom attended classes at UCLA. She stopped after two years, to be with my dad in Berkeley.

After my dad graduated, they travelled quite a bit, first moving to Cambridge, Massachusetts, then back to the West Coast to Venice Beach in Southern California. They went to India to follow Meher Baba. A month or so later they came home, sold everything, drove to New York, put their VW bus on a boat and flew first to Iceland, then to Europe. They had a flat in Amsterdam, where I was conceived. When they found out they were pregnant, they moved back to the Bay Area.

My father ran a landscaping business. I always found it interesting that although a large portion of the baby boom generation rebelled against the life their parents had lived, many of them still got married and started a family, often at a young age. A year and a half after I was born, my parents had an unplanned pregnancy. This time they had identical twins but didn't know it until my brothers were born – something about their heartbeats being in sync and no ultrasound. This added stress to my parents' marriage. They did their best, but ended up separating. They got divorced soon after. Instead of alimony, my dad took my twin brothers and my mother took me. They remained friends; to this day, they still are. I consider myself lucky. Growing up, a lot of my friends' parents were divorced, and most of them hated each other; many put their children in the middle of the whole mess.

My mom was a waitress at the famous Trident restaurant in Sausalito. A hip joint at the time, the restaurant sat on the bay and was decorated with heavily varnished wood, huge candles and murals on the ceiling. Woody Allen filmed a scene on the deck for *Play It Again, Sam*, and Robin Williams worked as a busboy while my mother was also working there. She says he had the staff in stitches constantly. It helped that everyone was high on blow – mom included.

When I was around six years old, my mother met a guy name Arty. He was also a single parent, with a daughter two years my senior. My mother introduced him to her girlfriend and co-worker, Linda, who was also divorced and raising a daughter. Linda and Arty became an item; they're still together.

One day, Arty suggested that we all move in together. I don't remember the specifics – and Mom's memory is worse than mine – but we all moved into a big house together. It was a loosely organized hippie commune with single parents sharing the burden, rent and a love of drugs. Random friends and couples also lived with us over the years, and on several different properties. We weren't allowed to eat sugar or meat or watch color TV. Vegetarian food was extremely limited at that time so we ate mostly vegetables, tofu, goat's milk and bread with tree bark in it. At least that's how it tasted. Needless to say, all I wanted growing up were Oreos, normalcy and a hot dog.

Arty was a drug dealer, which was no secret to us. In fact, when I was eleven or twelve, he called me into his drug den, pointed to two huge piles of blow and explained the difference between cut and uncut cocaine. None of the drug use was hidden from us kids. The adults didn't set out lines on the kitchen counter, but the doors weren't closed either. Some of our hippie rooms didn't even have doors.

Weed was commonplace. The adults smoked joints like cigarettes. I used to practice rolling them using loose tea. We were told not to tell the cops or talk about drugs when dealing with strangers. My commune sisters and I were given an early education in the drug life. Including all about the crappy parts.

I didn't really understand the exact effects of cocaine – except that it made you act like a giant asshole – until later in life. The first time I did blow, a few mysteries were solved, like the manic behavior. I realized why Arty would drag my sisters and me out of bed at three in the morning to do dishes, and why he was always blowing his nose. He used to do that horrible 'farmer blow' thing, where you hold one nostril and blow the snot out the other. It was disgusting.

In addition to his nasty nasal habit, Arty was a scary individual. He physically and mentally abused my sisters and me; the mental abuse being far more detrimental. Arty was a short, wiry fuck with beady eyes and veiny arms. He was erratic and unpredictable. As an adult, I could take him, but as a child, he was extremely intimidating.

He sold weed, cocaine and mushrooms. We grew the weed and mushrooms ourselves. I have a picture of myself, at around eight years old, wearing a jean jumpsuit and standing under a tall marijuana plant. Things were dysfunctional for sure. If I had a toothache, my mom would put cocaine on my gums. It was fine for the pain but didn't address the actual problem.

We moved a lot, but always within the Valley. I always assumed the drug dealing had something to do with our constant moving, but who knows? Maybe we kept getting kicked out.

Arty challenged us kids on everything; it was agonizing. He'd put his face inches away from mine and shout bloody murder, always testing and quizzing me on nonsense. If I gave him the wrong answer, he would get violent with me. I hated his bullshit games. They filled me with rage. Often, I would pray for him to hit me rather than to fuck with me mentally. I could deal with the pain, but the mental shit really did me in. My sisters gave him the answers he wanted to hear but not me. I knew he was full of shit, and I didn't want to play. Life may have been easier if I had played by his rules, but it wasn't easy either way, so fuck it. To this day, I don't like being quizzed. My mind tends to go blank, especially if it's about an emotional or heated issue.

One afternoon, Arty was furious with me for something – I may have set a bowl down wrong; it didn't take much to set him off. He was screaming bloody murder and he started choking me. I wished for death. This memory is crystal clear. I remember it as if it were yesterday. When he let go, I was crying and gasping for air. He continued to yell at me, telling me to stop crying while he hit me. My childhood was a lesson in controlling myself on every level. Those of you who were abused know exactly what I'm talking about. I walked on eggshells constantly, fearful of calling attention to myself, fearful of doing something wrong. It seemed I could do little right. Arty forced me to make some of his drug calls from pay phones and if I said something wrong, he'd deck me. What kind of jumbo jackass gets a fucking kid to make their drug deals for them?

I didn't sleep much during those years. Between people coming and going at all hours and the constant fear, it was difficult to find enough peace to shut down my brain. I was a horrible insomniac until I was about eighteen. When you live with a bunch of cokeheads, you don't eat much, either. A stranger once asked me if I had polio; that's how bony my legs were.

San Geronimo Valley was a hippie slash white-trash town. Most people knew that Arty was a drug dealer. Hell, my teacher and swim coach came to the house to cop dope. 'Bye, Gino, see you tomorrow,' I'd say as he left the drug den. I went to an open classroom, a student-centered format that was popular back then. We had one teacher for all subjects and we called them by their first names. There was no homework or grades. Even the building was a trip: an octagon with movable walls. I don't recall much of the curriculum, but I vividly remember Gino reading *The Hobbit* to us. He had the worst breath; I'm guessing the line horking was the reason.

Some time around 1982, Arty made us all go to an EST seminar. EST stands for Erhard Seminars Training and is named after the founder, Werner Erhard. The purpose of EST is to allow participants to achieve a sense of personal transformation and enhanced power in a brief time period. The weekend training was held at a hotel in the city. Clocks and watches were not allowed and the adults were separated from the kids. I was embarrassed because our vegetarian lunches had to be specially ordered. I just wanted to blend in, be 'normal'. Sugary peanut butter and jelly on white bread sounded pretty damn good to me. I didn't mind some of the main themes about having integrity, but the rest of it felt like brainwashing bullshit. Years later, it came out that Erhard beat his wife. Classic.

My mother never taught me any real parental lessons. Or perhaps she did and they just failed to make an impression. The only thing I remember learning from her was that I shouldn't litter; that lesson is embedded in me to this day. My mother was around, but she was young and going through her own shit. She witnessed Arty's abuse, but did nothing about it. Through teary eyes, I'd often plead silently for her to do something, to make it stop. Everyone was afraid of Arty, including the adults, although they may have been mostly afraid of being cut off from the candy.

I completely forgave my mother a long time ago, actually, and I found my peace with Arty as well. In fact, when I was about two years clean and sober, Arty joined Narcotics Anonymous. I was eighteen. Because we were both still living in Marin, I'd see him at meetings. It was a nightmare. Meetings were my safe place. And there he was – the main reason why I was there. The primary issues I dealt with in the first few years of my recovery were feelings originating from my childhood. It was infuriating seeing him acting aloof and making friends. I wanted remorse. I wanted a goddamn apology! But it became clear early on that I was never going to get it. He said some half-assed shit in a meeting once, something about how if he had ever wronged anyone in the room, he was sorry. Really, dude?

I eventually realized it wasn't about Arty anymore. I needed to forgive him for my own well-being. I needed to let it go and move on. It's possible he didn't remember the shit he had done – or maybe it was buried deep and covered with a thick blanket of denial. There's also a chance he didn't realize how much influence and effect he had on us kids, which is maddening to consider, not to mention unlikely. This wasn't the 1930s; everyone was well aware that child abuse was wrong and had a lasting impact.

I never approached Arty about my childhood. If this had happened today, I'd pull him aside and tell him exactly how I felt – not to instill guilt – but to honor myself. The mental and physical abuse Arty inflicted affects me on the deepest levels. I have an unnatural fear of being embarrassed, and I have horrible TMJ, a condition that causes pain in your jaw joint and ruins your teeth and gums from constant clenching. My tolerance for pain and bullshit is higher than that of anyone else I know. I often wonder if I could have stayed in the sex industry this long if my childhood had been different. On the other hand, it has made me an exceptionally strong, independent, self-sufficient woman. I wouldn't take that part back, but I envy the girls who were loved unconditionally, who felt safe and were told they were special. There have to be a few out there, right?

In addition to the drug dealing, Arty also trained dogs. We used to go to these uppity dog shows in a rented RV. Arty had Doberman Pinschers and then Standard Poodles. I felt bad for those dogs. He was ruthlessly mean and yanked hard on their spiked collars. Dog shows are a strange business. That type of training involves a bizarre regimen. It's deranged and perfect for a cokehead. Arty would be all gaked-out at these fancy dog shows, while my commune sisters and I would be running around, starving and dirty. God only knows what those people thought of us. Even at eleven, I knew life was a sham.

I remember going to a show in Carmel where there were all these rich people and us. We were eating at some upscale restaurant, and, like clockwork, as our second course arrived, Arty went ballistic over nothing and made a huge scene. Everyone was staring at us. I wished someone would say something, stop him, and save me from my life, but no one ever did. We'd barely touched our food when Arty dragged us out of the restaurant. I just wanted to eat one fucking meal in peace. Just once. My friends poke fun at me because I don't like to share my food. Trust me, if they'd been around during those years, they'd be the same way. Food was hard to come by.

My childhood wasn't all shit. The Valley was a great place to grow up. It was beautiful with lots of rolling hills and outdoor space to play. It was extremely safe; no one locked their doors. And although it hurt that my mom didn't protect me, she and I were really close. I loved that she was more like a friend than a parental figure. Professionals (and Oprah) would have something to say about that, but at the time, I really enjoyed it. I often skipped school to hang out with her. We played racquetball at the YMCA and went to Calistoga to get massages and mud baths.

My childhood was a great dichotomy. I spent it going to upscale restaurants, spas and uptight dog shows while living in one of the most exclusive locations in the country, but my home life was abusive and I lived in fear most of the time. Even so, there are people who have it much worse. I recognize that I grew up surrounded by beauty, and I'm grateful to have experienced some of the things I did.

9

I'VE BEEN WRITING for a long time. I should leave my tiny private domain and try to make some money.

Holy shit, it's slow. There are only a few guys in the club. It's pouring outside and people don't go out when it rains in Southern California. I need a sugar daddy. I look forward to the day when I can hang up my heels for good. Stripping is like being in the mob. As soon as you think you're out, it pulls you back in.

It's only 12.34 a.m. I wish I could pack it up, but I have three-plus hours to go. I better hit the floor and stay there for a while. I've only made ten dollars tonight!

Approximately four songs later, I'm back in the booth. Strip clubs are such a circus. The DJ was grabbing my boobs and moments later, the manager was hugging me and snuggling my neck while we watched a customer, wacked out on drugs, dance in the audience with his shirt off. Maybe that's why I like this business. I relate to the craziness. Crap, I'm down to the last drops of my stripper juice. It's 12.59 a.m. and I've already finished the sauce. I guess that's good, seeing as how I have to drive home. Maybe the DJ has something to drink.

It's 1.59 a.m. and I just danced for a young sushi chef who came straight from his restaurant. I do not smell good right now. It's making my stomach turn, but I can't shower, so I spray more cotton candy body spray in a lame attempt to cover up the fish stank on my skin. The DJ gave me some blue vodka something. Who knows what the fuck I slugged, but who was I to refuse mystery booze post-fish dance with more than two hours to go? The fish kid was nice but really skinny – our oversize chairs enveloped him. It made it hard to give him a decent lap dance. Strippers should be in charge of designing the dance couches and chairs; we know what works best.

The smell of fish reminds me of the time I danced in Japan in 1995. Nine girls and myself from Mitchell Brothers travelled to Japan with the help of an agency based in Los Angeles. They paid for our flight and accommodation and the Japanese clubs paid for us to come and dance. The plan was to work six nights a week for three months and make a butt load of cash. The agency told us we should expect to make anywhere from eighty to a hundred grand. Almost all of us were counting on this money as a means of retirement from the industry. Boy, did we have another think coming.

I had heard all the horror stories: rape, kidnapping, sex slavery. We were assured that the club in Japan was a trustworthy operation. I was getting pressure from my boyfriend at the time to quit dancing and figured this would be my ticket out. I would have the financial room to figure out what I wanted to be next.

We had to pack for a three-month stay that began in the summer and would end in late fall. Japan is exceptionally hot and humid in the summer and it snows in certain areas during winter. It was my first trip out of the country so, naturally, I packed way too much shit. The agency instructed us to hide our costumes among our belongings as it's illegal to work in Japan without a green card. We all sweated a little going through customs upon arrival.

We landed in Osaka and took the bullet train south to a town called Fukuyama where there was a brand-new strip club boasting all-American girls. The ten of us were the only dancers. We agreed on what we would and wouldn't do and how much we would charge for lap dances.

The small club was located on the third floor of a medium-size building. Everything was brand new and everything was mini. Mini chairs, mini tables, a mini stage and super-low ceilings. You could touch the ceiling as you walked on stage. We had brought CDs, so we divided them up and loaded them into the jukebox; the club didn't have a DJ. The place was busy as they'd been advertising the shit out of it, but after a few nights, it became clear that most of the customers were friends of the owner. I also noticed that a lot of the men were missing half their pinky finger; a sign of membership in the yakuza, the Japanese mob. It was no big deal as most of the clubs in the U.S. are run by the mob. You get used to it. I still had all my tattoos back then, and a few of the yakuza would pull back their long-sleeved shirts to reveal that they were covered in tattoos as well.

The men didn't speak a word of English and none of us spoke Japanese. We had a young interpreter who helped us get settled. He was only a phone call away if we needed something. He taught us how to say, 'big tip, please' in Japanese. I found that near the end of the night, I would be repeating the word 'please' in Japanese like a damn mynah bird.

Japanese men are quirky and extremely silly, like drunk eight-year-olds. If you keep them laughing, you keep them happy. Japanese men also drink like fish, which makes them fairly easy to entertain. Being a brunette with big tits and big almond eyes also helped. Unfortunately for me, I was clean and sober at the time.

Also unfortunate was the fact that we weren't making the kind of money we had hoped for. In fact, we were making even less than we'd been making at home. Japan is a non-tipping country, so it was nearly impossible to get the drunkards to part with extra yen, even when we begged.

We were staying in an apartment complex located about a mile from the club. The ten of us were divided between two apartments on the twelfth and thirteenth floors of a run-down high-rise. My pillow was made of rice! It was so strange. It took us a few hours to figure out how to use the space-age toilet. It was hot as shit outside, and we didn't have much to do during the day. The financial situation wasn't making us very happy, not to mention the lack of privacy, the heat and being around each other twenty-four-seven. All of it led to crankiness and ridiculous behavior.

After a couple of weeks, on a particularly oppressive and hot afternoon, our young interpreter came to the building and asked us all to gather in the larger of the two flats. He was visibly freaked out about something. He explained in his broken English that the owner of the club 'owned' us. That he had paid a large sum of money for us and would hurt us if we tried to leave. The kid had never been around the sex industry and was deathly afraid of the yakuza. He added that the man in charge also owned the apartment building and that we were being watched. He scared the living hell out of us.

This sent us into a mild frenzy. I called my boyfriend from a pay phone, told him the situation and asked him to call the American embassy if he didn't hear back from me the following day. The poor guy was crying on the other end of the line.

The ten of us devised a plan. We would work that night and act as if nothing was wrong. At the end of the shift, we would get our CDs and hightail it to Tokyo.

The manager seemed confused when we mimed and chirped about our CDs, but we smiled and acted as if it was the most natural thing in the world. We used lots of hand gestures and added 'See you tomorrow night!', not that he understood a thing we were saying. We acted like we had every other night at the end of our shift: a wild bunch of American girls. We arrived at the apartment building around three in the morning and started packing our gazillion heavy bags. We were crazed. The fear and the stress and the lack of sleep turned into major slap-happiness.

Around 5 a.m., we ordered four taxis and 'escaped'. It was hardly a stealthy getaway. Ten girls on zero sleep – nine of us on the downside of drunkenness – giggling from fear and insanity and throwing heavy suitcases down twelve flights of stairs, and a million elevator trips did not make for a quiet scene. We just wanted to get the fuck out of there alive. We managed to get ourselves into the taxis and to the train station, checking behind us the whole way. We were so anxious. Our interpreter had us believing that the whole town was in on this conspiracy. They weren't. He said that if we were caught, we would be turned into sex slaves. We even thought our cab drivers were going to call the owner and turn us in. They didn't.

When we bought our tickets to Tokyo and finally boarded the train, we felt ecstatic that we had made it, but we didn't feel truly safe until we were about an hour outside of town. As it turns out, we were never in any danger. It's common policy for international clubs to pay for girls to work and we made even less money working in Tokyo. Half of the girls went home. I stayed with another girl, but eventually we went home as well, long before the three-month mark. I returned home with broken dreams and with less cash than I would have had if I had stayed in San Francisco. So much for my grand retirement plans!

❧❦❧

It's too bad you can't see me right now. I'm wearing a fishnet top, my favorite pair of worn-out jeans and patent leather boots, and I'm lying on the floor of my tiny room with a writing pad. My left foot hurts. I drank too much. I took too many pain pills. I stink. It's nauseating. I just want to go home. I wonder if the DJ will let me leave half an hour early. Shit, he's calling another two-for-one.

IO

Since this is not a tell-all about anyone other than myself, I won't bore you with the tales of the famous people I've met and have danced for over the years. But I will tell you about one of my most disappointing and one of my most surprisingly fun encounters.

Both took place at Mitchell Brothers. The first story happened in the old Private Show, the one with the Formica island surrounded by water. The room was so brightly lit! I was twenty-five at the time. Only at that age would I be naked in that kind of light. I wouldn't be caught dead in it now.

Customers entered the Private Show through a second door. There was a chair, a wastebasket and a paper towel dispenser on that side. I was standing in the hallway, hawking my wares, and this guy walked up and asked me for a show. I recognized him immediately and said 'sure' as casually as possible, but I was excited. I'd been watching his movies since I was in high school. I'd venture to say that a lot of ladies had – and still have – a crush on this guy. He was in his early thirties at the time and he looked good.

We shut our respective doors, he gave me money, and the show began. I played with myself in different positions while he unzipped and jacked off. He had a huge dong! I'm a professional, so of course, I never let on that I knew who he was. Plus, famous people came to the club all the time; it wasn't that unusual. After he came, he asked me to go back with him to his hotel. I smiled and said I couldn't. I was still excited to have met him when he ruined it by saying, 'Don't you know who I am?' Ugh.

'Yes I do,' I said, 'and the answer is still no.' I was crushed.

The happy story – and one of my best friend's favorites – took place a few years later in one of the three Private Booths. It was a packed Saturday night. Our schedules were made a month in advance, and I had one of the Private Booths to myself for the evening. In between shows, I got word that a couple of actors from a popular TV show I had been watching shamelessly were in the club.

Unfortunately, I was so busy doing shows that I didn't have time to scout the place for a look-see. As it turned out, I didn't have to. I was escorting a customer from my little room, wearing nothing but heels, and while I unhooked the velvet rope, I scanned the club for my next victim. That's when I spotted the actors over by the Cabanas. The actress was pointing at me. I gestured for her to come over. She told me she had seen me earlier and that I was the one she wanted. I explained the price, and the four of them – the actress along with her fellow cast member and two of their friends – squeezed into my room. There was really only space for two on the couch, so the girls sat down and the guys stood. I got the cash from her and started the song.

They were surprisingly down-to-earth. The actress was even hotter in person. I knew a lot of my younger male friends had been jacking off thinking about her ever since her first hit TV show had aired and would be very jealous (and excited) when they heard I had danced for her. She saw that my tongue was pierced and asked, 'What's it like to kiss with that?'

'Would you like to find out?' I asked.

'Yes!' she said.

So I kissed her. I was in between boyfriends at the time and feeling shameless. I justified it on the grounds that a girl wasn't classic star fucking; I've prided myself on not sleeping with famous people just for the sake of doing it. But she was a really good kisser! The song ended and I asked if they wanted to stay.

'Is there anything more we can do in here?' she asked bravely.

'Honey,' I cooed, 'we can do whatever you want.' She handed me extra cash and the boys left. I was on top of her and her friend, gently smushing my tits in their faces, rubbing my thigh in between their legs and kissing both of them. It was a blast. Sometimes I'm amazed that I get paid to do what I do.

I pulled the actress's top down and licked her nipples. She had hard, fake tits, which isn't my cup of tea, but fuck it, I was having fun. She wanted to go down on me, but I told her sweetly that she couldn't. I'd been giving nude lap dances all night and hadn't had time to use the shower or the bidet in the dressing room in a while, so no way was I letting her go down on me. But I shimmied her pants down to her knees and licked her pussy. She put her head back and was smiling.

'It's hard for me to come from oral sex,' she said.

'Try putting a pillow over your head,' I told her. 'It helps block out any annoying thoughts or insecurities. You can just concentrate on the feeling or a fantasy.'

'I'll try it,' she said.

The song ended and the girls said their thank yous as they readjusted their clothing. With a devilish grin on my face, I asked, 'So, when can I come to Hollywood and visit you at *your* job?' That was the only time I alluded to the fact that I knew who she was. She flashed a starlit smile and hugged me.

II

IT'S FREEZING ON the floor and tropical in the dressing room, a cheap ploy on the part of the management to keep girls out of the dressing room and working on the floor. It doesn't work, of course. All it does is make us sweaty and cause our make-up to run. I'll never understand club owners. They always want to punish us when times are tough. On really slow nights the owner, Martin, will come into the dressing room and give us shit. But he doesn't get that stressing us out and running us out onto the floor won't get dances. Yes, there are lazy strippers, but those of us who've been doing this for a while know we need to pace ourselves, and we understand the value of disappearing for a minute or two. I'd rather a guy think I'm in the back dancing than see me sitting on the floor bored out of my skull and looking like I'd rather be doing anything else. Seeing a hundred lifeless girls doesn't usually get guys in the mood. Let us be goofy. If we could take pictures, shoot the shit, try on outfits, drink and laugh, we'd be much better at our jobs. We're here to project a certain image and fantasy, and sometimes taking a break from the floor and having fun in the dressing room is exactly what we need. Obviously if you have girls who *never* make money and are *always* in the dressing room, then the prudent thing to do is to pull them aside for a talk or take them off the schedule. But leave us gangsters alone!

Trust me, we want to make money too. We aren't here for our fucking health. I could be a million other places but I made the decision to drive forty-five minutes through traffic to Inglewood and sit in a dark, cold club wearing next to nothing, listening to ear-piercing music, getting judged by men and harassed by management, on a gamble that I'll leave with enough money to have made it all worthwhile.

❧

I'm suffering from what I like to call wet brain. I danced for a young guy a couple of weeks ago and he's supposed to come in tonight, but I have no clue what he looks like. It was late in the night when I met him and I wasn't sober. I made him lie on top of me – which didn't take any arm-twisting – I do remember that, but not his face. I'm pretty sure having a customer lie on top of you is not allowed, but I figure it's a far cry from letting a guy finger-bang me. And I get to lie on my back!

I have only thirty-odd minutes left on my shift. Should I stay or should I go? I'm tired and post-drunk, but still a little high. I don't feel like talking to any of the guys. This is the point where being too high can fuck my shit up. I want to be high enough to be flirty and happy (I call it my happy state) but not so high that I don't want to deal. It's not always an easy balance to achieve. I suppose people working normal jobs have their own burdens: How many cups of coffee? How many times should I jack off in the office bathroom? How many donuts can I eat? How many personal phone calls can I make? Can I get away with a nap at my desk today? These are just guesses, as I've never worked in an office myself, but we all have to find our happy state.

I haven't eaten since 1.30 in the afternoon and it's 8.30 p.m. I haven't made enough money to justify leaving, but sometimes it's nearly impossible to reverse the 'I don't give a fuck' state of mind. Let's see if I can do it.

Forty minutes later, I have a headache. Marvelous. I'm also a little too drunk to drive home. A girl I hadn't seen in a while offered me Patron. So, of course, I drank some. I'm such an idiot. Like I needed more alcohol. Whatever. I'm in my late thirties, I'm wearing patent leather boots, a silver mesh top and glow-in-the-dark panties. Who am I to start being responsible at this point? So, fine, I'll stay for a while, even though I stink of patchouli. Never in a gazillion years did I think I'd wear anything smelling remotely like patchouli, but I found this perfume at Rite-Aid and for some odd reason I like how it smells. Unfortunately, I've been here for too many hours, and since I habitually spray myself pretty much every time I go to the dressing room, I reek. I desperately need to shower and start over. I think I'll go to the bathroom and give myself a sink wash. My make-up, hair and perfume start out brilliant and beautiful, but after hours of reapplying, things get rough. However, here's a secret I've learned during my long dancing career: most men don't give a shit. In fact, I tend to make the most money after I've been at the club for a while and I'm worked and disheveled. I guess it's the post-sex look.

'You smell like a carnival,' a dude in a cowboy hat just said to me. I hope he meant candied apples and funnel cake, not cow shit and toothless carnies.

12

I CAN'T BELIEVE guys still come to strip clubs hoping to find a girlfriend. It's not the greatest idea. Love can and has happened in the club, but it's extremely rare. Most strippers are in relationships. Even when we're single, this is a job and we get hit on a hundred times a night.

This guy was nice enough. He started with the usual questions: 'How old are you?'

'Seventy-two, don't I look good?' I say with fake laughter and a smile. I lean in so he can smell my sweet skin.

'How long have you been dancing?'

'Only a couple years,' I lie.

'What time do you get off?'

'I get off all the time.' I wink and offer more contrived laughter.

'I just moved to Los Angeles and I'm looking for friends and a nice girl like you,' he says. I hold back the eye-roll and the word 'vomit' on the 'nice girl' part. He pushes, 'Can we have coffee tomorrow?' He says he 'doesn't expect anything'.

I mock contemplation. 'I don't really know you,' I say. 'Why don't we do a VIP first?' I flash my famous smile. He squirms and gives me the spiel about not getting dances and that he's really just looking for a lady friend. He tells me he'll give me money for my time, but doesn't want a dance and hands me a twenty. I let it go and figure I'll give him thirty more seconds and then make my exit. I tell him that I don't usually see guys outside the club (which is true), and that I would only consider it after I got to know him better (also somewhat true). In other words, I need him to come into the club and spend money on me first.

After a few more minutes of chitchat, I'm about to stand up when he says he's 'enthralled with me' and wants a dance after all. I take him to the VIP.

Just into our first song he seems a little crinkled up in the crotch area, so I ask him if he'd like to readjust. No need for him to be in pain. I stand up with my back to him, facing the curtain, since sometimes men are sheepish about this act. I'm not sure why. I wait approximately ten seconds and turn around. This guy obviously misinterpreted what I said because when I turn around, his pants are down and his cock is out and standing at attention.

'Oh no, sweetie, you have to put that away. I only meant to straighten yourself out *inside* your pants.'

He's embarrassed even though I don't mean for him to be. I wait for him to pack up his junk. He doesn't take this opportunity to make sure his stiffy is at a comfortable angle, but goes back to the crinkled dick for the remainder of our lap dance. Fuck it, so much for caring.

❧

What a night. I've been a busy girl. This cute twenty-year-old Marine has fallen for me. He's already spent about five hundred bucks. He gave me his dog tags to wear. I love walking around half-naked wearing an item that belongs to a customer; I'm not sure why, but it's fun. Maybe it feels like I've branded him for the night. I sort of feel bad taking his money; he's so young. But fuck it, he's able-minded and he's having fun. Even better, he's the one who keeps approaching me for dances. In fact, between him, a regular who came in earlier and a couple of other easy dances, I've barely had to scour the floor. And I've gone it all with zero begging!

I can lap dance all night. It's the walking around and selling that sucks. Despite my aching feet, I'm feeling marvelous. This is reminiscent of the Clinton era! I have to admit, I'm a little surprised that out of all the pretty, skinny, young girls here, I'm the one with the most dances. But I know that natural sex appeal and attitude are more important than youth and pole tricks.

Crap, Cargo Pants just walked in. I better jet to my locker for some mojito-flavored vodka.

Two hours later, I'm beat. I did four rigorous sets with Cargo Pants. I've also been here for well over my required six-hour shift, a rare feat for me. I figured we were done after our usual three sets. But he asked if I wanted to do another, and it was clear that he did. I hesitated, which I almost never do when it comes to making more money, but in this case, I knew that it probably meant he was spending my tip money on the dance. Not to mention I was running on empty. I'd much rather have the extra hundred bucks as a tip and call it a night, but I said okay. The customer always comes first, right?

❧

While I was on stage just now, a guy asked me how old I was. That's a first. I told him the truth. I'm too old to care and apparently too stupid to lie. He looked surprised and said I looked twenty-five, which is total crap, but I thanked him anyway. Maybe I should stop dancing to classic rock from the seventies. Nah, fuck that. I gotta have something that makes me smile. I think it's time to call it a night.

13

I ALMOST SOLD my teenage body to get a friend's boyfriend out of jail. Well before I was a sex worker, I knew the power I had as an attractive, sexually driven female. I'm not exactly sure how the idea originated, but I had been using sex as commerce for some time, so the idea that I could make money from it wasn't that far-fetched. This happened when I was living in an apartment with three delinquent boys in Fairfax. I had a short-lived friendship with a fourteen-year-old runaway. I couldn't tell you how I met her and I don't even remember her name, but she stayed with us for a spell in the spring of '87. She was tall and pretty. Her boyfriend had landed himself in jail for something petty and neither of them had bail money. I don't think I'd ever even met him.

One sunny day she and I got the bright idea to go into the city to trade sex for her boyfriend's bail. We were stoned, pill-ed out and on acid. As we were hitchhiking on highway 101 to the city – which was about forty miles from Fairfax – it dawned on me that I owned a car and that we could have driven. I used to drive on acid all the time. But these are the things that happen to people while on hallucinogens. We were already halfway there, so there was no point in turning back. We trudged on.

We got to the city and headed for a bar on Haight Street. Bars didn't ID everyone back in those days. We had a simple plan. Find a couple of guys and prostitute ourselves. Even at that age, we were very aware that men wanted us sexually. We'd gotten good at using that power to get all kinds of things, so why not money?

I found two German tourists who were interested. We were getting ready to leave the bar with these guys when I had an epiphany. 'Wait,' I thought, 'What the fuck are we doing?' I grabbed my adolescent friend and practically ran out of the bar. We left those Germans in the dust. Perhaps if I had known what I'd do as a profession later in life, I would have gone through with it, but I was young and under the impression that this sort of thing violated women's lib. It was only when I started dancing that I realized that owning one's sensuality and sex *is* liberation. But I don't regret our decision; we were far too young.

When we left the bar, it was around one in the morning and the trip home required several buses. The first one took us down Haight Street to Fillmore. On the second bus ride down Fillmore, the driver pulled over at Golden Gate Avenue, got out and didn't come back. The passengers consisted of one drunk middle-aged man, the two of us and a passed-out homeless dude. They didn't even notice that our bus driver had quit. We had no choice but to get off.

The neighborhood wasn't so great back then. The streets were dead. We didn't have any money, so a taxi wasn't an option. I saw a cop car down the street and, having no other choice, I waved it down. My nubile runaway was freaked, so I told her to keep cool and let me do the talking. I told the cops what had happened with the bus driver and they said it was pretty typical for drivers to up and quit before last call. They offered us a ride to Lombard Street. We got in the back of the squad car and told them we were eighteen. We left out the laundry list of illegal things we had done that day.

They were pretty cool. Looking back, they must have known we were underage, but who knows. When we got close to Lombard, they asked if we wanted to patrol with them for the night. The only rule was that we had to duck if they spotted their supervisor. Not ones for turning down adventure, we said yes. It was a blast! It felt like we were living in our own seventies television show. We were clockin' sixty miles per hour over the steep-ass San Francisco streets, catching air, and going on calls to handle domestic violence in the Panhandle, an attempted break-in in the Western Addition, a drunk tussle at a bar in the

Tenderloin. None of the calls ended in an arrest. That would have been weird. We stayed with the cops until dawn. One of the guys said he'd give us a ride home when their shift was up. Nothing about this was very smart. But it's not as if we were in our right minds, or cared that much.

We waited outside the station in the frigid dawn of the city and jumped into the black Corvette owned by one of the cops. He lived out by Ocean Beach and said he needed to get something from his house first. It was yet another red flag, but I was young, broke and coming down, so we went.

I'll never forget his apartment. It was ultra-mannish with one simple, black leather couch, empty beer cans everywhere and the tallest stack of porn magazines I've ever seen. I got an uneasy feeling and pushed for him to drop us home. I made up some lie about why we were in a hurry. We got into his car, and he drove over a hundred miles per hour up the Great Highway along Ocean Beach. I just wanted to get back to my dirty apartment in one piece. To his credit, he drove us all the way to Fairfax. As we were getting out, he asked my fourteen-year-old friend if she wanted to go to the beach with him. I said she couldn't and we got out of the car. I have no idea what happened to that girl.

14

What a night. I'm thoroughly worked: two weekend nights in a row. It's not just the hours and the physical exhaustion, it's that I give too much of myself. Even my colleagues have noticed this and mentioned it to me. But I can't help it. It's who I am. I like making people happy. I love being sensual in an environment where it's safe and encouraged. I enjoy the contact, the closeness, the love and attention I get to give. Even if it's fake, there's an element of realness for me. I've always been a highly sensual person. In fact, no one from my childhood was surprised when news got around that I'd started stripping. But sometimes my authenticity and open nature bite me in the ass.

The night started out like many others. I ate a BLT, drank cheap vodka and gave advice to a fellow dancer. I sprayed myself with vanilla body spray, asked a few guys for dances and talked shit with my girls. Dancing to The Clash was the highlight of the evening. Later, I regretted the BLT, got turned down by a couple of broke fools and talked to one really sweet guy who compensated me for my time. I drank more vodka, kept an old man's cock from peeking out of his shorts during a VIP and told a Jesus-loving regular to go fuck himself. That was the ass chomp.

I didn't want to work at the club tonight. I had recently met a guy who offered to pay me to have drinks with him. This happens from time to time with men who just want the company. I've gotten paid to go to events, dinners, et cetera. There's no sex involved in these transactions, just my time and winning personality. He was cute and I was looking forward to it, but I didn't hear from him. I don't usually notice or care if customers are good looking. Some girls won't dance with guys they think are ugly, which is utterly preposterous to me. Who cares what they look like? Do they have money?

That's what I care about. That and that they adhere to my rules and don't push me over the edge. A generous tip is also nice. And I'd like them to enjoy themselves. It's preferable if they don't smell like piss, but even that hasn't stopped me on desperate nights. Other than these simple things, the men get a lot of room to be weird. It's actually kind of amazing how much crap I can put up with for money. My tolerance for dysfunction and bullshit is ridiculously high. It's not just me – all dancers and sex workers are exposed to unique situations, which tend to come with a side of pain-in-the-ass. Strip clubs are circuses, brothels and wellness centers rolled into one. Men are paying to live out their fantasies. They take and take and it's our job to give. The giving sometimes gets taken advantage of. But since I'm really only here to make money, you know that when I tell a customer I'm done with him and will never sit with him again, the situation is dire. I doubt any well-adjusted woman could imagine putting up with some of the shit that comes our way on a nightly basis. What makes me different? Was it the coke-riddled childhood? Was I born like this? Both?

The final straw with 'Mr Catholic' was when he started talking about Satan. We were in the middle of a topless lap dance and he said, 'The dark Lord is coming through the techno music.' *What?* Of all the shit I've heard. I rolled my eyes and tried to pretend that he hadn't said that, mostly because I knew he was being serious and I didn't want to get into it. A few seconds later he asked, 'Did you read the books I gave you?' He had given me some religious books about a month ago, which I promptly gave to a fellow dancer.

'Uh, I started to read them, but then got super busy,' I said, hoping he would drop it.

'They will save you. You need help,' he said.

He had mentioned this before, but this was it. Something clicked in my mind and I went to the dark side. I was fucking over it. I stood up and announced, 'I don't need any fucking help. I'm just fine.' He was visibly shaken. I don't usually swear at my customers. The poem he had written for me fell to the floor. 'I didn't mean to offend you,' he said.

I couldn't take it anymore. His Devil talk, him praying for me, his craziness and rampant loneliness *and* his shitty poems – it was too much. I grabbed my top and walked away, feeling victorious. I never tell customers off. I knew girls who used to deck guys or cuss them out on a weekly basis, but this has never been my way.

About a month or so later, he came in and begged me to sit with him. I said yes because I needed money. But when he started in with the usual weirdness, I told him I needed to freshen up in the back – code for grab a drink. When I came out, the first thing he said was, 'I just saw Jesus in the sky and we talked about you.'

'Really? Jesus Christ? On the patio deck of a strip club in Inglewood?' I asked in a bitchy tone.

'Yes, he says—'

I didn't pay attention to the rest of what he said. I tuned out. I wanted to get more dances out of him and I knew that if I listened any further, I'd be too annoyed. So, I glazed over and got another dance and a nice tip, courtesy of my friends at Ketel One.

15

THE THING ABOUT anal sex is that there's poop in there! Poop isn't sexy. Why do people like this? I get the taboo factor, but it seems a little offensive to the vagina, as if you're telling her she's not good enough. I know the asshole is tight, but that doesn't make the situation any better for the vagina's feelings. In fact, it's worse. Leave it up to men to find a way to downgrade pussy.

One of my best friends loves anal sex. I tell customers about her love for butt sex during dances. I run out of things to say, and well, it's sexual. She knows I do this and it's a running joke with us. She'll ask me how many guys I've told this week. I've had good anal, but it's not really my jam. I like my men to resemble a twenty-four-ounce Colt 45 can, and that shit hurts goin' through the backdoor!

I have a bone to pick. Men, when you get a lap dance, you should anticipate us moving around. This means that in order to facilitate a better dance, you should fucking move, too. Nothing's more annoying than trying to slide my knee around the outside of a guy's leg and have him just sit there like a fucking lead potato. Do you *want* me to knee you in the meaty part of your thigh? Can't you feel me trying to put my leg in the crux of the chair? The slightest movement of your leg would be helpful. I just gave an extremely challenging lap dance for a man in his late fifties or early sixties with one of the worst toupees I've ever seen. He was sporting a pretty sweet button-up Doobie Brothers shirt, though, I'll give him that. In addition to him not moving in a helpful manner, his pants were hindering my abilities. Mid-lap dance he asked me if I liked his pants. He was wearing tracksuit trousers, so the answer was no. Slippery tracksuits are the worst type of clothing to wear to a strip club. Fashion aside, it's a challenge to stay on the guy's lap. It's like a Slip 'N Slide with a bump in the middle. I assume men think they're getting one over on us due to the thinness of the material, but in reality, it's annoying and earns them a shittier lap dance. Not to mention there's zero support for the man's junk, so it's all tube steak and wobbly balls. The best lap dancing pants are corduroy. They're soft and have just the right amount of support and leeway. Jeans are great, but often get too tight in the crotch area. Wool is bad and itchy. I've had guys come in on rainy nights wearing wool pants. You can imagine how much fun that is.

I kept my sarcasm in check; he was a nice guy. I just smiled and put my boobs in his face instead.

16

THERE'S A VERY sweet new dancer at the club. She's a twenty-three-year-old virgin. Can you imagine being a stripper and not having had sex? These are pretty wild times we live in. I was fourteen when it I lost my virginity. I was the poster child for the promiscuous teen girl. When I was a freshman and sophomore in high school, I'd go to bars to drink, play pool and find guys. My mom was often out of town for work, which gave me free rein of our apartment. I used the freedom to my full advantage. I had boys, men and girls over all the time.

Even if I was using sex for inappropriate or unhealthy reasons, I owned my decisions and never apologized for them. I never placed blame on the other party either. Including the few men who were well over eighteen. I easily passed for eighteen, and I lied about my age all the time. I believe in taking responsibility for my actions. In fact, of all my sexual exploits, I've only regretted a few – that's pretty good, considering.

I had been doing everything except penis-in-vagina for a year before I had intercourse. One of the guys I was doing everything-but with was a cute guy named Greg who had graduated from my high school and was in his first year of college. He either had his own apartment or his mom was never home; I can't remember which. We fooled around quite a bit, but only his fingers had entered me. In defense of the older men I fooled around with when I was underage, I was a strong-minded girl who knew what she wanted and rarely took no for an answer. Come to think of it, Greg may have said no to me when I wanted to lose my virginity, which is why he wasn't the one I lost it to. I *was* only thirteen for fuck's sake. It seems so young now, but I know how I felt, and I'm still the same headstrong girl.

I hated being a virgin. I thought the whole thing was bullshit. What the hell was I saving it for? So I gave it away to a senior and fellow drama department member. We had fooled around before, but this time I was on a mission. It was in the afternoon and my mom must have been out of town. It wasn't romantic; I wasn't in love. I just wanted to get it over with. I'm sure I put on a cassette tape, probably the soundtrack to *Purple Rain*. We were on my waterbed (awful). I'm ninety-nine percent sure he wore a condom, as there was no way I wanted to get pregnant. It hurt like hell and took a while to get in. He was pretty well endowed. He was also kind and patient. At some point the sheet came off the corner of the waterbed and my bare ass was on the plastic. That's what I remember the most. That and feeling like he could see right through me, which was a feeling I didn't like.

When he was done, I said, 'That's it?' I told him to get dressed and go. I was shocked at how exposed it made me feel and how little I felt about the actual act. I didn't even bleed. It was as if my pussy were already jaded. But I saw that I was going to have to add reinforcements to the wall that protected me from being hurt if I was going to do that again – which I did. Sex got better, but I wasn't coming. Orgasms scared me. The way people described them, it sounded so out of control. Being in control was everything to me. Sex felt good but not necessarily for the right reasons. I was using it to feel better about myself and have power over people. The next few boys I slept with all had big dicks and a size queen was born. My body got used to it, and I thought that was the norm. It wasn't until much later on when I had sex with someone who was less than huge that I realized all those boys were well endowed and I had been spoiled.

I did come later, but not until I was around eighteen. My first orgasm was with a woman I dated, named Riley, I think. I could be wrong about this; it may have happened earlier with my first girlfriend, Taylor. Either way, it was definitely from getting head.

Because I used sex to control people and feel good about myself, I was a good sexual performer. It was essential that I was the best a guy had ever had. I did tricks and gymnastics and I perfected my blowjob skills. I knew exactly how to act and what to do to turn men on.

My mom must have suspected I was sexually active because she gave me all of her condoms after she got her tubes tied. It was comical, because it was a pretty large box of rubbers she handed me. This was just before the AIDS epidemic became a thing everyone was worried about, so I was just trying to keep babies at bay. Soon thereafter I asked my mom if I could go on the pill. She said yes. I don't remember her saying much about it. We never had 'the talk'. She was just happy I was wearing clothes that weren't strictly black. The parade of boys I had over didn't seem to concern her much. I always thought her disdain for my attire was a bit hypocritical coming from a woman who wore velvet and seven layers of skirts when I was young (which *her* mother hated). I suppose we all turn into our mothers eventually. I didn't get the judgmental gene (I'm also not a mother), but I'm finding that, as I get older, I'm a lot like my mother in really funny ways.

17

I'M IN A surprisingly good mood tonight. I took my muscle relaxer earlier than I typically do. I've got to remember that trick. Of course, I also stopped by the liquor store and picked up a side of potato salad and a fifth of vodka; meal of champions!

All the usual suspects are here. We've got the drug dealers sitting by the ATM, the regulars at the bar, the semi-regulars in the audience and a few newbies sitting at the stage. A hockey game is playing on two of the smaller plasma screens. *Top Gun* is on the big screen in the far north corner of the room, and what looks to be a nature show is playing on the other big screen behind the stage. I can only hope the animals mate. At least there would be sex involved. Of all the programs showing, it has the highest chance of turning anyone on. Go pelicans!

Oh shit, the DJ is calling me to the stage. It's time to shake my moneymaker and hope I don't get a muscle cramp.

❧❧

Ladies, ladies, ladies. This goes out to you. I'm talking about the women who visit the club as customers. If you're going to get a dance and you're rockin' a micro skirt, please wear some underwear! I'm sure you can appreciate my not wanting your bodily fluids on my skin.

This couple fell in love with me while I was on stage (having a minor leg cramp). Female customers tend to like me because I'm fun and I smile. I also took her hands and put them on my bare breasts. It's something I do with the ladies. It's a crowd-pleaser. As I collected my tips, she told me that they'd like a dance. Dancing for couples is not my favorite, but I'm a professional and of course, I'd like the money. I used to like dancing for couples, but it's experiences like this that make it less appealing. Plus, it requires *a lot* more energy. I can't phone in the moves. But with our economy in the shitter and Los Angeles clubs taking more than half of our money, who am I to be picky?

I tell them to sit offstage and wait for me. It's poor form to speak to customers sitting at the stage while another girl is on stage. I gather the rest of my tips and journey to the bathroom to do my standard routine: wash my hands, inhale a tiny bit of speed, urinate, wash my hands again, apply lip gloss, unwrap a new piece of gum, then head back out to the floor.

I find the couple and become flirty Shannon. I talk them into getting a VIP. It's double the fee for two people, but he's down to pay it. They both seem pretty into the whole idea. I hold her hand as I lead them across the club to the VIP area. This always captures the attention of the other male patrons, which is good for business: both personally and for the club. Happy, participating customers lift the room's spirits. I walk up the three steps and into the VIP area, where I choose my favorite booth in the corner. It's not really a booth, just a cushy chair with a ledge behind it, walls with horizontal brass railings on each side, and a sheer curtain. I sit her down on the cushy chair and drag over a smaller chair for her man to sit on.

She's pretty, but not really my type. She's approximately my age or possibly younger, but she's got a certain pedestrian style and heavy, caked-on make-up that can add a few years. She has big boobs that are barely staying in her dress. I'm partial to small breasts considering that I've had big tits since I was twelve. The grass is always greener. Her hair is blondish and teased out, and she's wearing a short, barely-there dress with cheap boots you can find in shopping mall chain stores. I'm not opposed to cheap clothing, but I call these boots 'mall boots'. She ain't sober. In fact, I'd say she's bordering on sloppy. But none of this really matters because she's paying me and I encourage people to have a good time in the club. It beats sourpusses by a long shot.

Our song starts. Lap dancing for a woman is different than dancing for a man. It's much more demanding. You have to pay a lot more attention. You have to figure out where the hell to put your body. I usually go for the thigh-between-the-legs and boobs-in-the-face combo. That was the position I was in when I discovered that Mall Boots was rolling commando. As I backed away, I felt a cool sensation on my skin. Fuck, I've got her biscuit butter on my thigh. Outstanding. It's not the end of the world, but I can't say that I was thrilled. I resist the urge to say something. Instead, I continue to coo and flirt. I don't want to ruin the dance or my tip. But goddammit, why?

The rest of our time together becomes a strategic avoidance of her Bermuda Triangle, which was not as easy as it sounds. I become a circus acrobat using the brass rails on the sides of the walls like a damn monkey. Meanwhile, she's pulling me down on her, grabbing my boobs and reaching for my muffin. In addition to all of this, anytime my face is close to hers, she tries to stick her tongue down my throat. Women are generally worse than men. An old friend of mine was a male stripper, and he confirmed that the ladies went bonkers on them: licking, biting and tearing at their G-strings like wild animals let out of the cage. Just because we have the same parts does not give you permission to violate me!

I can also tell that this girl's looking to get off. She's arching her back and trying to grind her bare bits against me. Not at the expense of my leg, honey. There were a couple of female customers who had a happy ending with me back in the old days, but they paid a shit ton more money and they were wearing underwear. Let this be a lesson, ladies.

Our time was nearing an end, so while my butt was on her legs, I told her dude to lay on top of me, making a Shannon sandwich. He liked that. We were all laughing and squishing each other.

They were very appreciative and tipped me fifty bucks. I'm sure it would have been more if I had given in and had sex with her, but that's okay. Double VIP, a tip and happy customers are a good thing.

Next!

18

THE FIRST TIME I sold my body for money, I was twenty-six. I had been working at Mitchell Brothers for a few years. A guy came in one night and dropped a bunch of cash on me. During our last dance, he asked how much for sex – a fairly common question in this profession. Normally, I explain how I can't do that, but I was feeling glib and money happy, so I randomly told him twenty thousand. He said okay. We were standing in one of the Cabanas and he seemed serious. I looked him in the eye – he *was* serious. I was single at the time and twenty thousand dollars is a lot of money, so I did something I had never done before: I got his number.

A couple of weeks later, he wired me half the money and bought me a first-class ticket to Aspen. Or was it Vail? I can't remember. He gave me the rest when I arrived. This guy was obviously wealthy. He didn't balk at the money. Needless to say, his house was huge and it was just one of many. He was in his late thirties and average looking but with some funky teeth. He was interesting enough. He was well-travelled, intelligent and he collected wine. He brought his own bottles to the fancy restaurants we went to and each time the servers and managers would freak out.

I didn't tell anyone I was going because I didn't want to be judged or to worry anybody. Explaining my superb ability to judge people isn't usually enough to assure my close friends of my safety. So, as my protection plan, I told him that my best friend needed to hear from me at certain times of the day and that if she didn't, she'd call the cops. It was my only safeguard against him chopping me up into little pieces. I'd pretend to make the call, dialing my voicemail, and fake a conversation. Not quite ironclad but it was the only thing I could think of.

He obviously didn't kill me, but he did want an uncanny number of blowjobs. It's not like I could say no or claim that I wasn't in the mood. I was bought and paid for.

I cried in the bathroom at one point on the second day. Being intimate with someone you don't want to be with and the pressure of earning your keep is more difficult than I had imagined. I wanted to leave, but I sucked it up instead. The worst part – aside from the six blowjobs a day – was that he knew my real name. He needed it in order to purchase the plane ticket. He kept saying it over and over as I sucked him off. It was maddening. We use fake names for a reason. I didn't want to feel like myself; I wanted to feel like a separated piece of me. I concentrated on the money, making him come and the flight home.

About a month later, he paid twenty grand each to fly my friend and me to New York City. It probably seems crazy that I would put myself through that again, but it's hard for me to say no to that much cash. Plus, money is relative, meaning the more you make, the more you spend, which is why it's easy to be a dancer and always feel strapped for cash. Also, I'm willing to admit that there's a part of me that's willing to sweep my feelings under the rug in order to earn a living.

I figured this trip would be much easier because my friend and I could share the blowjob burden, and I was right. It was definitely easier having a friend along. The night before we left New York, he made us an offer: fifty thousand a month each to see him one weekend a month. It was a mind-blowing offer. Unbelievably, I turned it down. My ex-boyfriend and I had talked about getting back together just before I'd left for the trip. What a mistake. My friend continued to see that guy for more than four years and I can't even remember which boyfriend I had said no for! I've always been a sucker for love. I don't have many regrets, and although I don't regret my decision, that would have been a lot of money to stash away or invest. I guess it just wasn't in the cards.

Although having sex for money was more difficult than I had expected, I loved making large amounts of money in such a short time. The second time I hooked (after my relationship had dissolved again) was with one of my long-term regulars from the club. I had been saying no to him for years, but the minute I was single again, I yearned to make the same amount of money in hours that would normally take me months, so I put forth the idea. He jumped at the chance. This guy wasn't a real estate mogul so we settled on five grand. We had dinner first and then went to a hotel room he had booked. The sex took all of thirty minutes. It was sort of awkward, and I sensed he was disappointed. He was extremely shy, and we didn't have *any* chemistry in the sack. I had a tough time conjuring up a fake spark. The first guy was a sex addict; he didn't give a shit about chemistry. The regular stopped coming to see me at the club after that.

The next couple of men were all regulars from the club. They paid me five large. Getting twenty thousand on my first time out was incredible, but not every man can afford that – even five thousand is a decent amount of money – and if memory serves, they all seemed a little disappointed. The long build-up left me with an impossible fantasy to live up to. Or I'm just a shit lay.

19

ALWAYS GET THE money first. Lucky me, I learned this lesson the hard way. It was years ago, and I think it was only my fourth time doing extracurricular work. I had danced for a guy at Mitchell Brothers who had spent a ton of money on me and he asked if I would come down to Los Angeles sometime to see him. I said sure, for ten thousand. He said no problem. I had a good feeling about him, so I booked a ticket (which I stupidly paid for) and a room at the brand-new Mondrian Hotel on Sunset (which I also paid for). I flew down, checked in, called him and showered. I was nervous. He showed up and seemed nervous as well. We talked about how we were both inexperienced and after chatting for a while, I asked him for the dough, and he said he'd left it at his house. That's when I should have told him to go get it, but I didn't. I wasn't a pro and, for some reason, I trusted him. I didn't know the man, but I just couldn't fathom that a person would cheat me for such a personal act. He gave me his laptop as collateral and said he would bring the money by in the morning. This was well before I got into the computer thing and I didn't have a clue as to the value of laptops, so I assumed it was valuable and that he would definitely want it back. So we had sex, even though he hadn't given me a dime. It wasn't horrible and I even came.

Eventually, he left my room happy as a clam and full of promises about the morning. Did he come back? Nope. There I was, sitting in my expensive hotel room on Sunset Boulevard waiting for a man and a chunk of money that would never come. I was so embarrassed by my naïveté – I should have known better – I didn't tell anyone about it. Yes, I was new to the business of selling sex, but I wasn't new to the sex industry. I'm sure it's happened to almost every sex worker at least once, but it's humiliating nonetheless.

I was so bummed out. Ten grand! And I had paid for the whole trip! I tried to rationalize that at least I'd had a relatively good time, but it didn't matter. The whole episode still makes me cringe when I think about it. I can only hope that he felt guilty. Karma's a motherfucker.

20

I FEEL LIKE puking. I ate some fried chicken with one of my customers. He's been my regular for a couple of years. All the girls know he comes just to see me. He's extremely nice, and we usually spend a little time hanging out before we dance. He's intelligent and generally lightens my mood. He looks like a big, Asian teddy bear.

The Bare Elegance has a kitchen with a full menu. When I first started working here, I found it odd that guys were eating – sometimes, while sitting *at* the stage rail! But it's come in handy on long shifts or when I've botched my 'happy state'. However, fried chicken was not the wisest decision. I usually eat salads or the occasional BLT, but it smelled so damn good. It didn't taste the way it smelled. Now I feel like a greasy cow. Not sexy. Also, we hit the VIP too soon after our chicken. He was bugging me the whole time, which is rare because we usually enjoy each other's company. Maybe it was the grease, or maybe I wasn't drunk enough. The stupid chicken soaked up all my well-meaning booze. Everything he did irked me. His touch made my skin crawl. His attempted kisses made my stomach turn. It took all of my willpower not to yell at him and push him off.

A few minutes later, I danced for a weird dude. He looked like he'd rather be getting a root canal than be in the club, so I was surprised when he said yes to a dance, although I was not surprised when he said that he wanted the less expensive topless dance.

His energy was off. He wasn't into it in the least. It's not very fun to dance for someone who isn't into it, so I chatted him up. Apparently, I was too chatty because he said, 'You talk too much.'

'Oh yeah?' I continued talking.

He wouldn't touch me, which is better than groping my crotch, but not great when the man in question seems mad and uncomfortable, so I continued my nonsensical ranting. It was challenging, giving him a good dance. Near the end of the song he said, 'I'm giving this place a one star.' Is that right, strip club critic? Perhaps the dance would have been better if you weren't such a freak of nature.

Just before we finished, I lifted his shirt up and hugged him, figuring I might as well amuse myself. He looked at me like I had bed bugs. When I told the girls in the dressing room about the one-star comment, my friend said, 'I'm giving your dick a negative star.' I love strippers.

I just got a text for an outside job tomorrow. It's easy money. Or as easy as selling your body can be. This guy is a pretty breezy gig. I met him at the club one especially fun weekend night. We were both pretty buzzed. He got five VIP sets and was lots of fun to dance for. He also tipped me well. When we were finished, he asked, 'Can I see you outside of here?' Because he clearly had money and I liked his energy, I took his information. I told him how much it would be, and he said no problem. I prefer to discuss finances in person; it helps that I'm naked and a major plus that they're turned on. I hate talking amounts via phone, text or email. It's awkward, not to mention that it feels like entrapment. I like to agree on a price in person and then never discuss it again.

We've seen each other a few times, always at his house in Redondo Beach. He smells and tastes like cigars, which isn't my favorite, but I deal. It's basically a twenty-minute job. I walk in the door, we kiss, we take our clothes off and maybe start with a little sixty-nine. Then he puts on a condom and we have intercourse. He climaxes, then apologizes for coming quick. What he doesn't realize is that I prefer it. Sometimes I fake an orgasm just before he comes, so he doesn't feel too bad. Then we both pee. We make idle chit-chat as we get dressed, 'How's business been?' et cetera. I grab the cash he puts on the dresser and he walks me out. We talk about whether he'll be in town the following week and I tell him to text me. My friends call him Twenty-Minute Man. He's Italian, I think. He's a good-looking guy, but not really my type. He wears a chunky silver chain with Jesus on the cross. The cross often falls into my mouth as we're fucking. Insert obvious irony here.

21

IT'S 3.07 A.M. and it's been a long-ass day. I looked at a couple of lofts downtown around 2.30 p.m. then met a friend for a drink (or was it three?) at King Eddy's at 2.47 p.m. I left the bar at approximately 4.20 p.m., drove home, checked my email, made a salad, took two aspirins, washed the dishes, did some online research, got in the shower around 6.30 p.m., shaved, lotioned, rubbed one out, blew out and curled my hair and drove to work. I arrived at the club around 8.45 p.m., I applied my make-up, drank vodka and iced tea and hit the floor around 9.25 p.m. There wasn't much going on. I drank more booze and shot the shit with my friends. I gave my first lap dance of the night at 11 p.m., three VIP sets with a customer I met last Friday. He was a nice kid with an Iron Maiden T-shirt and a small dick. I took a short break then did two more VIP sets. More of the same. His penis lay to the left, which is unusual and makes my job more difficult. Most men lay to the right or they straighten themselves out, thus I have perfected a couple of different positions over the years to accommodate. The lefty took a little more ingenuity, but I worked it out.

I had a few more unmemorable dances and conversations, then a dance with a dude who smelled like cum. He was working my last nerve on the floor and being a jerk about getting a dance, but eventually I sold him. Halfway through, he tells me that it's the best lap dance he's ever had. Yes, sir. If I don't know how to please a man after fifteen-plus years in the biz, I should be taken out back, put down and buried in a stripper graveyard somewhere. During the third song, he adds that he loves me. I pretend to come close to climaxing. Upon hearing my superb breathing skills, he ejaculates, saying my fake name as he does. He hugs me tight and I kiss him on the cheek. It's not my job to make guys come in their pants. In fact, it's usually something I avoid doing, but if they do, I don't have to stay for the allotted time, which is a win for me. He was grinning ear to ear and handed me fifty extra bucks as I got dressed. I love when I'm able to turn a situation around. My mood improved a million percent in just three bass-y songs. He asked when I'd be working again as we walked out of the VIP and I told him Tuesday.

He said he'd be here. We hugged one more time and I pointed him to the men's bathroom as I scanned the club for my next mark. Unfortunately, he was wearing thin pants and my panties probably smell like jizz, which is disgusting. This was about forty-five minutes ago, and I'm still wearing them. Which is *really* disgusting.

Next was an Indian guy who came straight from an Indian dinner. He smelled like curry. He was beside himself and said he was in love. I've found that love and a good lap dance often go hand in hand. I could barely feel his dick through his pants. Now I smell like Indian food and ejaculate. I've got one more hour to go.

22

JEOPARDY IS ON. Fucking *Jeopardy*. This poor girl is working her heart out on stage and I'm trying to figure out 'What is _?' Ridiculous.

Asian Teddy Bear is coming in tonight. I'm ready for some good attention. Tonight will be his first visit to the club in more than a month. We've been going out for paid dinners and movies lately. He gives me the same amount he would spend on me at the club, which is better because I don't have to hand over sixty percent of it. The only thing that's strange about him being in the club is that it feels odd asking and flirting with other guys while he's in the audience. Most of my other regulars come to see me and then leave when we're done. Teddy Bear hangs out. It's almost like I'm cheating on him. Club life is so odd.

❧

Earlier, I had some weirdness with a girl in the dressing room. I usually get along with everyone. I don't like drama at work. The biz is tough enough. But this particular girl, Mila, is crazy. Actually, she's a woman – I think she's even older than me! Mila has started shit with almost every dancer and cocktail waitress. I don't get it. Why does she like the conflict? I generally stay clear of her, but tonight it was unavoidable. I was getting ready when she came in and asked if a duffel bag was mine.

'Yes, it is,' I said with trepidation. I smelled trouble.

'Well, will you move it?' the uppity nut said.

It was more of a command than a question. Bear in mind, the dressing room is small and works on a first-come, first-served basis. Every dressing room around the globe is like this. We have to be respectful of one another. Sadly, it doesn't always go down like that. I looked at her like she had spaghetti coming out of her head. 'Where do you propose I put my stuff?' I asked, sarcastically.

Completely ignoring my remark, she said, 'This is where I always get ready.' I swear I could see the tip of a stick protruding from her ass. She continued, 'I don't drink or do drugs, I work five nights a week, and I need this spot.'

I'm not sure what drinking or drugging has to do with where a person gets ready in the dressing room. I wanted to kick her. Like I need this shit while I'm mentally preparing for all the nonsense I'll be dealing with for the next six hours. 'Sweetie, we're all in the same boat,' I said. 'No one has saved spots here and you know that. But if you *need* this spot ...' I trailed off, afraid of what I might say next. Not wanting to deal with her, I moved my bag over for her highness. She didn't even thank me. What a cunt.

Then the bitch trapped me in physically with her shit! This sounds trivial, but I was pissed. I asked her to move one of her three bags so I could get out. She threw a fit and continued to sing the 'I need this spot' song and dance. I told her she was being ridiculous. She flipped out and started yelling at me. I moved her shit to one side and made a small pathway so that I could fucking move away from the counter. What a cow. I drank, undressed, ignored her and went to the floor. She's been throwing me vibes all night. What a joke. Fuck her.

❧

Asian Teddy Bear just told me that I'm the girl next door. He actually thinks this about me! He doesn't know that I'm drunk, pill-ed out and high on meth eight times out of ten when he sees me at the club. Or that I marched in the gay pride parade when I was fifteen, or that I've had sex with so many people I've lost count. He also doesn't know that I've had sex for money and once put pure dimethyltryptamine up my ass in an underground missile base. Also, that I was locked up in a mental institution for suicidal tendencies as a teen. The list goes on. I'm a good person, but I wouldn't consider myself the 'girl next door'. Unless being the girl next door means having a gracious heart. I have that in abundance.

A similar thing happened the other night at a friend's art show. A new acquaintance gushed, 'You're such a shy girl.' Me! Shy! She also said that she saw me as the girl next door. A 'good girl'. Not wanting to shatter her sweet but warped image of me, I just smiled. Little did she know that I had turned a trick an hour before I had arrived.

23

EVERY TIME I see pre-teens walking down the street, I always have the same thought: thank god my life is halfway over. My early teen years started out typical enough. At thirteen, I was a typical happy-but-could-turn-on-a-dime angst-y punk rocker. I hung out with friends. I drank. I inappropriately flirted with every boy I came in contact with. I used to take the bus to the city to see punk shows and play pool at the Palace on Market Street late at night. I'd walk from Van Ness to Fifth and Market, straight through the Tenderloin. I knew it was dangerous, but I walked with my head up and my wits about me. Fuck if I was going to let others dictate my life.

I loved that pool hall. It had high ceilings, unforgiving lighting and mirrored walls hugged by a row of raised theater seats. It was usually filled with hustlers, old-timers and me. The Palace was open twenty-four hours a day and for two dollars and fifty cents, you could shoot pool for as long as you wanted. Once, I walked out onto Market Street at 5 a.m. into the middle of a gang fight. They had *knives*! Even in the early eighties, it felt like the fifties.

High school was a brand-new start for me. I didn't know a single person, by choice. I was supposed to go to Drake High School, where all my childhood friends went, but I wanted to go to a school where no one knew me. My mom and I moved to Larkspur so I could attend Redwood High. I was on the cross-country team and joined the drama department. Life was relatively good, and, dare I say, normal.

Then sometime around the middle of my freshman year, my childhood hit me like a ton of bricks. I believe it was triggered when I lost my virginity. Suddenly I was pummeled by the feeling that my childhood had not been so kosher. The reason I suspect that losing my virginity may have unlocked Pandora's Box is because I had built up such a thick, protective wall around myself, that when I had sex for the first time, I was shocked by how personal it felt. I didn't like feeling so vulnerable.

Truthfully, I don't know what the catalyst was. For all I know, it could have been an episode of *Donahue*. But everything changed. A dark veil of depression and anger dropped over me. I stopped eating as a form of self-hate. I drank heavily at parties. I would get to a party and the first thing I would do is look for the most convenient place to puke, knowing full well that I would drink to that level. That's the planner in me. I also started cutting myself. I kept a razor blade in my jacket pocket and I'd cut myself secretly, and sometimes not so secretly, during math class, for example.

I loved feeling light-headed from not eating. Unfortunately, I gave myself heat stroke a couple of times during cross-country practice. I was taking a home economics class that was taught by a nice but slightly ancient teacher. He had us write down everything we ate for a week. He told us to be completely honest, and he promised he wouldn't get us in trouble. My list consisted mostly of Hot Tamales, vodka and the occasional turkey sandwich on a French roll from the cafeteria, with the turkey removed. That dear old man pulled me aside and gave me his best Marin County 'Are you okay?' talk. My female history teacher handed me a suicide prevention card once. Ah, high school.

It was around this time that I met a girl named Taylor. She was two years my senior. She wasn't like anyone I had ever met. We were both in the drama department and we hit it off right away.

After a couple of months, Taylor told me she was gay and that she had a crush on me. She was the first gay person I had ever met. I said, 'That's cool, but I'm not, so let's just be friends.' I was a bit of a hussy already and was fucking my way through the junior and senior classes, so we remained friends. But I flirted with her nonstop. I was such an asshole. I had zero boundaries. I used sexual attention to feed myself; it made me feel powerful. This may sound strange for me to say when I make a living using sex, but I don't hate myself or have anger toward others as I did back then. It makes a huge difference. I'm not using my clients to boost my self-esteem or play mind games; it's a mutually beneficial exchange. Although I suppose if you asked the boys I crossed paths with in high school, they might say that my sexually deviant behavior was beneficial to them. But I was callous back then, and I know I wasn't careful with people's hearts or minds.

Taylor and I grew very attached and spent a lot of time together. We'd do this thing during class where we'd take turns lightly touching each other's arms. The sexual tension was palpable. I was falling for her. And as life would have it, the day I professed my love to her, she told me she had given up and found someone else. This infuriated me. Now the tables were turned, though she had the decency not to shove it in my face. Her girlfriend was the captain of the rowing team, and naturally I hated her. I wanted Taylor, and I wasn't used to being rejected. Her feelings for me hadn't changed, but she had someone else. My infatuation only heightened.

The summer between freshman and sophomore year, shit hit the fan. Taylor had been dodging me, and I wasn't responding to it well. I missed her something awful. I had been away for the month of June working at a county fair in Southern California selling crystals with my mom (more to come on that later). I was home for about a week before another month-long fair started in Sacramento. I called Taylor, and with very little persuasion on my part, she gave in and came over. My mom was with her boyfriend, so I had the apartment to myself. We drank jug wine and chewed Juicy Fruit gum. I sat between her legs while we watched a movie. My body was ablaze with hormonal electric current. She rubbed my shoulders. I knew she wouldn't make the first move, so when I couldn't take the tease one second longer I turned around and kissed her. It was my first female kiss, and it was breathtaking. We had waited so long, and our connection was so intense. We made out for a while. It was incredible. I took her into my room where there was a red light, music and my waterbed.

Taylor was on top of me, licking and kissing my neck and caressing my breasts. She took my pants off. I couldn't get enough of her. She kissed my stomach while pulling my panties down, and the room started spinning from too much cheap wine. I turned my head and puked over the side of the bed and directly into my cassette tape case. That's the last thing I remember. My first lesbian sex and I blacked out.

Taylor felt guilty about cheating on her girlfriend and blamed it on me. The next couple of months were torture as I tried to win her over. All my thoughts were consumed with Taylor: nothing else existed. I was away for a month working with my mom at the Del Mar County fair, but barely a minute went by when I didn't think about her. I drank and fucked older guys to try to get her off my mind and out of my heart; it didn't work.

Sophomore year started. I continued my sexual spree. Taylor broke it off with her rowing captain, and then we were finally together. From that moment on, my life consisted of nothing else but Taylor. We were attached at the hip. We'd lie in her bed for hours holding hands and listening to Bread, Mozart and a lot of Cat Stevens. I adopted all her likes and dislikes. I was more of a punk, rock and soul girl before, but after Taylor, I was listening to America and Joni Mitchell. We even started dressing alike: army pants and wife-beaters – the lesbian uniform.

We marched with the Gay and Lesbian Youth Group in the San Francisco Pride Parade in 1985. It was mind-blowing. Three hundred thousand people cheered for us. We were young, out and proud. It was one of the best days of my life.

Taylor and I barely attended classes at school. If we went to school at all, we'd hang out in the drama department and make out on the couch or in the theater. We didn't hide our relationship. We didn't give a shit. We'd challenge anyone to fuck with us and very few did. Now remember, this was before being a lesbian was cool, before *Will & Grace*, and before straight girls kissed each other in bars to turn men on.

A few 'dykes!' were shouted from cars or second-story classroom windows, but this was Marin County, home of the hot tub and wine spritzers. No one really messed with us. Also, I had a lot of friends in every clique in school. In fact, no one seemed all that shocked when I started going out with a girl. I guess I've never been very conventional.

Unfortunately, my mom caught us kissing on the couch one night and my life changed. I hadn't told her about my relationship with Taylor. Instinctively, I knew she'd have a problem with it, although part of me argued that because she used to be a coke-snorting, velvet-wearing, weed-smoking hippie, who was she to judge? But she did.

Here's how it went down: my mom and I lived in a modest two-bedroom apartment. Mom was in her room with the door shut, getting ready to go out with her boyfriend, and Taylor and I were in the living room. Taylor leant over and kissed me, and just then, I heard a door slam.

'She saw us,' I whispered.

'I don't think so,' Taylor said.

'She did,' I replied. I knew.

A few tense minutes passed, then my mom came out of her room and walked out the front door, barely saying goodbye. About thirty minutes later she called on the home line.

'Taylor needs to leave,' she said.

'Why?' I asked.

She wouldn't say. I wanted to hear her say it, but there was no way those words were going to pass her lips. She just insisted that Taylor leave the house. I said fine and hung up. Taylor and I devised my runaway plan. Everything was so dramatic back then. I packed some shit and we left for her place. I don't think I even left a note. I was gone for two weeks. The funny thing is, I don't remember my mom trying to find me. I'll attribute it to her faith in my ability to survive.

We lied to Taylor's mother. 'Absolutely, it's cool with my mom that I stay here,' I told her. It was the best two weeks; we never separated.

Taylor was the first love of my life. I had told boyfriends before her that I loved them – and I did – but it wasn't anything like this. This love consumed me. Of course, with that type of unhealthy obsession comes utter dysfunction. We had loads of issues. What teenage couple doesn't? Jealousy, pride, trust and low self-esteem were problems. We fought a lot.

Eventually, Taylor's mom found out that I had run away and forced me to call my mother. As a form of punishment, she didn't allow us to spend our last night together. It worked. We had a wall between us and could hear each other crying. Teenagers. You couldn't pay me to go back.

I went home. My mom and I were fighting worse than ever. I had to get out. She was fine with me fucking much older men just a bathroom away from her, but a girl? Absolutely not. In fairness to my mother, I don't think she was all that thrilled with the male action either, but she tolerated it. The Taylor situation was just too much for her. We scheduled an appointment with my old therapist.

My mom was concerned that I was choosing a difficult life. I explained that it wasn't a choice and that I believed I was born that way. It went on like this with neither of us understanding the other. Some of it was typical mother-daughter teen stuff, but being gay compounded it considerably.

During one session, I put forth a good argument (one of my strong suits) for moving out on my own, and my therapist begrudgingly gave it the okay. They weren't fans of the idea, but when I set my sights on something, there is very little anyone can do to change my mind or stop me.

I was about to start classes at the delinquent high school down the street from my regular school. Taylor dropped out and got a job fighting fires with the Marin Conservation Corps. We got a two-bedroom apartment with one of her co-workers, a nice twenty-one-year-old boy named Josh. Although I was the youngest roommate, I was the one who talked the friendly older couple into renting to us. I moved out of my mom's place just after my sixteenth birthday. I was psyched to be on my own.

Life was good. Our roommate was awesome. We made cheap dinners, listened to music and smoked weed. None of us had much money and the rent was high, but we were young and our needs were low. Top Ramen, generic food and cheap chili from the deli down the street were satisfying in a way that only the first taste of freedom can be.

I always thought that school was bullshit, and since I had no plans of going to college, I took the proficiency test before winter break and was done with high school. This allowed me to quit pumping gas at night and get a full-time job. Looking back, I'm not sure why I was in such a rush to be a tax-, rent- and bill-paying slave, but I was.

Honeymoons don't last forever, and soon Taylor and I began to have some serious issues. We had nasty fights. We tried to make it work, but we were young and not very healthy of mind. During the previous summer, when we had marched in the gay pride parade, we had become close friends with another teen lesbian named Riley. Riley had intense energy and a magical pull. Taylor and I both had secret crushes on her. The three of us hung out a lot, and it became pretty dysfunctional. This happens quite a bit in the lesbian community.

One weekend, we drove down to Santa Cruz to stay at Riley's dad's house. The three of us shared a bed. Riley slept in between Taylor and me, and while Taylor slept, Riley and I fooled around a little. I felt guilty and tried my damnedest not to flirt with her, but as I've mentioned, I needed a lot of sexual attention from people back then in order to feel good about myself.

The sexual tension among the three of us increased over the next couple of months. I had a sneaking suspicion that Riley and Taylor were up to something. One night, Taylor took off mysteriously, and on a hunch, I drove over to Riley's house where I caught them kissing in the street. I was heartbroken and envious at the same time. Later that night, Taylor and I had a huge blowout fight. It was really ugly. I had thought I was going to grow old with her, but instead, I moved out.

I rented a bedroom from a nice couple and cried every single night for a month. It felt as if my heart was breaking inside my chest. It was awful. Riley and Taylor became a couple and it wasn't long before they moved to Seattle. This was especially devastating because Taylor and I had always talked about doing that together.

About a month after Taylor moved out, Josh suggested that I move back in with him and his new roommate. So I did, and the debauchery commenced. I drowned myself in alcohol and drugs to get my mind off Taylor. I also started fucking Josh for the same reason.

Life was bizarre. We lived in a beautiful, sleepy little Marin town called Fairfax. It was spring, the air was warm, and the scenery was beautiful. The smell of pine and loneliness permeated the air. We went to punk shows. I got into physical fights and did a lot of hallucinogens. I remember long, hot days, high on acid, the afternoon sun filling the living room, making a mockery of my struggle to be happy. I was depressed, to say the least. I wallowed in and cherished my bad feelings. I gave them parades. I made my roommates listen to the *Liquid Sky* soundtrack way too many times. I rarely showered and I didn't eat much. I just didn't give a fuck.

At around this time, I had breast reduction surgery. Thanks to both of my grandmothers, I was blessed (or cursed) with enormous boobs. Being anorexic with huge boobs is a bummer. Large breasts can make you look and feel fatter. After the intensive surgery, I gobbled up all my painkillers in a matter of days. When I kept asking for more, my doctor caught on and reduced my prescription to some lame non-opiates. But I wasn't taking care of myself and one of my scars got infected. Even so, I'm so grateful my mom had figured out a way to get insurance to cover the surgery. I loved having smaller breasts. The female surgeon had removed only fifty percent, so I still had enough to work with, but I felt a hundred times lighter. Unfortunately, that was only physically. Mentally, I still had the weight of the world on me.

One afternoon, I was slumped on our filthy couch feeling like a shell of a human. I didn't want to feel anything anymore and I didn't want to live. I went to the kitchen and found the sharpest knife I could. I pressed that old, heavy blade to my wrist. As trickles of blood appeared, a friend of mine walked in the door. She took me to the Marin General Crisis Unit. I was too exhausted and broken to put up a fight.

24

IT'S DEAD AT the club right now, so I'm writing. My manager is on to me. He just gave me some light-hearted shit about sitting in the audience with a composition book. Fuck it. There's not much going on. Earlier, I had some swigs of a customer's Jack and Coke. He didn't want any dances, but thanks for the free hooch. Our club doesn't serve alcohol, but some guys are savvy and sneak mini bottles in. I just finished a dance with an older black gentleman before I sat down with my composition book. He moved like a turtle but smelled really good. He wanted me to pinch his nipple. He was surprised when his dick got hard. I guess it doesn't happen that often anymore.

❧

Word vomit is a hazard brought on by booze and boredom. I get this at work sometimes. We have to be chatty and interesting, and let's face it, I run out of things to say. That's when I get myself into trouble. Often I tell customers my real age (strippers aren't supposed to be closing in on forty), or that CDs didn't exist when I first started dancing, or that I remember when color televisions and answering machines came out. None of these things are sexy, but they fall out of my mouth like I was given a shot of sodium pentothal. This is generally the point when I can see my potential lap dance fading away.

❦

I can't seem to get fucked up enough tonight. I've been drinking and drinking and taking pills, and I still feel sober. It's a phenomenon that happens from time to time. If I ingested this much crap outside of work, I'd feel utterly wasted. There's something about a strip club. It's like a casino; you never know what time it is and everything that happens in here stays in here. Sometimes the drugs and alcohol will hit me all at once, and I'll get way too fucked up. I'm always trying to achieve the perfect state of mind at work. I want to feel the effects enough to flirt, but I also need to stay present enough to make money and drive home. I know driving isn't the smartest thing. I usually stop drinking halfway into my shift, or at least I try to.

❦

I worked out a deal with a guy to go to his hotel room after my shift tonight. I don't want to, but I can use the money. It's less than my usual fee, but considering it'll be after 2 a.m., I'm not expecting it to be a long one. Truthfully, I didn't have the energy to negotiate or say no. I'm secretly hoping he doesn't call. My eyes are already the same burgundy shade as the VIP curtains. I made a margarita concoction to drink tonight and it's clearly run its course. I look like shit. Do I really want to go to this strange guy's hotel room? That's a resounding no.

It's moments like this when I'm jealous of my friends with family money. They've never had to ask themselves these kinds of questions. They can turn to their parents if times get tough. They have that support, that knowledge. Not that you need a trust fund in order not to hook. I'm just saying it must be nice to know there's a safety net if you need it. I have the opposite. I have given my mother more money in our lifetime than she's ever given me. I'm happy to do it. I love her. I'm just praying that by the time my mom is too frail to work, I'll be able to support her. Either that, or that she stays healthy, grows old and dies suddenly. I like my life and I stand by my choices, but once in a while – like at 1 a.m. when I'm dead tired and putting myself in a possibly dangerous situation for money – my choices seem less glamorous.

What're the odds of him calling? Five to one? It's so late already. I bet he got to his hotel room and passed out after the magic of the club's inner sanctum wore off. I can see it being easy for a man to lose sight of why he'd pay a stripper to come to his hotel room. This guy doesn't know me. I could be a complete nut, a con artist, a bitch or a bad lay.

An hour later, he calls. I'm going. I'm trying to remove some of the blue eyeshadow before I leave the club so I look a little less hooker-y walking through the hotel lobby. That's always my favorite. They must know. Thank god I wore a cute shirt tonight. I don't usually look cute when I go to work. I have a forty-five-minute drive in stop-and-go traffic and a late-night drive back. The last thing I want to be is uncomfortable after a night in skimpy outfits and body contortions. Plus, after a night in high heels, I'm usually dying to slide into my Chuck Taylors.

After one last trip to the ladies' room for a pick-me-up, I drive my tired ass over to the hotel by the airport. I self-park and begin my walk of shame to room 702. The lights are bright and my eyes are bloodshot. He opens the door with a big smile. He doesn't seem to notice or care that I'm exhausted. He's a lot taller than I remember. I suppose it's because I'm no longer wearing my platforms. We hug. He hands me the cash, which I shove in my pants. I left my purse in the car. I have nothing but my car keys. This way he can't jack me for what I earned at the club. He can kill or maim me, but he won't get my purse.

I give him my usual speech about a friend who's waiting to hear from me by a specific time. He says no problem. I suggest a shower, partially so I can wash off the night and as a good way to start the deed. Two birds, I figure.

His cock is average: short, but with decent girth. Not that it really matters, but of course, I notice these things. We kiss. Yes, I'm a hooker who kisses. I'm not sure why I do or why I didn't implement a no-kissing rule when I started, but it's natural for me to kiss. Plus, if there's anything I can do to turn a client on, it only ensures that the deed will be over faster and I can go home.

We wash each other and as I get out to dry off, I make the mistake of looking in the mirror. Yikes. I'm quite the sight. Jesus, I look ragged. I lay down on the bed and he follows. It's a bit awkward. Being intimate with a stranger can be strange, but it's my job to ease the tension. Then again, I'm basically a crackhead at this point, so who knows how calming I'm being? He goes down on me. I fake a small orgasm. There's no chance for the real thing even if I wanted it. I go down on him.

'Damn baby, you give good head,' he tells me.

'Why, thank you,' I purr and go back to the job. I'm dehydrated from the tequila and pills, so I make an excuse to jump up and drink some water from the sink. He's ready to fuck me. He reaches over to the box of condoms he purchased and hands me one. Apparently, I'm supposed to do it. Fine. I open it with my teeth, place it on the head of his dick, and roll it down. But it won't fucking roll. It's too thin. I open a new one. Same thing. It gets wrapped up in itself. Shit. The condoms he bought are ridiculously thin. I make a mental note of the brand so I'll never buy them for work, realizing at the same time there's no way in hell I'm ever going to remember. I grab a third one. He says he's never worn a condom before, which seems ludicrous, but maybe he's been married for thirty years (*if* he got married when he was five years old).

I finally get the fucker on. Third time's a charm and whatnot. Now if only I had some damn saliva or moisture – anywhere. I try to straddle him, but I'm not wet enough and of course, I don't have any lube. I suppose I should carry tiny packets in my purse like a good ho. I usually just use my saliva, but not tonight. Crap, it's becoming troublesome. I explain that I need to give him head in order to stimulate my saliva glands. I have a crazy physical response to giving head. Slippery, lube-like saliva forms in my mouth. I'm not lying. It's totally different from my regular spit, an entirely different consistency, and I only get it from giving head.

I go down on him, condom and all, which is yucky but it works. It's not Niagara Falls, but it's better than nothing. I use this spit on the outside of my vagina. He gets on top of me. I wouldn't put this on the 'hottest sex' list, but he seems relatively happy. After about ten minutes, I turn over on my stomach. It's a little better. I tighten my pussy muscles, hoping this action will aid him in getting off, but he pulls out after maybe eight minutes. I'm parched like a motherfucker. I giggle and drink more tap water. He must think I'm out of my mind, which, of course, I kind of am.

'I want to jack off and come on your tits,' he says, as I'm sauntering back from the sink.

Excellent idea! I lick his hairy balls and he moans. I haven't met a guy yet who doesn't like his balls licked.

'I'm really close,' he says.

I jump up and lay next to him. He sits up and strokes it faster and comes on my breasts – a decent amount for an older guy and almost no smell. Now I can go home.

I wash off and make idle chit-chat while I get dressed. We're both exhausted, but he's happy. It pleases him to hear that I had two orgasms (wink, wink). He can sleep soundly now. We thank each other and hug again at the door. It's 3.30 a.m., and I'm walking back through the lobby a little richer than before. The best feeling in the world is driving away from a john.

Shit, I forgot to pee.

25

IT'S UNCOMMONLY DARK on the floor tonight. I've complained in the past about it being too bright (no one wants it to look like a 7-Eleven), but I can't even see across the room! I sprayed perfume in my face earlier by mistake, and now it's up my nose. It's all I can smell. I suppose it could be worse.

Riddle me this. Why the hell is there a super-bright, yellow halogen spotlight shining from above, traveling around the floor? Do you know what a bright-as-fuck yellow light looks like on a naked girl? Jaundice, that's what. I'd love to make all the male employees, owners and managers get naked and walk on stage and around the floor for an hour. I bet the lighting would change the next day. It's mind-boggling. Isn't the idea to make us look our best? Of course, I'm probably the only weirdo who notices. It's a curse to notice everything. I exhaust myself. If you spent a day inside my head, you'd need a nap. My eyes sting.

There's a new sign up in the dressing room that reads, 'No two rap songs in a row'. I've been sitting here listening to at least twenty-five minutes of rap. Who are those signs for? I get why they have to put the ones up about no prostitution, but everything else seems to be ignored. Yes, that's right, we need signs in the dressing room reminding us *not* to be whores. I'm grateful this is a clean joint, but I've always assumed those signs were mandated by law, like the 'Employees must wash hands' signs in restaurants. There should be signs in the men's bathroom that say, 'Ignore your urge to ask for a blowjob' and, 'These girls are strippers. If you want more than a lap dance, check Craigslist'. I wouldn't mind adding one more that reads, 'If you don't plan on spending money, please get the fuck out'.

26

I HAD SPENT three nights at the Marin General Crisis Unit when they contacted my mother. I was living on my own and supporting myself financially, but because my parents didn't bug me, I had never bothered with a legal emancipation. Unfortunately, this meant that I was still legally under their jurisdiction.

I was young and disgruntled and being held in the Crisis Unit against my will. I was wearing a torn Clash T-shirt and jeans held together by safety pins. My mom called the psychologist I had seen when I was fourteen and she suggested sending me to Gladman Memorial Hospital. On a visit to the Unit, my mom told me that Dr What's-her-name suggested I go to this place in the East Bay for the weekend. She added that there would be other kids my age there and that it would just be for the weekend. I didn't want to go, but I had no other options. So I went along with their little weekend getaway plan.

My mom drove me to East Oakland. We pulled up in front of Gladman on East 27th and Fruitvale Avenue. Upon entering the facility, it was pretty clear that it was a mental institution and that this would be no weekend getaway. I protested, but it was pointless; they already had a bed with my name on it and were drawing up the bills to the insurance company. I was powerless, which only added to my state of mind. I was simultaneously enraged and empty.

They stuck me in Unit Two. Unit One was for people who were less insane or less likely to hurt themselves. I was with the psychotic and endangered teens. It was surreal, to say the least. The endangered and bored messed with the loony. They were endless entertainment. Some of them had been locked up for well over ten years. We were angry, and they didn't know better. Most of the kids were around my age, but some were much younger. There was a sweet twelve-year-old who had tried to hang herself – she still had the mark around her neck. I got the distinct feeling that some of the really young people were locked up due to the fact that their parents couldn't or didn't want to deal with them. I suppose the same could have been said for me, but I was living on my own and was therefore a burden to no one.

Inside this cement circus in the hood, we were forced to attend a billion meetings and therapy sessions. They were trying to fix us (or heal us . . . tomato, tomahto). We had to earn points in order to move to Unit One, which was more relaxed and where we weren't on twenty-four-seven watch. Earning points meant you had to have a good attitude and follow the rules. I had a shitty attitude and was anti-establishment. I stayed in Unit Two for a while.

None of the shared bedrooms had locks, which meant that the nutrolls had free rein to go through your shit. One of the female lifers would leave messages for me on my nightstand that said things like, 'God called for you'. She was a schizophrenic kleptomaniac. I think her name was Judy. Looking back, maybe she wasn't as crazy as it seemed because her notes usually made me smile, which was a rarity.

One monotonous day I was walking down the hall and saw her wearing one of my T-shirts. I got one of the guards. She had on five or six T-shirts, all safety-pinned to her bra straps. We went to her room and found all kinds of items in her drawers, none of them belonging to her. Who knows how long she'd been working at that collection? That's institutional living for you. The lithium shuffle. Kids on Ritalin. Cancer in the small enclosed smoking area with the only television. Peach walls. No hope. And the sound of gunfire outside the barred windows. I wasn't getting better, just more morbid. I wrote down the lyrics to Phil Collins's '*In the Air Tonight*' and sent it anonymously to Arty, my mom's old drug-dealer friend who had left his mark on my soul. Classic teen move.

Coupled with losing my freedom, I was in extreme pain for the first week. Apparently I'd had a serious urinary tract infection that I had ignored. I had wondered why it was difficult and painful to pee, but I had just assumed it was the mushrooms or acid. I was put on antibiotics, a mild painkiller and cranberry juice. They'd call me up to the nurses' station and watch me take the pills and drink my juice. It was very *One Flew Over the Cuckoo's Nest*.

The only thing I liked about Gladman was bingo night. Every Saturday night we played bingo in the dining hall. Playing bingo with the mentally unstable is comical, but also frustrating. Someone yells, 'Bingo!' every five minutes. You don't have bingo, freak show, so stop yelling it. I won a pair of striped tube socks. I kept those socks for years.

Then there was the old Rorschach test. Of course, I lied like a good little girl. I told Dr What's-his-name that I saw butterflies and lollipops when in reality I was seeing death and decay. I wonder what he wrote down about me? Probably something like: 'This girl thinks she's so smart, but she's not fooling me.' I wonder if that's part of the test – if the answers are categorical bullshit. It's not what you see, it's what you lie about seeing.

My doctors eventually decided that my problems didn't stem from a mental disability, it was the drugs and the alcohol – so they sent me to a teenage rehab center in the small town where I grew up. Of all the rehabs in the Bay Area, I ended up back in San Geronimo Valley, the birthplace of my angst and torment.

I begrudgingly went through the intake, and when my mom left, I made the rookie mistake of mentioning to a fellow 'camper' that I was going to kill myself as soon as I was alone. It was stupid. I just assumed she would be on my side, but she wasn't. She told the counselors and they called my mom. They said they couldn't keep me because it wasn't that kind of facility; they couldn't place me under twenty-four-hour watch.

After being there for a total of five hours, a police car came to take me back to the Marin General Crisis Unit. The cop made me remove all the safety pins from my jeans so I couldn't hurt myself. I'm not sure how I could have managed that, seeing as he handcuffed my hands behind my back for the long ride. The poor cop. He wanted to be shooting at criminals, not escorting miserable teens, but that's the action in Marin.

So I was right back where I started. There was more talk among the adults, and I was shipped back to Gladman. This time I put up a fight. They literally had to drag me out of the hospital. It was all *very* dramatic. My dad was there this time. We weren't close, and I wasn't thrilled with his presence, which only added to my chagrin.

I was crying and making a complete scene the whole way to Oakland, saying the meanest shit to my mom. When we got close to the freeway exit, I tried to jump out of the moving car. My dad was doing eighty miles per hour and I was halfway out the window. My mom was screaming and trying to grab me. I was thinking if I could reach the tire, it would pull me under. I wanted to die before we hit the exit; I didn't.

After a few more weeks of the same bullshit inside the peach walls, my yearning for freedom replaced my need to rebel, and I came to the realization that I needed to play their game in order to get out, so I started behaving. I eventually earned enough points and made it to Unit One.

My delinquent high school graduation took place while I was locked up. The hospital gave me a six-hour pass to attend. I had stopped going to school in January and I was only a junior, but the school invited me to graduate with the seniors in May. It felt incredible being free, although it was bittersweet knowing I had to go back to the hospital. The ceremony was held at a beautiful location in San Anselmo, surrounded by trees and peacefulness. After the ceremony, when my friends were going to party, I had to return to the fucking mental institution in East Oakland. However, before going back I did manage to sneak off to have sex with my roommate Josh, who was now my boyfriend.

Gladman was affiliated with an adult rehab center next door. I spoke to one of my counselors, who set up a meeting with the head of the rehab center. I convinced him to let me join the twenty-eight-day program. I was two years younger than the minimum age, but they admitted me anyway. I had no intention of joining Alcoholics Anonymous or staying clean; I just wanted to get the fuck out of that hospital. I missed my friends, my boyfriend and the acid I had in my freezer.

Two weeks into rehab, I broke my hand while playing volleyball. Don't ask me how. After waiting for a few painful hours at the Alta Bates ER with a counselor, they put my hand in a cast and gave me pain meds – which I was to take under very strict watch. I pretended to take a pill one day so that I could double up on the next. That night when I took both pills was the first time I didn't like being high. The pills made me feel sick and cloudy, and I wanted it to be over. It was a breakthrough moment. I didn't tell anyone. I had already found out the hard way that authority figures often used things against you. Instead of hearing what this meant to me, they would likely concentrate on the doubling up. But the significance of it was not lost on me, which was the only thing that really mattered.

As in Gladman, the rehab center had lots of groups. We watched classic 'Don't Do Drugs' movies, which was ironic because I had been in a 'Don't Drink and Drive' after-school special a couple of years before. We were hooked up to biofeedback machines and made leather bracelets. We went to local AA and Narcotics Anonymous meetings, where I was a minority in age, race and background. I thought the meetings were bullshit, but I kept my mouth shut. I was counting down the days. When it finally came time for me to graduate, my counselors said I was never going to stay clean. That bugged me. I didn't like being told what I was or wasn't going to do, so being the stubborn person I am, I set out to prove them wrong. I wonder if that tactic has worked on other people?

27

I WAS ECSTATIC to end my stay at Gladman. Time in a psych ward feels like an eternity. Once out, I did everything they told me not to do and nothing they suggested. They wanted me to attend ninety meetings in ninety days: nope. They suggested I get a sponsor: nah. Keep away from friends who were using? No. No relationships? Yeah, right. Don't drink or use: yes!

The boys had lost our apartment while I was locked up so I was sleeping on the couch at my boyfriend's house. He had a roommate who drank a case of beer a night. But since I was out to prove the 'know-it-all' counselors wrong, I didn't partake. A few months out and still sober, I was introduced to a girl named Jennifer. She was fourteen and had been clean for a year. She showed me the heart of NA. I had hated meetings before, but she took me to an amazing NA meeting in San Anselmo, which became my home group for a very long time. It was then that I fell in love with the program. I never did ninety-in-ninety, but I started doing all the other stuff. My home group was full of ex-convicts, hookers and society's rejects. They were my kind of people. Even though I was only sixteen and hadn't lived as much as my peers, I fit right in. Everyone was sarcastic, had a dark sense of humor and had big hearts. Besides the overuse of drugs and booze and the propensity to be an asshole, that's what you'll find in the twelve-step program. The people in AA and NA taught me how to love myself, how to be honest and have integrity. I grew up in the program. I never had the compulsion to drink or use – staying sober was easy for me. I saw people struggle and relapse and I always felt extremely lucky.

I spoke at tons of meetings and was even selected to tell my story at a young people's convention in front of sixteen hundred people. I chaired meetings in jails and prisons. I spoke at a meeting in San Quentin when I was eighteen, and I held a weekly NA meeting inside a jail cell for two years at the Marin County Jail. Nothing makes you feel more grateful than leaving a jail cell. I attended classes at junior colleges and eventually made my way to San Francisco State University. I changed my major from psychology to pre-law with a minor in criminal justice, and the topic of my senior thesis at SFSU was prison reform. The program was my life. I never pushed it on others or judged people who drank and used. I'd go to bars and clubs and say, 'No, thank you' if someone offered me something. It was a non-issue.

28

IT'S FRIDAY NIGHT and I'm with my first guy. We'll call him Lazy Eye. He has a lazy eye. I sit down next to him in the audience. 'Hi baby, how are you?'

'I'm good.'

'Have you been to the club before?'

'Yep.'

'Welcome back!'

'Thanks.'

'I like your shirt.'

'Thanks.'

'Do you live in Los Angeles or are you visiting?'

'Visiting.'

'From where?'

'Outside of California.'

This guy is giving me fuck all to work with, just answering my questions and not elaborating. 'What do you like to do for fun?' I ask, trying to get something going.

'The usual things.'

Okay, fuck the small talk. 'Do you know how the dances work?'

'Yes,' he says, followed by an awkward pause.

'Would you like one?'

'Sure, but I want the cheapest dance, and let's wait for the next two-for-one.'

I mentally donkey punch him. 'Okay.'

Lucky for me, a two-for-one comes up quickly and I take him to the topless area. It's not *the* cheapest dance, but fuck him. The song starts and almost immediately he tries to touch my boobs. I tell him no.

He frowns. 'You're the only one in here who won't let me touch her breasts during a forty-dollar dance.'

Yeah, right. I know this isn't true. He keeps trying. He's seriously annoying me, but I just smile and hold his hands down.

Then he says, 'Just because you have the best tits in the club doesn't make you special.'

I literally laugh out loud. 'Did I say I was special?' I ask.

'I think there was a compliment in there somewhere.'

I smile. He gives me a blank, one-eyed stare, and our two-for-one ends. I get off his lap and reach for my top. The fucker says he wants me to stay for another dance. They're doing back-to-back two-for-ones. Lucky me.

Lazy Eye tells me how much he loves my body and how he 'normally dances with skinny girls'. I laugh again. Thanks, Lazy Eye. He elaborates and says, 'Anorexics.'

'Yeah,' I said. 'I got your point. I'm not super skinny. I like food, and I don't starve myself from self-hatred anymore. Sue me.' Of course, I happen to be feeling icky about my body that day, and now I have to listen to this crap from a lazy-eyed piece of shit who probably hasn't had sex with a woman in ten years. I often wonder if men get off being mean to dancers. They pay admission and unload a lifetime of resentment onto pretty girls. We let it slide, night after night.

There's a young, new girl mouthing the words to the song on stage, which is a major no-no. She doesn't even know all the lyrics. Oh honey. The club has been hiring new girls at an alarming rate. They've never hired so many girls in such a short time before. It's as if Martin, the owner, is shipping them in from Nebraska. They're seriously young too, fresh off-the-bus types. Even though I'm old enough to be their mom, they aren't taking any money away from me. These girls have the conversational and hustle skills of a houseplant. We don't really have the traffic to justify them, but I get the concept of having fresh meat. But what if they're flushing out the old girls? Nah. Why would they? We still make money. It's good to have a balance of teen pussy and women who can carry on a conversation.

It's a couple of hours later and I've just been with a man who told me he got a dance from me a year ago and was wondering what had happened to me. Then he said that I was much more fun the last time. Sorry, boo boo.

The next man said, 'You're the ideal woman.' Really? Is it because I'm wearing sheer panties, or because my boobs are popping out of my top? Or, maybe it's because I'm smiling and flirting with you. The requirements to be the ideal woman are pretty remedial for this crowd.

29

MY FIRST SERIOUS relationship after I got sober was with a man named Eric. I met him at a meeting in San Rafael. Eric was only twenty-three or twenty-four at the time, and I was barely eighteen, but he seemed so much older to me. He ran his own asbestos removal company and made a decent living. Eric was from Arkansas. He loved Harleys and Elvis. Our apartment in Novato was drenched in Elvis memorabilia. In my chameleon-like nature, I got a perm, wore acid-washed jeans and cowboy boots. I was biker chick Suzy Homemaker. I tried to make tuna casserole, and I even hand-sewed oven mitts!

Eric was a good person. He was newly sober, a Christian and a member of a sober bike club. We went on lots of motorcycle runs. It was so much fun! Riding down a two-lane highway with three hundred Harleys is a powerful feeling. You'd never know by the look of us that we were all clean and sober. I even went to Eric's church service a few times. It was actually really nice. I didn't spontaneously combust, and the preacher spoke mostly about love and family.

Eric and I lasted for about a year and a half. In the end, we were just too different. It ended and I moved out of his Elvis house. About a week after I moved out, my teenage crush Riley called to say that she was back in town and single, and since I still harbored feelings for her, I jumped at the chance to see her. The spark was definitely still there, and we immediately fell into a relationship. I don't waste time in this department. I lead with my heart.

Riley and I stayed together for a little over four years. She saw me deal with a lot of my childhood shit during my early period of sobriety. It wasn't always a pretty sight, but she stuck by me, for which I give her a lot of credit. Riley wasn't in the program, but she was very supportive, and we had a good thing for a long time. We were the ideal a lot of our young gay peers wanted to be – the all-American lesbian couple. Everyone loved our long, romantic story: that we had met while still in high school and then ended up together years later.

Of course, Riley and I had our share of problems. We both had bad tempers. There were huge bouts of jealousy on both sides. When I was young, jealousy infected my love life tremendously. Near the end of our relationship, in a last-ditch attempt to make things work, and thinking that we just needed personal space, I moved out of our Castro Valley flat and rented a room with other lesbians just two blocks away. It ended up being a stepping-stone to the demise of our relationship.

During this time, I met a young man named Ryan. We met at San Francisco State University. We had a couple of classes together and struck up a friendship. Ryan was tall, smart and super funny. I loved being around him. Riley and I were having our issues and it was nice to have a break from all that. I never thought I'd date a man again, but Ryan and I would pass fun notes to each other during class, and after a while, they started getting a little sexual. The taboo factor was high. The note passing was a fantastic aphrodisiac. I don't think a criminal justice class has ever turned anyone on like that.

It became clear that I was falling for Ryan, and never having cheated on anyone, I broke things off with Riley. It was hard and I was conflicted, but in my heart, it felt right.

Around the same time, a new lesbian roommate moved into our railroad flat. She was cute as a button and worked part-time at the Lusty Lady. She was my stepping-stone into the industry. Ryan was less than thrilled when I got hired. It was a lot for him to stomach. We had many, many late-night discussions about it. I loved Ryan, so we tried to make it work. I thought the fact that I was behind Plexiglas was a good argument against him being jealous, but it didn't matter to him. I was naked in front of strangers, and they were jacking off looking at me. When I was finally hired at Mitchell Brothers, it was the nail in our relationship coffin. There were nights when I'd be on the pay phone in the dressing room fighting with Ryan about my work. It's so difficult to fight with someone you love about what you do for a living and then hang up and go flirt and hustle. By the same token, work often functioned as a way for me to escape my problems at home.

While I was still working at the Lusty Lady, a bunch of my gay friends, including my roommates, said they could no longer be friends with me because I had become a 'breeder'. They even asked me to move out. My roomies didn't want to hear our 'het sex'. Never mind that one of them was a self-proclaimed vampire, another was a witch, and I loved them regardless; they still wanted me out. It was painful and unfortunate. I had fought for the gay community since I was fifteen. It was shitty and unenlightened to shun me like that. However, it did eventually make me realize that I didn't have to choose sides. 'Bisexual' was no longer a dirty word. I could be myself. I didn't stop myself from falling in love with a girl when I was a teenager, so why should I stop myself from loving a man?

After Ryan, I dated and slutted my way around San Francisco for a while. I had real money for the first time in my life, and I felt like I was on top of the world. Life was sort of magical. I was living in a stunning flat on the hill near Buena Vista Park in the Haight Ashbury neighborhood, overlooking the city. I had brand new furniture and I ordered delicious food from Waiters on Wheels. I felt like the luckiest girl in the world. I had a diploma from SFSU, money and long-term sobriety under my belt. Life was good.

I had been going to an AA chapter on Union Street for a while and one night, I met a cute boy named Jacob. He was a trust-fund baby and the only fellow Jew I've ever dated. Our relationship was a little controversial at first because he was living in a halfway house. Halfway houses are set up to support addicts and alcoholics post rehab, before they go out into the real world. I had been sober eight or nine years whereas Jacob had only a month and change. Dating a new and more vulnerable member in the program is known as 'thirteenth stepping', and it's frowned upon in the sober community. But it happens all the time.

Jacob's family was very loving and treated me as if I were a member of their tightknit family. He was by far the wealthiest person I've ever been with. I went to school with rich kids during my two years at Redwood High, but I was unaccustomed to that sect of society. My mom and I shopped at Goodwill and shared a bathroom with seven other people. Being around that kind of wealth was a struggle for me at times, but I had graduated from college, was making good money and held my head high. It's amazing what money can do for your self-esteem.

Jacob's mother paid for almost all of our outings. You wouldn't believe how many events wealthy people are expected to attend! There are cotillions, restaurant openings and vineyard parties. It was such a drastic departure from anything I had ever known, yet somehow, it felt natural. I've always had a knack for fitting in.

I never lied about who I was or what I did for a living. Jacob's family knew and I was honest when anyone asked. I'm sure more than a few people at these events had opinions about strippers, but they never let on when I told them what I did for a living.

Jacob didn't love my job but he loved me, so he dealt with it. It's very 'program' to work on things. Not to bag on my sober years, but I probably wouldn't have stayed in some of my relationships for as long as I did if I hadn't been so entrenched in the 'make it work' philosophy. Granted, I was in my twenties then, so it may have been an age and life experience thing. I'm guessing it was a bit of both.

Although Jacob's family was beyond lovely to me, I felt pressure to do something else for work. Although she never said anything, I know his mother was conflicted when someone asked her what her son's girlfriend did. To her credit, I don't think she lied. I tried to start other careers while we were together, but nothing fit. I bought my first house while I was with Jacob – a beautiful Victorian home in Berkeley. Both my mother and Jacob's mom were very proud of me. I wanted to show the people who loved me what I could accomplish by being an exotic dancer. I earned most of the down payment in three grueling months of double shifts at the club.

Jacob and I hinted at marriage, but never really got there. At one point, I quit dancing and worked at a fancy new restaurant in the city. It was a disaster. I was miserable whereas I had been happy dancing. Straddled with a mortgage, not making enough money and feeling resentful, I went back to the club. Ultimately Jacob and I parted ways.

After Jacob, I had a short stint with a nightclub owner. He loved that I was a stripper. I was his first, and he acted as if he'd won the jackpot. It was a refreshing change. We had a lot of fun together. He visited me at the club a couple of times. It was exciting to perform for him and we even had sex in one of the Private Booths. Unfortunately, he was one of those loves-to-be-in-love types and the affair was short-lived. We broke up in

Venice, Italy, of all places. I wouldn't recommend it. We were a casual couple – our understanding was that we could sleep with other people as long as we used condoms. After being in Rome and Florence together, he told me over a romantic dinner in Venice that he'd started sleeping with a girl back home and was pretty into her. I was vexed and irritated. Why was he telling me this? I didn't want to hear about it while we were in one of the most romantic cities in the world. My feelings for him ran a little deeper than I would have liked and although I didn't want to admit it, this news hurt. Also, why couldn't he have told me over the phone or after our fucking trip! I just wanted to laugh, eat, see Italy and screw. It put such a damper on things that we cut our vacation short, took a train to Milan and flew home. We kept it civil but were distant with each other for the lengthy travel back to San Francisco. It sucked. To this day, I don't understand why he chose that moment to bring it up. Timing is a motherfucker.

Shortly after our untimely breakup, I slept with another AA member named Robert, a friend of Jacob's I had been attracted to. Every woman and gay man thought Rob was a hunk. It was risky sleeping with him because I didn't want to hurt Jacob. Also, during Rob's ten years of going to meetings, the longest sober time he'd ever put together was a year. He was a chronic relapser. But I slept with him anyway. I never thought it would turn into a relationship, but we fell in love almost immediately.

Rob was a wonderful but deeply broken man. He was gorgeous, tall and strong with the most incredible green eyes. Everybody loved Rob. He had charisma in spades. How could I not fall for him? Even though the huge, waving red flags were there, I loved everything about him, even his beautiful, broken soul.

We were together for about a year and a half when he proposed. I knew he was going to; I designed the ring. I didn't know when or how he was going to do it, although I had an inkling of what was going on when he booked us a room at a hotel on top of Mt Tamalpais. We had dinner at the hotel's beautiful restaurant and I could barely eat from nerves. I was worried he was going to pull the cliché move and drop to one knee in front of everyone. I don't like that kind of attention; it makes the bottoms of my feet itch. Naked on stage with blue lights and cash? Yes. A whole restaurant staring at me during an intimate moment? No. But the meal went by without any kneeling and we went back to our room and made love. Afterward, Rob asked me to get his lighter from the fireplace mantel. I walked up to retrieve it for him and there it was: my ring in an open box among all the candles. He had pulled it off. I turned and gave him the biggest smile. I grabbed the box, bounced over to him naked and flopped down on the bed. I put the ring on and kissed him. I don't think he even asked me the traditional question, but I didn't need it. I had him and that was all that mattered.

When we got back to the city, I told him that I wanted a long engagement because he'd already gone through a couple of horribly painful relapses during our time together, and I didn't want to go through that again, especially as husband and wife. It was incredibly naïve of me, but I thought if I could stay clean and sober, so could he. I think he had only six consecutive months of sobriety when we got engaged; I had over eleven years.

Rob and I had troubles, but we also had a great love for one another. Unfortunately, he hated the stripping and brought it up during every argument, even when the fight had nothing to do with my job. He would call me a whore and a bad person. It was extremely painful. I wanted his approval and acceptance and craved his understanding that it was just work and he had no reason to be jealous. Dancing didn't change what we had or the way I felt about him. I couldn't understand why he didn't see that. On the flip side, I hated seeing him struggle, and although *I* know it's just a job, I understand that it takes a lot of trust and confidence to date a stripper.

Just as I did when I was with Jacob, I looked for other work so that I could quit dancing and salvage my relationship, even though it wasn't what I wanted. Looking back, it's clear that Rob's treatment of me was unfair, and it wasn't my issue to bear. He knew I was a dancer long before we were intimate. Had he been honest with himself, he would have acknowledged that he wasn't equipped to handle it. Of course, that's easier said than done.

I had been saving money and sold my house in Berkeley after renting it out. I hated living in Berkeley and had moved back to the city. I had enough to buy a beautiful two-story condo on Clayton Street. I bought it from Rob's sister and her husband. They gave us a great deal, and even though I put all the money down and my name was on the loan, I put Rob's name on the deed. That turned out to be a terrible mistake.

30

THAT SUMMER, I met a man named Todd. He came into Mitchell Brothers periodically with a friend whom we all called the Hundred-Dollar Man because he gave each girl a crisp one-hundred-dollar bill when we were on stage. As you can imagine, the duo lit up the place every time they came in. We were making good money at the club at the time, and the stage was a whole different animal back then – guys actually tipped the girls – but for a man to give every girl a hundred dollars for as long as he was in the club was rare. These two had been frequenting the club for a few months, and although they were extremely generous with everyone, they only bonded with a few of us. On very special nights, one of them would hand wads of hundreds to me or to one of my lucky friends. It was insane! Neither of them ever got lap dances or private shows. Todd didn't even like sitting in the front row. I talked him into sitting at my stage once, and although he covered the stage with hundreds, he looked away when I spread my legs. We struck up a friendship of sorts. I had no idea who he was, save for the fact that he was atypical, had money to burn, seemed to have a kind soul and was extremely intelligent.

Todd called me one night as I was walking down Polk Street on my way to work and asked if I would like to do some nutmeg compound with him. I had no idea what he was talking about. He said it was like ecstasy. I said thanks but no thanks and explained that I was clean and sober. He told me to think about it and said it was a fantastic experience.

I didn't think much about it at first, but his description would occasionally creep into my thoughts, and one day I made the decision to try it. I had been clean for a very long time, and I was ready for a new chapter. I was also feeling disenchanted with the program. I had been working on myself diligently for so long, yet I still felt impatient and controlling. I'm on anti-depressants now and probably should have been on them all along, but I was determined not to take what I referred to as 'the easy way out' when everyone and their mothers started taking them in the nineties.

I called Todd and said that I wanted to do it. We made a date. He got a room at a fancy hotel and suggested that I call a friend to take it with me. He wanted to make sure I felt safe. I called a girl I knew from the club because most of my non-dancer friends were in the program. Maybe this decision to break my sobriety should have been a much bigger deal, but honestly, it felt right and I was at peace with it.

The big night arrived and I must have told Rob that I was working. I was both nervous and excited. I was the type of sober person who wouldn't even drink cough syrup – it had been a very long time since my state had been altered. Never having done ecstasy, I had no idea what to expect and no one to ask about it. Obviously, some of the girls at the club could have told me, but I wasn't ready to air my business, so I just went for it. I was putting a lot of trust in Todd.

I arrived at the hotel and tried to make myself comfortable. Todd had the ability to create a sense of calm, which helped, but I was in unchartered territory and my stomach was doing backflips. My friend showed up a short time after me. Todd explained what I was about to do, but he was something of a master chemist and most of what he said went over my head. It turned out that Dawn had done ecstasy, and she assured me that it was fun. Todd lit candles and played music for us. It took a while to kick in, but my stomach started feeling wonky and sort of puke-y. They both said it was okay and that the 'nutmeg' was starting to work. Dawn ran a bubble bath in the huge tub for the two of us while Todd stayed in the living room and acted as trip DJ. He was such a gentleman. The nutmeg started hitting me during our bath. I was surprised at the giddiness I was feeling. It felt spiritual and as if my heart was opening. I had never experienced anything like it. The acid and mushroom trips I'd experienced as a troubled teen were negative and riddled with anger. They were full of blood and darkness. But this was light and love.

When I got home late that night, I immediately told Rob what I had done. He wasn't mad at all. Instead, he was excited because this meant he could use with me. Foolishly, I said okay. I knew his problem was alcohol so I thought it would be all right if we tried something else, which was pretty naïve of me. Of all things, he said he really wanted to get stoned with me. I said sure. He procured a joint in surprisingly short order, but I guess bartenders have all the hookups. I drove him to his dealer, and then we parked on the Embarcadero by the Bay Bridge and got high together. I hated it instantly. It was then that I realized that the copious amounts of weed I'd smoked when I was young was a form of self-punishment. It was never a good high for me, but I had smoked it because I thought I deserved to be miserable.

I begged Rob to drive us home and I crawled into bed. I wanted it to be over. I was fine the next day, but it started Rob on a downward spiral. I told all my sober friends and sober people that I sponsored about breaking my sobriety. I had nothing to hide and I was not ashamed. I explained that I was trying something different and that if it became a problem, I would promptly take myself to a meeting. Since I loved meetings, I knew this wouldn't be difficult. I continued to attend meetings, but eventually it didn't feel right. I still wanted a safe place to talk about my feelings and problems, but it just wasn't appropriate after a while. No one struggling with addiction wants to hear about a person 'going out there' without it being a problem. Not that I was advertising, but it became strange when people asked how long I had been sober. Plus, I didn't want to influence anyone or be the cause of anyone else's relapse.

I didn't announce myself as a non-addict in the beginning. I said that I would see what happened before making that call. A couple of years later, some of my sober friends admitted that they had never thought that I was an addict or an alcoholic but that I was just a young girl with emotional problems who ended up in the program.

A month or so later, Todd came into the club by himself. Rob and I had been fighting something awful, and I was feeling pretty down. Todd could tell something was wrong. He asked for a private dance, which was a first, but told me to keep my clothes on because he just wanted to talk. We sat on the little couch in the small, mirrored room, and he asked if I was all right. I didn't speak about my relationships with customers, so I skipped that part and just said that I was stressed out. He asked me how much money I would need to take a month off from work; he assumed it was my job that was bringing my spirits down. I said I would think on it and give him a figure.

Two days later, I told him the figure, and he said okay. I was astounded! I was making good money at the time, but I had tacked on a little more to be safe. Todd clearly had it to burn. I lied to Rob and said that I wanted to take some time off work. Even though it was completely above board, he would have thrown a fit if I had told him where the money had come from. Rob was extremely jealous and hostile about *everything* concerning my job. I loved him something fierce, but honestly, it was exhausting.

A week after I took the money, Rob and I got into a raging argument. I don't remember how the fight started, but one afternoon we were in our living room, screaming bloody murder at each other. He was standing in front of the sliding glass door to the back-deck smoking when I took off my engagement ring and threw it at him. The ring sailed through the open door and out over the ledge; never to be seen again. I instantly regretted the move. Rob had worked his ass off to buy me that ring and it wasn't cheap. He was livid. He picked up a chair and crashed it into a side table next to where I was sitting, shattering glass everywhere. I grabbed my purse and left. I knew he would drink. I knew it with all my heart and soul. I stayed at Dawn's house that night and brought her with me the next day to pick up some of my things. It wasn't that I thought Rob would hurt me – I knew he'd never lay a hand on me – but I just couldn't face him alone.

As I suspected, he'd been drinking. When he drank, it was like the movie *Leaving Las Vegas*. There were gallons of vodka, convulsions and tears. It was agony to witness. I knew our relationship was over. I had made it clear that I wouldn't stay if he relapsed again. Rob was the last man I dated who couldn't handle my dancing career. He was also the last alcoholic.

Todd offered to let me stay with him in his huge, two-bedroom hotel suite near Union Square. Todd and I were going to fancy dinners and talking for hours while my ex-fiancé was holed up in my house, drinking himself into oblivion. It would be an understatement to call Todd eccentric. We would sit down in a restaurant and he would immediately rearrange everything on the table and order five non-alcoholic things to drink. Todd didn't drink much alcohol. At that point, neither did I. I thought he was wonderful. I saw a kindred spirit in him. We had a lot of fun together.

Todd had to leave town, so he booked and paid for a room for me at the Mandarin Oriental Hotel. I was living out of suitcases in a nine-hundred-dollar-a-night hotel room while paying for an expensive mortgage on a condo less than three miles away. I couldn't kick Rob out since I'd added his name to the deed. It was a mess, and while it was one of the hardest things I've had to go through, the following months were also among the most remarkable times of my life.

I had never met anyone like Todd. He had the most magnetic energy; it felt good just to be near him. I wasn't the only one who felt that way. Over and over, I saw how people were drawn to him. At one point, he told me that I was one of the few people who rejuvenated him in this way. He said it was rare for him to find a strong energy like mine. Todd wasn't especially good looking. He was six foot six and weighed approximately two hundred and fifty pounds. He had hair all over his body, except for his head, and he wore glasses. However, his hair was baby soft and he always smelled like soap. But none of it mattered; I was falling for him.

My month off work turned into several months. Todd had some secret business in Santa Fe, so off we went. I had no idea where all his cash came from, and I found that I didn't really care. He told me that he'd made money early in his life and had investments. I didn't ask questions. I just wanted to be around him and was grateful for his financial help. He paid all my bills and gave me extra spending money. He was extremely generous with me. In turn, I spoiled the people around me – including a couple of expensive shopping sprees for my friends. Todd made me feel like his money was my money and I felt very comfortable spending it. At one point, we even discussed buying my mom a house.

We stayed in two gorgeous, members-only, full-service casitas just outside of Santa Fe. I had a whole house to myself. At that point, we hadn't done anything more than hug. Todd was tremendously respectful of my personal space. One night we took a bunch of pure MDMA (ecstasy in powder form). It was the same as when I had tried the 'nutmeg'. We lit candles and listened to Native American music. The air was cold, so we built a fire in the chimenea on the back patio of his casita and lay on chaise lounge chairs with blankets, looking up at the endless bright stars. We talked until the sky started turning pale. I loved our connection. It wasn't just the ecstasy; I couldn't have picked a more perfect person with whom to break my sobriety. I gathered right away that I'm not one of those sexual types when I take ecstasy. In fact, it makes me so sensitive that I can barely stand to be touched at all. I tend to go the more metaphysical route: connecting with high-frequency energies that are around us and within us. I want to heal people when I'm high.

But something was clearly amiss. Todd and I had to speak in code over the phone and often used burner cell phones purchased at convenient stores. Even so, I didn't ask questions. He was a mystery and I was happy to be along for the ride. It was the polar opposite of the life I'd been living, but I felt happy. I felt as if I'd been speaking in code my whole life. The drug dealing I grew up with prepared me for the type of lifestyle I was living with Todd. We traveled a lot. We always stayed in the best accommodations. Todd rented a house on the hill in Stinson Beach and had a hundred-thousand-dollar sound system installed in the living room. We took crazy, off-the-market drugs and blasted new-age-y techno music.

One especially memorable night at that house, Todd, myself, three master yogis, a philosopher and a famous singer took acacia, a bush and/or tree that contains small levels of psychoactive alkaloids. We tripped our balls off for fourteen hours. I had been out running errands, and when I walked into the house, a singer I had listened to my whole life was standing in the kitchen. I tried to play it cool. I'd encountered lots of famous people over the years, but it's rare to find one standing in your house. Todd saw me and gave me a bear hug.

'This is ____,' he said.

Like I needed an introduction! 'Hi, nice to meet you.'

The singer gave me a warm smile and said hello in his British accent. Then Todd said, 'We're going to take acacia.'

I had no clue what he was talking about, but I assumed it was a strange drug. 'Okay!' I said. I went to put my stuff away in one of the bedrooms.

Todd cooked up an unholy concoction. It smelled god-awful – a bubbling, brown witch's brew. I got settled and watched Todd work his strange science. It was the worst-tasting shit. We had to keep this liquid of death in our mouths for as long as we could before swallowing it. One of the yogis spit it up immediately, and Todd had to make her another dose. It was extremely difficult to keep it in contact with my taste buds as every single one was yelling at me to spit it out. But I held fast for as long as I could and finally swallowed. Twenty minutes later, I ran to the bathroom and puked. I barely made it to the toilet in time, which is rare for me. My visuals were already up and running – it was like being on acid and ecstasy at the same time – which made the dark-brown liquid swirling around the toilet bowl a lot more interesting than it should have been.

A couple of hours later, music filled the whole house. Naked yoga masters were in high-level yoga positions. Todd was meditating and I sat cross-legged on the floor with the singer's head on my lap, playing with his hair. He kept telling me how special I was and that I had a gift for healing. Sometime around nine or ten in the morning, my vision turned black and white. The whole world was in black and white. It was such a trip! Then things went skeletal. The trees, the clouds and the falling leaves – everything looked like pieces of white bone. It was time for Valium and sleep.

31

TODD AND I became intimate during our stay at the house in Stinson Beach. He was cautious at first, wanting to make sure it was something I wanted. I did. I wanted to be close to him without boundaries. He had a young girlfriend who was studying organic chemistry at UC Berkeley. They had a non-traditional relationship. She wasn't thrilled about Todd and me, but she liked me and she understood that I could give him things she couldn't, like companionship when he traveled. We spoke openly about the arrangement and tried to make a three-person affair work. Todd and I spent most of our time alone, so it wasn't much of an issue, but feelings are feelings and I knew she wasn't crazy about the whole thing. Todd was a free spirit. I think she knew that his happiness affected hers.

Todd owned an underground missile base in Wamego, Kansas. I think he told me that it was built on one of the Native American energy hot spots, which was a factor in his decision to purchase it. He had converted it into a living space. Todd's base was surrounded by farmland and a few scattered homes and was located down a small road off a two-lane highway, guarded by an electronic gate. The silo was covered by tall green grass. A large metal door sat at the bottom of a wide cement slope. The door opened to the four-thousand-square-foot missile bay. A standard-size metal door sat to the right of the bay and led to the living quarters and hidden rooms. The base had a beautiful marble kitchen and wood-paneled sauna. The living quarters – which included an eleven-hundred-gallon hot tub, three large, carpeted rooms and a massive bath complex made out of jade and imported marble with several showerheads – were connected by a one-hundred-twenty-foot cement and metal tunnel to the missile bay. A large dark room with a lower ceiling sat in between.

Todd had the sound system from the Stinson Beach house shipped to the base and installed by professionals. In the center of the bay sat a Chattam and Wells king bed. There were hundreds of glass candles and with a flick of a switch, you could open the horizontal, titanic, sliding metal door to the outside world.

One night, during another one of our massive, pure-MDMA escapades, we opened that enormous metal entrance late at night and sat on the driveway, music cascading out of the bay and into the misty Kansas air. This was my life for a little while, taking strange and powerful drugs at all hours and recovering for two days. On our recovery days, we'd drive to the nearest big town (ironically called Manhattan) to eat steak and ice cream.

Dimethyltryptamine (DMT) is what makes certain mushrooms more fun than others. Ingesting pure DMT is nothing like eating psilocybin mushrooms; it's a million times more intense. But that was just another Tuesday night at the base in those days.

Todd had a big chunk of pure DMT. He chipped a small amount off the gold-colored, crystal-looking rock, mixed it with butter and put it in the microwave. Once it had melted into liquid form, he sucked it up with a plastic syringe and handed it to me, 'Insert this up your ass. It should hit you quickly,' he said.

I went into his bedroom, lay down on my back on the cushy carpet with my legs in the air and emptied the syringe. A few minutes later, I lost self-consciousness – in the most literal sense. I simply was not aware of myself. What I remember is a visual of dark greens and blues. It looked as if I was in between the sheets of a tightly made bed, facing the fold. Near the far corner of the fold was a being. It didn't say or do anything. It just existed. I wasn't scared. I didn't feel or think anything. It was purely visual.

When I came back to reality, it took me a minute to get my bearings. I looked at the clock. Only twelve minutes had passed. It felt more like hours or days, or like time hadn't existed at all. Then it hit me that my inner voice had not been present during the elapsed time, something that had never happened before. No matter what drug I was on or how bad the trip was, I always had my inner voice to soothe or guide me. I'd tell myself, 'The walls aren't actually moving' or 'Bruce Hornsby's head isn't really four feet around – it's just the drug'.

Todd had tried to explain what it would feel like, but he couldn't have prepared me for what I experienced. Todd believed in my ability to handle large doses, so he had a heavy hand when it came to me.

When I regained my senses, I rushed into the kitchen, 'It's too much, don't mix as much for her!' My use of the English language was extremely simple.

'You should see your pupils; they're huge,' Todd said with a smile. I didn't care about my pupils. Losing my inner voice had shaken me to the core. I didn't speak to Todd or to our friends – all of whom were tripping – for the next two hours. I sat silently in the bathtub, reflecting on what I had just experienced. I wasn't sure if I would rush to do that again, but I was glad to have done it once.

32

TODD INVITED ME to spend New Year's 2000 with him at the silo. He said it was the best place to be if the world was going to fall apart. Unfortunately, he didn't tell his other girlfriend that I would be there, and after my thirty-some-odd hours of travel and little sleep, I arrived to one of the worst nights of my life. I had been in Mexico with my mom, and by the time I landed in Kansas City and drove to Wamego, it was 10 p.m. I was exhausted. It was cold. I drove down the big driveway, parked my car, got my luggage and opened the heavy steel door. I walked down the tube to the living quarters.

Emily and two of her childhood girlfriends were in the kitchen. She was not pleased to see me. Things had become a little more strained between us. Todd was telling her too much. He had told her about how he could come when I gave him head – something he rarely did and that she hadn't been able to make him do. For such a highly intelligent man, he came up short sometimes when it came to intimate relationships. Emily barely said hello to me and her friends said nothing at all. I could hear them whispering as I left to find Todd. I knew instantly that he hadn't told her I was coming. I was furious.

I found him in the bay. He was constructing a huge movie screen. I tore into him. I was a maniac; I couldn't stop crying. My whole body was shaking. I couldn't believe this was happening. I knew my sleep deprivation was affecting my reaction, but I couldn't help it. He said that he was dealing with highly electric shit and couldn't stop to talk to me yet. I told him to fuck off and left.

I walked back down the long hallway, grabbed my stuff, said something derogatory to Emily and got the fuck out of there. I drove toward Manhattan, Kansas. It was almost midnight. I was freezing and couldn't stop crying. I was a mess. I needed to find a hotel. Happy fucking New Year. The new millennium, no less! I called my mother and gave her an abridged version of what had happened. My call waiting beeped; it was Todd. He didn't know I'd left. When he found out I had, he had laid into his counterpart and she had taken off, too. Now he was alone. He convinced us both to return to the silo. We did, and the lot of us took a shitload of MDMA, salvaging what we could of the most significant New Year's Eve of our lifetime.

33

I WAS STILL dealing with Rob at home, but I was miles away, in every sense. Those months after Rob relapsed would have been unbearable if it hadn't been for Todd. It was also the first time since the age of eleven that I wasn't working. But I wasn't with Todd twenty-four-seven, and as the months went by he became more and more difficult to get a hold of. It frustrated me endlessly and hurt my feelings. Not to mention, he was my financial lifeline. He was always changing cell phones, and during a two-week trip I took with friends to Thailand, he dropped off my radar completely. I was sad and confused and out of money. It was time to go back to work.

Rob was in a dark place. His father flew out to try to pick up some of the pieces. But I'm not a savior; patience with his soul-crushing sadness and liver-damaging relapses had grown paper-thin. It was clear that a reconciliation was not in the cards. There was an unfortunate fight between us while his father was in one of the guest bedrooms, during which I punched Rob in the face in a fit of rage. It wasn't a proud moment for me. I decked him while he was detoxing and shaking from alcohol withdrawl. No one could make me see red like Rob. This was pre-Wellbutrin; aka my 'happy pills', and I had almost no control over my anger.

Perhaps a month later, after much deliberation and tears, I finally worked out a deal with Rob to buy him out and get his name off the deed to my house. I gave him a large sum of money and the deed was done. After everything he and I had been through, I just wanted to move on. By the time he moved out of our house in Cole Valley, I had fallen in love and gotten my heart broken by another man. But I moved back into my house.

Heartsick and without hope, Rob struggled to stay sober and find peace. Four years later, in the spring of 2004, he took his own life. The trip to upstate New York to attend his funeral was one of the most heart-wrenching experiences I've ever been through. I drove a rental car from JFK airport directly to the church and sat in the parking lot, weeping. Rob's father almost collapsed when he saw me. Rob's sister said that her father hadn't cried until he saw me. I hugged him and we sobbed together. The funeral was unbearable; I couldn't stop crying.

Rob will always have a piece of my heart. He was an incredible human being.

❧ ❦ ❧

When I went back to work at Mitchell Brothers, things were very different. I was no longer clean and sober. The club served champagne to the girls at the beginning of the night and now I could partake! Dancing buzzed was a whole different ballgame, and needless to say, I loved it. I suddenly understood why most of my fellow dancers drank and used drugs on the job: it's so much fun!

I hosted a big party at my house after our club's annual Christmas party. It was the first time I ever did crystal meth. The Mitchell Brothers' Christmas parties are infamous and over-the-top. They have live bands, food, booze, male strippers and people hooking up all over the building. This was my first adult party with drugs and alcohol. My friend had given me a little crystal at the club, and I was having a blast. She brought more to my house. At one point, I tried to eat some toast and chewed on it for ten minutes. I couldn't swallow it! Eventually I spit it out, laughing my ass off.

I was hanging with a new crowd at work. I had known them for a long time, of course, and had loved them all along, but now that I was partying with them, I was in their secret world. I was also partying with Jim Mitchell and his famous guests. I had always known that drugs existed at the club, but I had been so naïve. I had an image in my mind of what people who did uppers looked like: strung out with no teeth and twitching. This was what I'd heard from the recovering addicts in Narcotics Anonymous. I had no idea that half the girls I was working with were on drugs. They looked good and weren't wasting away. They ate! They were perfectly functional.

I was single and, for the first time in years, was not feeling guilty about stripping. I was feeling good about myself and my life. It's strange that drugs and alcohol were big players in my freedom.

The club often hired cute, young male techs. I'd heard stories about girls hooking up with these guys on the down-low – if a manager or Jim found out, the tech would be fired – but I had always been in a relationship. But now, mama had a brand-new bag! I was trying to decide between two new baby techs and went with the dumber of the two. He was a sweet kid with big blue eyes and ratty, dime-store-bottle-black hair. He also had what is still one of my top ten all-time favorite dongs. He didn't really know what to do with it, but I didn't care. He was fun, and his cock felt good. We carried on for about a month until one lazy shift, I caught eyes with the other tech, Jonny. We started talking, and I discovered that he actually had some depth. He also wasn't quite as shy as I'd thought.

We started hanging out. It was magical. I felt like a teenager – only this time, I was happy. The fact that he was ten years my junior helped in this youthful feeling. He was still living with his mother! A wonderful woman from Ireland, she was warm and friendly, although I imagine she wasn't thrilled that her son was dating a thirty-year-old stripper.

Jonny and I had been seeing each other for a couple of months and during an afternoon cocktail in the Mission, I asked him to marry me. He said yes and twenty-four hours later, we were in Vegas. We checked into the Hard Rock Hotel, had a fancy-ass dinner and followed it with a strip club outing to the Olympic Gardens. It was Christmas Eve, so the action was a little slow. After a couple of drinks, it was time to get hitched. We got into a taxi, but marriage joint after marriage joint was closed. Closed! In Vegas! I hadn't even considered the possibility. I was leaving for a three-week trip to India in a couple of days, and we really wanted to do this before I left. Our taxi driver was kind and patient, and we finally found a place that was open, the Silver Bell. The nice man at the chapel told us he'd wait for us to get back from the courthouse. Our cabbie took us downtown to the courthouse, and back to the chapel. He signed as our witness.

I got married in jeans and Chuck Taylors. I wouldn't have changed a thing. Jonny was the first man I had been with who not only accepted me for who I was but who also really understood what it was like to be a stripper. He was there in the trenches with us. It was incredible not being made to feel bad about dancing. Jonny was mature beyond his years. We had a wonderful chemistry and lots of fun together.

Jonny was in a band and they were getting some attention. Los Angeles was the place to be, so in 2001 I moved to Los Angeles with him to give his band a chance to succeed. My friend moved into one of the bedrooms in my house in Cole Valley and Jonny and I moved to Hollywood. I had never, ever thought I would move to L.A., but it turned out to be a welcome change. I had no idea how much I needed to get out of the city. I was such a San Francisco girl. But with every square inch of the Bay Area home to a hundred memories, it was nice to start with a clean slate.

After living in L.A. for about a year, the shine wore off for me, and I asked Jonny to move out. Although he was mature beyond his years, he still didn't have the life experience and independence that I had. In fact, I had supported us financially for most of the relationship. I was happy to do it as I was making more than enough, but as my love haze dissolved, I felt more like his parent and less like an equal. Jonny moved into a studio down the street. I filed and paid for the divorce. Considering we had gotten married on a whim, I thought it was a miracle that we had lasted for two and a half years. The break-up was much harder on Jonny than it was on me. I was his first real love. We remained friends for years.

I had been living in Los Angeles for a short time when I got a disturbing call from Todd saying that our friend the 'Hundred-Dollar Man' was in jail. He had been caught outside the missile base with an estimated ten million hits of liquid acid. It seems that they were in the business of making acid. I had known they were business partners in something, but I had had no idea what it was. Suddenly, all the cash and speaking in code made more sense. After that bust, there was a ninety percent drop in the availability of LSD worldwide. But the story wasn't clear, and Todd wasn't telling me much over the phone. I hated the fact that such a sweet and tender soul was sitting in prison. He was later sentenced to three life sentences. It's abhorrent. All drugs should be legal. Our jails and prisons are overflowing with men and women who shouldn't be there, and hard-working, tax-paying citizens are paying out the ass to warehouse them.

Not long after Todd's call, I was up at my house in San Francisco when the DEA came knocking on my front door. Two agents came inside and questioned me. I lied about some small things but for the most part, I told the truth. I had had no idea that they were manufacturing LSD, nor had I been involved. Turns out my phones *were* tapped – I had always taken Todd's paranoia with a grain of salt – and I had been on their radar for a while.

They contacted me a few more times, but I wasn't super nervous; I knew Todd wouldn't put me in any legal danger. The DEA eventually decided that I wasn't a key player and left me alone, which was a relief. But the fact that I was even peripherally associated with the largest acid drug bust in the history of the country is nuts.

34

I'M DRINKING VODKA from a cleverly disguised bottle, staring at myself in the dressing room mirror. Just zoning out. It's been a tough night. I feel like a used car salesman. 'Only two hundred miles and she rides like a dream!' Beyond that, the owner is here bugging us again. Are you fucking kidding me? Is he grinding on strangers? Is his ass being squeezed? Is he evading tongues and fingers? I think not. It took all my willpower not to headbutt him when his short, coke-y ass came up to me and tried to tell me how to be a stripper. I did, however, say a little something about how pressuring us was not the way to get his next Ferrari. I tried to say it tongue-in-cheek. He followed me into the dressing room and asked the girls to gather and listen up. It was the same speech he always gave. They know times are tough, he's spending thousands on billboards and advertising, but he needs our help. It's not a flawed concept; it's just a little lost on forty broke girls when there are only five men in the club.

I was bursting at the seams with opinions (and hooch). 'There isn't any money out there, Martin.' He shot me a glance, which I read as, 'I'm not talking about you.' Martin knows I'm a hard worker. Instead of keeping quiet, I followed it up with a slurred, 'You know I'm a hustler, but there ain't shit out there. We can't pull ass from a bush.'

Way to go, Shannon. He pretended not to hear me, which I suppose was best for both of us. It's not the smartest thing to point out the obvious to club owners. But what's he going to do, fire me? It doesn't cost him a dime to have me here. I only make him money. But he could if he wanted to. The system doesn't make a lot of sense. It's backwards on a lot of levels.

Plain vodka. What bullshit. Disgusting. The smell of it reminds me of high school. I threw up a lot of beer and cheap vodka in high school, mostly on purpose. I wanted to reach a level where my mind could shut up, but not drink so much that I'd black out, appear too drunk, or get the spins. I was a 'boot-and-rally' gal. I'd readily put my finger down my throat if things weren't working out the way I wanted. One of my other drinking tricks was to put vodka in an orange juice bottle, skip class, walk to Piper Park just down the street and drink under the willow trees. It wasn't until years later that I realized the police station was also located in the park and that I was actually drinking on their front lawn. Silly girl.

I had to take a break from the sugary-flavored shit for my girlish figure. So that's what I'm drinking tonight, plain Smirnoff out of an Arrowhead water bottle. I guess some things don't change between the ages of fourteen and forty.

None of my regulars can make it tonight, but I danced for Peeping Tom earlier. I consider him a semi-regular; I'm one of about five girls he sits with. Although he's harmless, he's sort of annoying. He gets his nickname from the fact that he tries to sneak his four-inch dick out the bottom hem of his shorts. He's been doing his shorts trick for years and it's always the same. He's gotten gutsier with this move over time by wearing shorter shorts. I spent the whole dance giggling and pulling his shorts down. He was telling me how sexy I was and kept repeating 'Ooooh mannnnn' and 'You're so hotttt' in this elongated, nasal voice. He does it with all the girls. We do impressions of him endlessly in the dressing room.

I can barely stand. I feel a hundred years old. The crowd is horrible and the sad thing is I don't give a good fuck about money right now. Maybe it's the vodka talking. Or it might be the tropical papaya body spray. Or perhaps it's the fact that I've had this very same thought about a thousand times before.

There's a young couple in the audience. She seems nice. I ran into her in the bathroom, and she was pleasant and only a tiny bit freaked out. That was about an hour and a half ago. Now she's by herself and when I get closer, I notice that she's crying. I sit next to her and ask if she's okay. Her stupid boyfriend pressured her into getting a lap dance, not so he could watch, but so he could get one as well. He got a dance in the chair next to hers in the topless room, which has red Plexiglas between the chairs. She watched in horror as he enjoyed his lap dance. Then, when the song was over, he gave her money to pay her dancer and stayed to get another dance! What a dick. Some relationships can handle this kind of thing while others can't. I feel bad for her. She was trying to be strong and rise above the feelings she was having. I told her how lame he was being and gave her a hug. She wiped away her tears as he walked up. Then the DJ called me.

35

FOR FUCK'S SAKE, I hate when grown-ass men whine. I had two pen-worthy dances this evening. Irritant number one was a classic over-fifties guy. He smelled like Brut and was wearing a Tommy Bahama shirt. I could tell right off the bat that he didn't respect women. I peddled a VIP set. We walked back and he sat in my preferred booth. We chatted while we waited for his first song to start. It began and I closed the curtain. As I slid out of my pretty but scratchy top, I descended onto his lap, putting one of my legs in between his and draped myself across him –

placing my chest against his and my mouth near his ear. I told him the rules. He immediately started in with the complaining and whimpering.

'You sold me with false advertisement,' he said, flashing me his best little-boy smile. He thought he was being cute. I ignored his comment and maintained a smile, fearful of the flowing obscenities that would come out of my mouth if I engaged in his childishness. So I danced. Dance, monkey, dance. Good monkey.

Despite his response to my guidelines, he was clearly enjoying himself but testing my boundaries with his grimy fingers at every turn. When I couldn't stand it any longer, I said, 'Sweetie, you can't touch between my legs.'

'But I want to,' he said.

'I know you do, honey, but I've had these rules for a long time, and I'm not changing them for you.' As I was saying this, the fucker grabbed at my pussy! I slapped his hand like he was a two-year-old. After a deep breath, I explained with a tight smile that men who fucked with the rules tended to get a shittier dance due to my lack of trust in them. The concept was lost on him.

Then, into our third song, a stream of whining commenced. Tommy Bahama said he was real tired as he had just flown in from Atlanta. Like somehow this bit of information would change everything and I'd let him touch my box. He was bewildered that his so-called charm wasn't working. For the record, whining is *not* a turn-on. Men, you need to know this. Let me say this again: whining is *never* a turn-on.

The fucker continued to breach my lines. Finally, in frustration, I got on my knees and hugged him. This accomplished two things: it put my pussy out of reach and gave me the opportunity to pat him on the back and be utterly condescending. 'Ah, you tired baby? There, there,' I said, as I rubbed and patted him. He said it felt good. What a joke (although I'm not sure which one of us the joke was on).

I've been addicted to the television show *Mad Men*. Set in the mid-sixties, the men drink like fish, smoke cigarettes like wake-n-bakes and treat women like pencils. Walking away from this guy, it occurred to me how antiquated stripping is. Not the act itself, but the attitude I have to adopt. This demeanor consists of smiles and boobs and switched-off grey matter. Men over sixty-five are generally the most aggravating customers. They're the first ones to go straight between your legs. This fact crosses my mind every time an old-timer solicits a lap dance. It's obvious that a lot of this demographic has little to no respect for women. It's best to act really dumb with these guys. 'How do you boil spaghetti?' dumb. I know this goes against everything feminists have stood for, and everything I've fought for personally in my life, but I'm a hustler with a high cost of living. I would never get a second dance or a tip if I were myself with these pups. Can't teach an old dog not to grab my vagina. I do my part to educate the small-minded men I sit with, but most of these over-the-hill pooches are a lost cause.

Wow, it's an extra special night for Shannon. I just finished dancing for a man in his late thirties or early forties. He was tall, had dirty-blond hair, big hands and a thick Dutch accent. And he was drunkety-drunk-drunk.

'I luf you,' he slurred, as I approached him.

'Yay! Let's go to the VIP!' I had just come from my locker, where I had imbibed three huge gulps of vodka and was therefore a tad more armed for tomfoolery.

'Huh?' he asked as he leant into me and almost took me down.

'Lap dance,' I said.

'Wha?' he asked, confused.

'Free pizza,' I said. Why not?

'You're beautiful.'

'Thank you. Let's go play,' I motioned toward the VIP.

'Where?'

'Come with me.'

'Where?' he was still confused.

'To the VIP. It's only a hundred bucks. It's fun.'

'What are we going to do?'

'Have fun!' I knew I was being evasive, but I also knew that logic and reason didn't apply here. The booze was coursing through my system, putting me on the same level as this gem. Also, he had the biggest smile. I'll take happy drunk over disgruntled man-child any day.

'You're really, really plitty,' he slurred.

'It's a lap dance. You'll like it. Come with me,' I said, as I bounced up and down. I was killing him with my persuasive silliness and my boobs. He stumbled and followed me.

I wasn't overly convinced he understood how much it cost, but I didn't care. I could barely understand a word he was saying and vice versa. I danced and dodged his kisses; the usual. He was a chatty motherfucker, but between his broken English and the slurring, it was a lost cause. So I giggled. When in doubt, always giggle. And put your tits in their faces. He was driving me bonkers with his squirming and his roaming bear claws. Of course, the DJ chose that moment to play the longest song known to man. His breath was bad to boot. I'm sure mine would smell similar if it weren't for the three packs of gum and mouthwash, I go through each shift. One more song to go. I trudged through.

We went to the bar to pay. He was jabbering on about something, but I didn't know what he was saying. He was happy, that much was clear. Allison and I exchanged 'ugh' looks. I sort of gathered that he wanted more dances, so I told Allison to charge an extra VIP set on his credit card. I figured he'd either want to do another set or it would serve as my much-deserved tip. He signed and we went to sit down. He started going on and on about how beautiful I was and that he was in love with me. A bunch of time passed. I was getting ready to leave him and take my extra money when he said he wanted to do a Sky Box! This semi-private dance is upstairs and costs five hundred dollars for roughly thirty minutes. I hadn't seen that coming. Funny thing is, my first reaction was, 'shit'. I wasn't thrilled to spend a solid half hour dealing with this guy, but of course, I was happy to make the money. So I acted excited and told him that I'd be right back. I definitely needed to guzzle more patience and take a trip to the ladies' room for this one.

Bar again, credit card again. The Sky Box is the only dance men have to pay for in advance. Allison looked as surprised as I was, but gave me the way-to-go-sister look. I took him up to the 'Sky Lounge'. The staircase is prominently placed in the club, so all the patrons see you walk up the stairs – it's great advertising. It says, 'yes, my dances are that good.' Our club is large, but it's pretty easy to keep track of which girls are getting dances. And trust me, the men watch.

The dance was unbearable. He couldn't understand why we couldn't have sex. He stuck his tongue out every time any part of my flesh got within close proximity of his mouth. I got on my hands and knees and had him kneel behind me (this room is bigger and has a love seat-chaise lounge combo). Much like with Tommy Bahama, this position kept his mouth far away from me and his hands on my hips (instead of other places). But he was so drunk, he couldn't stay up like that for long, so I moved to the side and he plopped down in my place, on his stomach with his butt slightly up in the air. Fuck it. I climbed on top. I held his hips and ground my pelvis into his backside. It's silly, but easy. His face was smashed into the corner of the probably-never-been-cleaned chaise lounge. He started to roll over, and I decided our time was up. The floater usually tells the dancer when the half hour is done. I'm notorious for going over, but not this time. I couldn't stomach one more minute. I knew drunkie-pants wouldn't have a handle on how much time had passed, but I was fairly certain we had danced for most of the half hour.

'You should come home with me,' he garbled.

I completely ignored the comment. The music was pretty loud, so there was no reason to address it. This whole event will feel like a dream to him tomorrow anyway – until he gets his bank statement.

While zipping up my boots, I sang a happy, 'Let's go, sweetie.' He almost fell coming down the stairs and had to use me to steady himself. At the bottom of the stairs, I gave him a big hug. 'Thank you, honey,' I chirped. 'Have a good night!'

36

IT'S ALMOST 1 A.M. and my left foot is killing me. It shouldn't be; I've taken enough painkillers to kill a small dog, but it's nerve damage, and that shit is no joke. The joke is that I did it to myself. I was perfectly healthy, with two working feet, and then in July of 2005, I tried to kill myself and all I got was some lousy nerve damage. It was my second suicide attempt as an adult. The first took place in San Francisco in 2001. Jonny and I were living in Hollywood, but we happened to be in the city for a combination work-friend visit. One of my nights off was spent with my Mission District group of friends, my non-sober gang. We were out drinking, eating, laughing and having a great night. Near closing time, Jonny and I got into a big, stupid fight. I couldn't tell you what it was about. I left him at the bar and drove up to Twin Peaks (not far from my house in Cole Valley), cranked some meaningful and depressing music, cried my eyes out and decided to kill myself. Suicide has always been my ace – my way out. It's my go-to solution when my life feels like too much to bear.

I downed twenty Valiums and eighty Somas, then wrote a letter in a mini notepad. It was nothing too cynical, or poor me, just a goodbye of sorts. I still have that notepad. There's an obvious decline in my handwriting as the pills started to kick in. It trails off into a sad, illegible scribble.

Post scribble, I drove down the hill to my house. I parallel parked and stumbled into the house. That part is hazy; the rest is unknown.

Jonny and my friend Dawn found me a day and a half later, passed out, sitting on my upstairs toilet, leaning against the wall with my roommate/renter's dog staring at me. They didn't know what was wrong with me. Having no knowledge of the pills, they thought maybe I had shot up dope (which I've never done) because my eyes were completely bloodshot and I was really out of it. They took me to the ER.

The doctors said that too much time had passed, so pumping my stomach wouldn't do much good. The doctor added that he was surprised I was alive. I was asked what I had done and why. I lied. I made something up. I knew not to say the 'S' word. They told me to get rest, and I was released. I slept for another twenty-four hours.

Jonny was only twenty-one at the time and scared shitless. He told my friends, and in secrecy, they met with some hack psychologist who advised them to stage an intervention. Everyone was instructed to write a letter and then read it aloud to me at the intervention. Good times.

My friend tried to trick me the day of the intervention, but I knew I was heading into the lion's den. I spent over twelve years in the program. You don't think I could smell an intervention a mile away? But it didn't matter. There was no getting out of it. I had to suffer through it.

I understand that suicide is painful for friends and loved ones, so I sat like a good girl and let them read their heartbreaking letters to me. I didn't protest but I didn't make concessions either. God forbid a person fight for what they believe in or point out that maybe it's the person who wants to kill themselves that needs love and understanding, not punishment. Call me crazy.

My friends made the obvious points that they loved me and didn't want me to die. I had lots to offer the world. So on and so forth. I saw that I wasn't getting out of this scot-free, so I asked what I could do to make them feel better. Them! They had done their homework. They wanted me to check into the Kaiser psych ward, so I did. My doctors were perplexed. The main man said that he didn't think I needed to be there. I agreed. I was appeasing my friends and getting them off my ass. I never said the word 'depressed', but I participated in the groups. Talking about my feelings has never been difficult for me. Truth be told, I wasn't depressed. I had had a moment and then it was over.

During my week-long stay, I read books, wrote and kept mostly to myself. The one great thing that came out of my stay on Geary Boulevard was Wellbutrin. I've been taking it ever since. It helps me function better. Most of the time I can actually think before I act. I'm also far more patient now than I've ever been in my life.

Interestingly, a short time after my stint in the psych ward, I was hanging with the Mission crew, and the topic of suicide came up. I asked the room if anyone had ever considered it, but I was the only one who had. Up until that moment, I had assumed that everyone considered suicide. It was eye-opening, and I realized that maybe I really did need the meds after all.

A couple of years after Jonny, I was seeing a chef. It was an intense and tumultuous relationship from the start. We fucked and fought like crazy. I loved him, but man, could that guy hurt me. Cash was tall, skinny and handsome with thick brown hair. I called him the anorexic chef. He was a brilliant cook, but he preferred booze to eating.

I had met him about a year before we started dating. He worked with my friend Frannie's boyfriend, Link, and was married at the time. I was attracted to him, but he was off limits, so I paid him little mind. Many months later, on a Sunday evening, the girls (Hattie and Frannie, my two closest friends in Los Angeles – neither of whom are in the sex industry) and I were having dinner at the fancy restaurant where the boys worked.

Cash was the sous chef and within my line of sight for the entire meal. He was extremely sexy. Over dessert and Moscato, I asked Frannie, 'So what's up with Cash?'

'I don't know, let me check,' she said. She texted Link and two minutes later, Cash was sitting next to me.

'Hey,' he said.

'Hey yourself,' I shot back. 'How's tricks?'

'The wife and I split. She moved out today,' he told me.

'Oh yeah?' I could feel the energy between us.

'Yeah, and I got a new mattress that arrived just before I left for work.'

'You want me to come over and help you christen it?' I flirted.

'Yes,' he said without hesitation.

Done. We made out like teenagers in the back of Link's car on the way to Cash's place. Both of us were already buzzed when we reached his flat, but the real drinking had yet to begin. He needed to shower. Would I join? Fuck yeah! I'll never forget it. I undressed, said a little prayer and stepped into the sixties-style stand-up shower with him. His stiff cock hit my stomach. Way above my stomach! My prayer had been answered; I had hit the jackpot. We locked lips and explored each other. Half-wet and on his new bed, we drank tequila out of the bottle, listened to death metal and fucked for hours. It seemed like a natural fit … for disaster. We were glued together from that moment on. Cash and I drank copious amount of alcohol and copulated everywhere we went. The electromagnetic pull between us was so strong it was almost visible.

But then there were the fights. Colossal fights. I even gave him a black eye once. To say that our love was volatile would be a gross understatement, but to say that it ran deep and wide would also be true. Cash was the classic unavailable man. He told me he loved me and was extremely affectionate, but he would never refer to himself as my boyfriend even though we were a couple, and he kept parts of himself at arm's length. It's not that I need labels, but it felt as if he could drop my fragile heart and crush me at any moment. Cash also had this shitty principle about not telling me that I was beautiful. He said to me early on, 'You hear it all the time, so I'm not going to be like all the other men.' Such bullshit. It didn't matter if I heard it a hundred times a night. I wanted to hear it from *him*. I hadn't had much experience with this. I usually choose partners who are all-in and full of compliments. But I was in too deep. His reserve left me wanton and breathless. I couldn't get enough. Our friends likened us to Sid and Nancy. I was smart enough to understand the implication, but in deep enough to love the comparison.

I had never drunk booze in the morning, but I did with Cash. We'd kill a fifth or more simply watching a movie together; we slayed lots of bottles. I thought it was all rather romantic. Cash, myself, Frannie and Link were a great foursome and had a lot of fun together. Cash and I had been dating for about a year and a half when Frannie threw a big birthday bash for Link at their house on Kingswell Avenue in Los Feliz. Everyone drank, did drugs and tore it up until the wee hours of the morning. There was even an all-out squirt-gun fight! Cash and I left their house as the sun came up and drove to my place on June Street. Not five minutes after we entered my apartment, we got into a massive, nasty fight about nothing. In the middle of the yelling, Cash threw his copy of my apartment keys on the floor and stormed out, saying it was over for good.

I was a disaster. Sobbing and heartbroken, I made the decision to end my life. Death would be easier than feeling like this. I gathered up my porn and sex toys and threw them in the dumpster. I didn't want my mother finding these things when they cleaned out my place. Once I felt that my place was people-ready, I grabbed a bottle of Crown and went into my bedroom to assemble all my pills. I like to hoard pills and I had quite a collection. I opened the bottles and started swallowing twenty or thirty at a time.

Through tears I wrote 'I'm sorry' on a piece of paper and laid it next to me. That's the last thing I remember.

Cash called me all day and started to get worried when evening came around and he hadn't heard from me. He knew something was wrong, but couldn't get into my apartment since he'd tossed his keys so dramatically. He called Frannie and asked if she had a copy of my house keys. She did. At around 10 p.m., the three of them found me in my bedroom, passed out in a pretzel position on my bed. An empty bottle of Crown sat on my nightstand and many, *many*, empty pill bottles were strewn about. Pandemonium set in. They picked me up, put me in the car and raced to the hospital.

In the emergency room, Cash wouldn't leave my side and even watched them pump my stomach (just what every girl wants her boyfriend to witness). He told me later that when the doctor was asking me questions, all I said was, 'Fuck, it didn't work'. Link and Frannie had to go back to my place to collect all the empty bottles so the doctors could figure out what they were dealing with. I have zero recollection of any of this. I was in a complete blackout for the first few days in intensive care, which is probably a blessing.

My friends were in distress. They called my mom and she flew down from the Bay Area. Talk about the worst time for a mother to meet your new friends and current boyfriend! I had tubes in every orifice. Hattie told me that when I started coming to, I kept pulling at them and mumbling, 'annoying'. When I finally gained consciousness, I asked the nurse if the tube down my throat could be taken out. She said yes and that she would get the doctor, but I couldn't wait, so I pulled the fucker out. I had no idea how long it was. It made my mom's and Cash's stomachs turn to watch, but that goatfuck needed to go!

None of this was easy on anyone. It is never my intention to stress people out. It's just an unfortunate by-product of attempting suicide – or succeeding.

My mom was driving my Jeep while she was in town. I assume she also stayed in my apartment, but in all honesty, I don't know. One afternoon, she came storming into my ICU room in a huff. Apparently, she had found an old bag of my friend's weed in my car and focused all her anger on it. I don't even smoke weed!

'What the fuck is this?' she asked.

Cash was lying next to me on my bed-slash-gurney. We looked at her like she had rabbits coming out of her ears.

'I don't know. What is it?' I asked.

'It's a bag of drugs! Why do you have drugs in your car?' She threw the baggie at me, but because it was so old and dried out, it swished back and forth in the air until it landed softly on my legs, not giving her actions the impact she had intended. Her rage over something so inconsequential immediately pissed me off. Lovers and parents have a special way of pushing your buttons in milliseconds.

'Are you fucking kidding me?' I said. 'Sit the fuck down and shut up. That's not even my weed. And this coming from the woman who gave me mushrooms when I was a kid? That's a real fuckin' hoot.'

She sat down. She instantly looked defeated. It was a strange thing for her to be angry about. I had recently swallowed some three hundred pills, but this old-ass baggie of weed was what set her off? I recognized the misplaced stress, but I was not willing to be yelled at, especially by a woman I used to roll joints for when I was eight.

They finally moved me out of intensive care and to a different floor. I wasn't out of the woods and I certainly wasn't sharp yet, but my body was healing and doing much better. Years later, we still joke that I'm a cockroach.

I had strange burn-like lesions on my face and body. One doctor told my friends that I must have burnt myself with an iron or the stove while I was pill-ed out. Another doctor later said that a chemical overdose sometimes causes these kinds of marks on the skin.

Soon after they moved me, Hattie noticed that I was using my hands to move my left leg. She asked the doctors about it, but initially, they didn't know why. My liver had healed itself quickly, which astonished the nurses. I was not surprised, which is why I had tripled the amount of pills this time. But something was wrong. I had pain in my left leg and foot. The doctors had been so focused on my internal system that no one had noticed that the underside of my thigh was swollen and blood had pooled. As it turned out, my vital organs had made a remarkable full recovery, but the way I had passed out had cut off the blood circulation to my leg, causing permanent nerve damage to my left foot. When I stood for the first time (with help from the nurses), it felt as if my foot sank into the earth, as if the floor didn't exist. It was the weirdest sensation. And then the pain set in.

It was a long, slow and extremely painful few months after I left the hospital. I have a pretty high pain tolerance, but this was unlike anything I had ever experienced. Sometimes it felt like my foot was on fire, and at other times it felt like shattering glass. The oxycontin I was prescribed, which I took five times a day, didn't even touch the pain.

I had what they call 'foot drop'. My left foot was useless. It was all floppy. I couldn't walk, and my bed was too high, so I lived on my couch for about a month. I couldn't sleep because of the pain and I couldn't eat because of the pills. I just cried. I wasn't even sad about being alive, but I had done this to myself. If only I had lain down flat, this wouldn't have happened. I used a walker to go to the bathroom but couldn't stand for long periods of time. Even being on the toilet hurt. Some days, even the walker was too difficult to use, and I would just drag myself to the bathroom.

Eventually, I graduated to crutches and could leave the house. I had to wear a plastic device to keep my foot in place. It was eight or nine months before I could put my foot into a sneaker. My doctor switched me to methadone to help with the pain. It was the first and only thing that gave me a modicum of relief. Once I could put a little weight on my foot, I moved up to using a cane. The canes at Rite-Aid are seriously ugly, so I found a bad ass, dark wood one with a red dragon curling around it. The handle was a phoenix head with a marble in its mouth! I figured if I was going to be a gimp, I might as well do it in style.

My limp went away a little over a year after the event. But I wasn't able to work for ten months during this fiasco. I had to declare bankruptcy, which ruined my perfect credit. C'est la vie. The moment I could walk without the cane and put my foot into a shoe, I went back to the club. I could no longer wear my pretty stripper heels. I have to wear boots now, which sucks because they aren't as feminine, but now I look like a superhero.

Cash stayed with me throughout the healing process, but our relationship was unhealthy (clearly), and we finally called it quits in 2008. He's still in my life, and I see him from time to time, but I'm no longer in love with him.

37

HOOKER OVERSEAS. I'M off to Europe to spend a week with a man I barely know. It's on his dime with my services rendered, of course. I'm going to Paris, London, Amsterdam and Vienna, all in one week. It's a business trip for him, so I know I'll get some alone time, which is key for my sanity. It's been a while since I've been to Europe and I'm excited to travel. Luckily, he lives in New York and had to fly to France a day ahead of me, so I'll be traveling alone. Time spent with a john means being 'on' and therefore it's exhausting.

Now that I'm single again, I can take advantage of opportunities to earn a better living. Money at the club has been declining, so I put an ad in the adult section on Craigslist. Ah, Craigslist, it's like the inappropriate uncle. It's a bit tricky though, since prostitution is illegal (which is dumb), so you can't come right out and say how much you charge and for what. The word 'donation' is used, as well as other ridiculous verbiage for sex and company. I met this guy only a couple of weeks ago. We spent a total of five hours together. It's pretty insane to spend a week traveling with a man I've only met once, but my instincts are good. And fuck it, you can't live your life in fear. If I get chopped up into bits, at least it'll be in Europe and not in some mini-mall on Western Avenue. As long as I keep myself properly lubricated – with wine, I mean, not KY – I should be fine.

The first time we met, we had dinner in Santa Monica. I wanted to get a read on him before I went to his hotel room. We actually had a fun night together with lots of laughs. He's smart, and we have a similar sense of humor, which is to say quirky and a tad dark. He's forty-seven, has dark olive skin, thinning brown hair and hazel eyes. He wears designer glasses and his wardrobe is in black, navy or a deep green, olive color. He's the type of man who, when he finds an item of clothing he likes, buys six just like it. 'Craigslist' is quite the talker. He likes to repeat himself, too, but considering I remember very little, it's a good match. I'm feeling optimistic. Granted there's the whole he-owns-me issue, but drinking should aid in this dilemma. Also, he seems rather wealthy, and if the trip goes well, this could be the beginning of a beautiful relationship.

Sleeping pills are the only way to survive overnights with clients. Lord, please don't let him be a snorer. Nothing is worse. Crap, I ordered a Bloody Mary and I'm flying British Airways. I forgot that Brits use plain tomato juice instead of Bloody Mary mix with spices and such. Yuck. I don't want it on my tiny fold-down tray. I have two words for Craigslist: business class. I was bummed when he didn't book it, but I think I'll have earned an upgrade by day seven. Or I'll be dead, in which case it won't matter. It's cramped here in coach. I should be laid out with glass stemware in the next cabin. I'm such a little prostitute princess. I was born into dirty hippiedom and came out with champagne tastes.

I absolutely love airport life (sans the lines, shitty travelers and security). It's a suspended mini-life. You have autonomy. You get little meals and random packaged needs. It's fascinating watching people on planes, each one a master of their tiny space. Airplane bathrooms are also great, not because they're nice but because the plane is so loud, it makes passing gas easy, so long as it's just sound and not smell. Being in such cramped quarters, I care too much about the passengers and flight attendants to ever leave a smelly bathroom in my wake.

Something about being on a plane makes me want to get fucked up and do bad things. I blame Hattie and Frannie; those Midwest girls can party. The girls and I have gotten tanked and high on pills on every plane we've ever been on together. Getting fucked up on a plane is good. But being hung-over on a plane is very bad. Hattie and I went to New York for an art show and got completely shitfaced the night before our 10 a.m. flight home. It wasn't smart. I was shaking and puking for almost the entire five-hour flight. It's my shittiest plane ride to date. The only positive note of being hung-over in a plane lavatory is that it's easy to brace yourself with the handles, and you can generally lean against the wall in between heaving.

Of course, I would get my period a couple of days before the trip. Luckily, mine don't last very long, and it's almost over. That's a hooker's nightmare, or savior, depending on how you see it. I guess I should milk it and earn myself one sex-free night. I just hope he doesn't insist on me having orgasms (real ones). It didn't seem to be an issue the night we met. An old client of mine got upset with me once for faking it. He said that he was old enough to know when a woman faked it – something about the clit being engorged. He was dead set on making me come. He was a handsome black man and gave decent head, and eventually I did, but I felt like shit right after. It was too much: too real, too personal. You'd think the act of sex would also be real and personal, but for some reason, I've always been able to compartmentalize it. Faking orgasms is so much easier and far less emotional, although it sets a horrible precedent for women and men sexually. Men think it's so easy to make girls come, and I'm just reinforcing the myth. I never faked it before I was a hooker. I guess I gave up my social cause for five-star restaurants and travel. But how much time is believable before I come? How much noise? I wish they didn't give a shit. When did johns start caring about our orgasms, anyway? Just get off, dude. I don't want to come with you. This isn't my fantasy, buddy, it's yours.

38

WEDNESDAY IN PARIS. I was thoroughly exhausted and in pain from the traveling. Craigslist arrived at the hotel from work just as I arrived from the airport. Bad timing. I was hoping to get settled in and have some time to myself, but no such luck. He said he was starving, which worked out because I was, too. So, we left immediately to find food. I don't know why, but he didn't bother making reservations, and we ended up walking *all* over town. Walking miles around Paris is fine as long as you aren't ravenous and don't have nerve damage to your foot. On top of the walking and the hunger, he kept stopping randomly and jamming his tongue down my throat. Nothing was natural or consensual about it. I'm sure it looked romantic from a distance: a couple kissing on a bridge in Paris. Upon closer inspection, though, you'd have noticed the pained look on my face. He was a horrible kisser. I guess I hadn't noticed in Santa Monica. He was nothing but a strong, stiff tongue rammed to the back of my mouth. It's a wonder he couldn't feel my head pulling away. How can a forty-seven-year-old man kiss like that? It's not as if he didn't have kissing experience. What woman actually likes that? Interestingly, I've noticed that all of my johns have been shitty kissers.

We finally found a cute little bistro and I ordered a bottle of wine before our waitress could finish a sentence. In the middle of dinner, he started talking about marriage. Can you imagine? Not to mention that I'd met him only a few weeks ago. Aside from the absurd marriage talk and my earlier annoyance, the rest of the dinner was nice. The food was fabulous, and by the second bottle, I was feeling much nicer and more pliable. Time to go. Luckily, he hailed a taxi back to the hotel so I didn't have to walk.

I had told him about my period being on its last legs, so he knew sex was going to have to wait, but as soon as we walked into the room he was *all* over me. I didn't have a moment to relax. Or pee. Or breathe. Nothing! Just tongue thrusting and a body attack. It was awful. Give me a second to chill, motherfucker! At least let me take off my goddamn socks first, the ones I've been traveling in for the past twenty fucking hours. I finally tore myself away to take a shower. I felt like Penelope struggling to get away from Pepé Le Pew. Must adjust attitude. Must adjust attitude, I told myself. Deep breath. Repeat.

After my shower, I was a smidge calmer but still aggravated and exhausted. Pepé wouldn't leave me alone. It was quite clear that my bleeding wasn't a deterrent and that I was going to have to give this guy a happy ending in order to get any sleep. So I gave him a blowjob, and he finally chilled out – for a minute. Then he got hard again almost instantly. Luckily, this was also when all the wine and my magic sleeping pills kicked in and I passed out. I should have gotten more money. What was I thinking? How was it okay to put myself through this? The crazy thing is, I thought it would be all right. Mere hours before I had been thinking that we might have fun. I'm such a dumbass. Prada would have soothed the fact that I settled for less money than I wanted, unfortunately, Craigslist didn't seem keen on taking me shopping. When I had mentioned something about it, he had mumbled under his breath and changed the subject. I'm in fucking Paris and I don't get to go shopping? Merde.

The next morning, I sensed him wanting to wake me up for some action before he left for work. I pretended to be asleep. I would have to explain that mornings are a no go. I am not a morning person; not by a long shot. I used to throw things at my mom when she would try to wake me up for school. I figured I'd mention it that night, post-coitus. I had also realized I'd have to keep my foot pain to myself somehow. He simply didn't care. Again, like the shopping, he had ignored me and kept walking when I told him I had an injury and that I was suffering. I wasn't being a baby; nerve damage is painful. I would have to suggest a taxi or a horse and carriage. Anything would be better than walking ten miles on cobblestones in leather soles. In terms of shopping, I decided I would say something like, 'Chanel makes me wet', or 'How about a blowjob in the Dolce & Gabbana dressing room?' That might work. I knew I needed to get creative.

I had successfully fallen back asleep after his sex attempt in the morning. When I woke up, I saw that he had left me a check and cash totaling the remaining half that he owed me for the trip. Nothing extra, it was exactly the amount we had agreed upon. I can only assume it meant, 'spend your own money while I'm at work'. Jerk. If he were a gentleman, he would have given me additional run-around money. He had given me fifty fucking euros the previous night. Do you know how much fifty euros gets you in Paris? It's barely enough for a niçoise salad and a Perrier. The waiter brought it to me ten minutes ago, and it's horrible. I pushed the smelly tuna to the other side of the table and ordered a glass of save-me wine.

39

I TOOK THE train to London and you won't believe this, Pepé Le Pew had the audacity to tell me that I couldn't order the risotto with white truffle at dinner the night before because it was too expensive. True, it was eighty euros, but I didn't know that at the time. I wasn't checking the prices because one would think I shouldn't have to budget with a wealthy client. Plus, I was seriously hypoglycemic because, just like the previous evening, he hadn't made reservations (on a Friday night in Paris!), and we had spent two hours looking for somewhere to eat. Again, my foot was killing me (my prescription pain meds were no match against hours in boots on cobblestones). We had to wait for a table and by the time we sat in the beautiful bar area, I was shaking and fighting back tears. It took everything in my power to be nice to him. I must be the best actor on the planet or this guy has ice in his veins because he asked me to go check with the hostess on the status of our table. Pain or no pain, isn't it gentlemanly for a man to do those kinds of things? Whatever. I got us a table and ordered a bottle of wine from the hostess. As it was warming my belly and returning my blood sugar level to normal, I noticed that the only thing on the menu that sounded good to me was the risotto. I must have given him the look of death when he told me it was too expensive because he seemed to register immediately just how wrong he was. I was fuming. I was tipsy already, due to the lack of sustenance and pills and the emotional roller coaster I was on. I went dormant.

'I'm sorry, babe,' he said. 'You should order the risotto.'

I looked him dead in the eye. 'No. You don't want me to,' I said. It was a childish move, but I didn't care. The tension was palpable. I wanted to kill him. I'm sure it wouldn't have been the first murder in Paris at the hands of a prostitute. A few minutes passed as I guzzled more wine. He reiterated that I should order the risotto. So I did, as well as another bottle of wine.

The risotto was really good. Pepé ended up eating half of it. I was full on booze anyway. We finished dinner and went back to the hotel. I was feeling better after the wine and the food but was still out of sorts. Like clockwork, Le Pew was all over me the second we walked in the door. He even hurt my neck with his forceful kissing. He went down on me and was way too rough with his tongue. I faked the fastest orgasm of my life. We fucked, he came, I peed and washed myself, took a sleeping pill and passed the fuck out.

Cheapnut woke up early the following morning and took the train to London where he had a meeting, so I followed him a few hours later. Being by myself was heaven. Starting that night, until the end of the trip, I would be with him nonstop. On one hand, I knew that would suck, but on the other hand, it would save my pocketbook. He hadn't even given me enough to cover the train ticket to London. I would have to keep my eyes on the prize: I would be flying home on Monday.

Pepé clearly didn't understand that the better you treat a woman, the more you'll get in return. This is true even for someone you're paying. It's not rocket science. None of his behavior made me feel amorous. Granted he was paying me, but he barely treated me like a human. He had told me there would be food on the train, but I didn't find any. I hadn't purchased water or snacks before boarding because he said there would be food. So I was starving (again) and dehydrated (again). Starving in Europe! I was the hungry hooker. It looked like Kansas outside.

40

THINGS GOT BETTER in London because there was a lot less walking and a lot more drinking. We stayed in a beautiful suite at the Savoy. We had fabulous dinners, saw *Wicked*, got stinking drunk in some great pubs and laughed a bunch. He seemed more relaxed once he had left Paris. He still did things that irked me, but it was a far cry from how I had felt before. Then off we went to Amsterdam, the place where I was conceived. We even found the flat where my parents had lived. I loved Amsterdam. It was my first time there. Again, we had great meals, found some really cool bars and smoked a little hashish, which isn't exactly my thing, but you know, when in Amsterdam. That was how I had originally envisioned the trip going. The kisses were the same, as well as the sex drive and lack of shopping, but I was having more fun. Get this, he bought me a blouse in Amsterdam. One blouse. He kept telling me how great the shopping was in Vienna. 'Wait till we get to Vienna,' he kept saying. Okay, boss.

I'm a person who's used to spending a lot of time by myself, and I enjoy it. One of the reasons I had agreed to go on the trip with him (besides the money and going to Europe) was the fact that he had said he'd be working. But I hadn't known that it was really only in Paris and London that we would have time apart. He may have canceled meetings in Amsterdam and was getting work done on his laptop, but this meant zero me-time. By day four, it was catching up with me. He woke up much earlier than me, which meant that he got time to himself, but the millisecond my eyes opened, he was there wanting a hug.

On our last night in Amsterdam, I decided that I didn't want to have sex that night. I wanted one night off – one night out of six. I felt this was fair. I had never guaranteed sex every night! In fact, sex wasn't even discussed when he had proposed the trip.

I told him early in the evening that I wasn't feeling well and that I wasn't in the mood to fool around. He acted like such a baby. At first he said okay, but he kept tossing out backhanded comments. 'Can't believe I'm in Amsterdam, city of brothels, and I'm not going to get laid.' You can't imagine how much restraint it took to keep my mouth shut. Just smile, I told myself. Only two nights left. You can do it. This was my mantra. In between his whining he would bear-hug me, which was just his excuse to thrust his pelvis into me.

Early on in the trip I had realized that every time I dressed or undressed in front of him, it caused arousal and sexual comments, so I had started changing in the bathroom like we were at a truck stop and not in a five-star European hotel. We didn't have sex that night, but he made me pay for it in verbal harassment.

We arrived in Vienna on a Sunday. All the shops were closed. I swear he had planned it that way. He had been to all of these cities multiple times, so he must have known all the stores would be closed. My flight was scheduled to leave early the next morning, so there wouldn't be time to shop for a pair of stupid boots. He kept telling me about a pair of boots he was going to buy me. To be totally honest, I had completely lost interest in shopping by that point.

Vienna is beautiful. We saw some gorgeous architecture and walked through a beautiful park. Our hotel was spectacular as well. Pepé Le Pew definitely liked nice things. I just wished I had been there with a lover and not a client.

That night we had dinner in one of the most stunning spaces I've ever seen, but it hardly mattered. I was done. I had had enough. He was clueless and going on and on about our next few years together. He didn't even notice that I wasn't speaking. I was afraid to open my mouth, lest the wrath rain down upon him. I really didn't want to get into a huge argument on our last night in Europe. I had made it this far, and I'd be damned if I screwed it up because however annoying he was, he had money and I didn't. The really crazy thing is that I'm set to see him in New York in a couple months. What's wrong with me?

41

I JUST READ this article in the *LA Weekly* about a Miss Hooker contest. I get it; people love to throw that word around. But I read it and *this* hooker got annoyed. It says, 'Of course, the pageant girls are not "real" hookers. Just like the rest of us writers, lawyers, bartenders, accountants, waitresses and secretaries with clients to please and bosses to appease aren't hookers either.' Are you fucking kidding me! I'm seeing a man tomorrow at 1 p.m. for anal sex. This is not the same as answering the fucking telephone or taking orders. True, you couldn't pay me enough to wait tables again, but until someone has sold their body, soul and mind for money, they'll never know what it's like to be a real hooker. I'm so sick of people thinking they're cool by poaching my profession. Oh, and tomorrow I'll get more money if I 'enjoy it'. That's what he actually said. Of course, I'll 'enjoy it'. That's what we're paid to do. No one wants a prostitute who complains.

I have to remember to do an enema first. Although, maybe I shouldn't since it might cure him of his anal fantasy. It's been years since I've had anal anything, and this guy's dick is hefty. I'm definitely going to need a couple of drinks before I see him. And lots of lube. Do you need anal lube at your desk job?

42

IT'S SO SLOW tonight. I'm dangerously broke. Why are strippers always broke? Why is life so damned expensive? The Choker is coming in tonight, thank god. At least that's some guaranteed cash.

Did you know some girls lie to their boyfriends, husbands and parents about being a dancer? This has always baffled me. How the fuck can these people not know? Parents, I get, they're not a part of your daily life; but someone you live with? I've certainly hidden aspects of my job and minute details like handjobs, but I've never tried to pull off the I-work-at-a-restaurant-that's-open-until-four-in-the-morning-and-we-have-to-wear-a-shit-ton-of-make-up-and-smell-like-cupcakes deception. It seems like a huge gamble, especially for the married dancers. Although I will admit that not having to deal with all the bullshit that comes with people knowing what I do for a living does sound appealing.

Crap, an old French customer of mine just walked in. I haven't danced for him in a long time. He doesn't dance with me anymore and I sense that he feels bad about it. It's a bit of a tricky situation. I don't want to be rude, but I also don't want to get stuck in an awkward conversation or make him feel bad for being here. I want him to have fun and spend money. I just don't want to talk to him.

Honestly, I don't know why he keeps coming to the club. He's smart, charismatic, handsome and wealthy. And he's got a huge cock. I know this because I can feel it during our dances, and also, I've seen him outside of the club. He plays sports and is in really good shape for his age. It seems like he could easily find a woman. Maybe he's a sex addict? Or a strip club addict? Is he afraid of intimacy? Or a woman taking half of what he owns? Perhaps one already did.

One of his investors was also a client of mine. Manhattan Beach is a small community. I met Frenchy first and the investor about a year afterward, but I wasn't aware of their connection until much later. Mr Limo – that's what my friends and I called him – was an investor. He had racehorses, played the stock market and owned his own limo (hence the nickname). Mr Limo and I had fun together. He was down-to-earth, smart, in his mid- to late fifties and had a good sense of humor. He was also only five-foot-two. I wore flats most times, and did what I could with my clothing so as to not scream 'hooker' when we went out. He never seemed to care, though. He treated me as an equal and was good to me. He had me on a monthly salary, which was nice because we didn't have to deal with it every time we saw each other, but I had settled for less than I wanted. He was a bit of a tightwad with his money, which is one of the reasons why he had so much of it.

I went with Mr Limo and a few of his friends to opening day at the Del Mar Racetrack – that's a spectacle and a half. I was not prepared. The Turf Club was chock-full of sugar daddies and working girls, most of them looking the part in skimpy, trashy outfits. I was dressed in a modest but stylish polka-dot dress and hat, yet there I was, with my sugar daddy, just like the rest of them.

Mr Limo hinted at marriage once. He said I would be set for life. I'll admit the idea sounded appealing, but I just couldn't do it. I respected him and had fun with him, but I couldn't imagine living with him. Though it would have been nice not to have to worry about bills and to have a retirement plan. I don't always make the wisest decisions when it comes to money. I hail from financially delinquent Jews. Actually, my dad is good with money, but he didn't raise me. Ah, here's the Choker.

Approximately an hour and forty-five minutes later, there's been an interesting turn of events. The Choker did only one VIP set, but he tipped me well. He told me that he had recently had a procedure done on one of his testicles, so we took it easy. After the Choker left, I was on my way to the dressing room when Frenchy motioned me over. He asked me for a VIP. During the dance, he confessed that he had just broken up with his girlfriend and asked if I would come to his place after work. So I'm going to his place after work. He said he was 'dying to eat me out'. Ugh, I hate that term. Thank god my period ended yesterday. I'll try to keep the visit short. It'll be late, and I know he gets tired. Whoa, no more alcohol. I just looked up from my composition book and felt pretty tipsy. I can't believe I'm going to drive to Manhattan Beach after work – the opposite direction from my apartment in Hollywood – and be sexy. Fuck it, I need the dough.

It's about 4 a.m. and I just got home. I'm beyond exhausted. I got to his house, and he wanted to talk. Why do men want to talk? Can't we just have the sex and get it over with? I mean, I understand foreplay, but how does us talking about your soccer practice get your dick hard? I suppose it's the simple act of someone showing interest.

He poured some pear brandy he had recently brought back from France, which was pretty yummy, I'll admit, but I had ants in my pants. There was more chitchat on the couch and then I finally got him upstairs. I did a mini crotch wash in his bathroom. I reeked of used vanilla and lap dances, but I didn't feel like taking a proper shower. I wanted to get the show on the road. I had to fake like six fucking orgasms before he would leave me alone. He finally came, but really he just wanted me to. I was lying there on his bed, naked, thinking, how long is enough? No man wants you to get dressed the second after they come. Maybe some do, but I never seem to get those guys. After what seemed like plenty of time, I started putting my clothes on.

'You're leaving?' he asked.

I could see that he had half a chubby. He wanted to go again. Shit. I knew he was tired and he is older than he is young, so it was going to take extra time and effort to get him to come again.

I reluctantly took my clothes off and joined him. I am way too nice sometimes. I faked some more orgasms and did my best to work with what he had. He wasn't even close to coming. I pulled out all the tricks – even in my haggard state. I talked dirty. Put a little finger up his ass. Tongued his balls. Tweaked his nipples. Did Kegel exercises. Nothin'. Finally, I stopped because I'm no spring chicken either. He told me how beautiful I am.

'Not a typical Southern California beauty, much more natural and exotic,' he said. Yeah, yeah, can I fucking go home now? I couldn't take much more. Strenuous sex work after working all night at the club is bonkers. I told him I needed to get up early and that I really should start my long drive home.

'You can stay here,' he said.

'Thanks, baby, but I've got to go.' I kissed him and made a mad dash for the door.

43

I AUDITIONED AT a new club earlier tonight. A girl at the Bare told me about this place that had just opened and said I should check it out. Apparently, they aren't charging the girls a stage fee, or taking a portion of the dance price, due to the fact that the club is brand-spanking new. That's music to my ears. Unfortunately, I loathe auditioning. It's completely nerve-wracking, no matter how many times I've done it. It's especially distressing at this point in my career (because I'm no longer tween flesh), but it comes with the territory, so I get over myself. One of the things I hate about auditioning is that I have to get dolled up before I leave the house. I prefer doing my make-up in the dressing room as it gives me time to drink, catch up with my friends and settle into work mode. And since I don't usually drink before I get to the club, I'm extremely sober and hyper-aware of each humiliating moment of these auditions.

I arrive at the new club and it turns out I know the door guy. He used to work at the Bare. He tells me that they have a stack of applications and that I should come back in six months when they have customers. He says it's been slow. But I'm already there, I've psyched myself up for it and look the part, so I decide to go through with it and fill out the application anyway. Should I say how long I've been dancing? Do I put down *every* club I've ever worked at? Should I tell them that I worked at Mitchell Brothers for nine years before it turned into a full-blown brothel? Is that an asset or a handicap? The application also asks for my age, and I write down the truth assuming they'll photocopy my driver's license like most other clubs. But they don't. Damn, I could've lied. Now they have this piece of paper on file that says I'm a hundred and forty and that I used to work at a whorehouse. Awesome.

The nice door guy tells me that the manager is ready to see me. He takes me on the nickel tour; the club isn't very big. We sit in the VIP area. It's a separate room, approximately five feet wide and twenty feet long with a built-in, high-backed bench running along one side. This is where we're supposed to give sexy, nude dances? Right next to another girl? And I'm not kidding when I say it's bright enough to study calculus. Anyway, he's nice enough. He gives me the rundown. I just sit there with a dumb smile, thinking, 'let's get this over with'. Throw me up on the stupid stage already. I've been stripping for a thousand years. He's not telling me anything I don't already know. Even better than dancing on the stage, let me take off my clothes and give you a lap dance. I'll be a shoo-in!

He finishes his spiel and shows me the dressing room. I thought the dressing room at the Bare was small, but it's the fucking Taj Mahal by comparison. This so-called 'dressing room' is a walk-in closet with mirrors and bright, fluorescent lights. There's only enough room for two opposing countertops and four folding chairs. There's also one young girl giving me dirty looks. What the fuck am I doing? I'm way too old for this shit. Whatever, I just need the manager to see me naked. I auditioned at a club in Vegas once where they skipped the stage and just had me walk up and down a hallway in my sexy outfit for the manager. It sounds degrading, but honestly I preferred it to this. Isn't our business based on looks? Plus, how a girl is on stage isn't a guarantee that she'll make money.

I get undressed and put my boots and outfit on. I look green under the fluorescent light. I don't fake-tan anymore, and I hate the sun, so my complexion looks vaguely gangrene-y and shiny from my shimmer powder. That's how I try to hide my changing body and age. I wonder if I'm fooling anyone. Did I mention that there are only two men in the club? Yep, two men.

I choose two safe classic rock songs and go on stage. The stage is brand new and made from a strange material. It's sticky and difficult to slither around on. I can actually feel my knees bruising from the weird stage. The lights are also super bright. The bitchy girl who went on before me got gorgeous lights, all dim and sexy. Not me. Not for my debasing audition. I get the goddamn house lights. Fine. I expect this. All clubs do this for auditions. So I do my shit. I smile at the only two guys in the audience and try to pretend that I'm sexy and not miserable. I accidentally roll my eyes (at myself and this life) when facing away from them and then realize that there is a big mirror behind me. Oops. Both guys tip me well. The Asian one looks familiar.

The second song finally ends. Thank god. I walk down the three stairs to get offstage. I'm not sure what their naked cash rule is – some clubs don't allow girls to touch money while totally nude – so I put my panties on while standing there. I stand there, naked and sweaty, leaning against the wall trying to get my lame foot into the panty hole while everyone is watching, and knowing the wonderful things this position is doing for my poochy belly. Yay me.

I head over to the DJ and realize that I didn't see the manager until the very end of my set, meaning I don't think he even watched me. The DJ tells me to get dressed and wait for the manager. I already know what this means: I'm not hired. As I'm getting dressed, I wonder why the hell I put myself through this. And why didn't I wear stockings? I've been working a lot lately and my knees show it, plus with my pale skin, I must look like a crackhead.

I come out of the dressing room, give the DJ all the cash I made on stage and wait for the manager. After ten minutes and much self-reflection, he tells me they'll call me. Uh-huh. I smile, grab my shit and leave. Outside the club, the Asian guy from the audience tells me he'll see me at the Bare. So I take my humbled, bruised ass to my club to work a long, hard Friday night. And here I am.

44

MONDAY NIGHT IS contest night at the Bare. The 'amateur' contest is a way to win some dough, but it's also how most strip clubs facilitate their hiring. I don't usually work on these nights.

It's too chaotic – too many men in the audience who are there just to watch the show and not spend any money. While the contest is amusing, it's gotten longer and longer over the years, making it difficult to get lap dances before they announce the winner. The amateur contest attracts all shapes, sizes and varying degrees of professionalism, including some ladies fulfilling a fantasy for their husbands. Are you getting a mental image yet?

A friend and I were watching the parade when I noticed a cute blonde in the audience. I went over to her and sat down. 'Why aren't you in the contest?' I asked.

'I was going to,' she said. 'But I left my ID at home. The girl who was just on is my friend.'

'Cool,' I said. 'I hope she wins. She was pretty good.' We exchanged names and chatted for a bit. After another song passed, Jessica asked me for a lap dance. The request took me by surprise, but I happily took her slender hand in mine and led her upstairs for a bikini dance. She was obviously young, had an extremely pretty face, a pierced lip and long, wavy blonde hair. I could tell she liked girls. It was evident in the way she held me and moved in time with my body. It was a hot lap dance. I gave her extra time and when it was over, she gave me her number, saying we should hang sometime.

'Yes, we should,' I replied with a deviant grin.

Five days later, we made a late-night date. She had plans with friends to go out in Hollywood, so I told her to come by my place after. She called while she was out. Apparently, her friend had driven and she asked if I would mind giving her a ride home to Long Beach after we hung out. It's not something I'm prone to doing, but I told her I would. Around one in the morning, her buddies dropped her off. She was dressed up and ridiculously adorable. During our couch flirtations, she mentioned that she had told all her friends about me. It's nice having a hot girl gushing over you.

We took it to my bedroom. She was fun, sensual and relaxed. I was right about not being her first woman. She had known she liked girls from a young age. She had the tightest little body and was a really good kisser. The natural end to the hook-up had arrived. She didn't want to leave my bed – and I certainly didn't feel like driving to Long Beach – so I gave her one of my softest concert T-shirts from my stagehand days, and we passed out.

When I woke up, I cringed at the reality of having to drive her home, but I'm a woman of my word. Not used to having a one-night stand spend the night, I was in a hurry to move it along. On the drive, she said she was missing school. When I asked her what she was studying, she got real quiet. I looked over at her. Her gaze was fixed on the beautiful scenery of the crowded 405. 'I'm in high school,' she said.

'Holy shit! Are you serious?' I asked.

'Yeah, please don't be mad?'

'Wow,' I said, shaking my head.

She started to explain, but I didn't hear a word of it. I couldn't get the words 'high school' out of my head. We finally arrived at her house. She asked if I wanted to come in and meet her mom. What? One thing I do remember her saying is how old her mother was; two years *younger* than me. I suppose that should have been the warning bell, but it was silenced by her pretty face. 'Uh, no baby, I'm good,' I said. She kissed me goodbye.

As she walked up to her house, she turned around and yelled, 'Call me!' I almost ducked, afraid her mother was watching from the window and about to call the cops. I drove away, chalking it up as another random experience.

In the days that followed, Jessica called a couple of times and texted me, including sexy pictures of herself. To be an upstanding citizen, I avoided her. But then – and I can't say for sure how it happened – we were sitting in a booth at my local dive bar. The owner/bartender is a buddy of mine and would never card anyone who was there with me. He assumed and trusted that I wasn't bedding an underage teenager. Jessica and I weren't hiding the sexual spark between us. She even finger-banged me under the table, the naughty little minx. We stumbled back to my place before the bar closed. I knew it was morally questionable, but it didn't feel unjust. I'd rarely adhered to common views on morality anyway, so why start now? If anything, it felt like she was taking advantage of me. Not buying that? Yeah, me either. Did I mention she was really hot? I know, I know, you can spank me later. We only saw each other once or twice after that. Although she was a lovely girl, we lacked things in common. Plus, she didn't have a car and the distance acted as a conscience barrier. I'm just lazy. Long Beach is too far to risk jail time and a rape charge on my record. It was something sweet and fleeting. I'm glad she walked into my club that night.

45

IN ALL MY years dancing, some of the wildest stories are still from the first place I ever stripped, the Lusty Lady. Something about the anonymity and Plexiglas attracted all sorts. I witnessed hundreds, maybe thousands of men jack off during the time I worked there, which was a trip because although I was dating Ryan at the time, I had just come out of a four-year relationship with a woman. I was surprised by how much I liked watching men stroke their cocks and release. It was dirty and intoxicating.

The main stage (which was actually a room) at the Lusty was a medium-sized, mirrored fishbowl with a red carpet. In this fishbowl of flesh were five naked girls gyrating and posing provocatively to music from a jukebox. Customers stood in narrow private booths and paid by the minute. Sometimes, guys would try to talk to us through the thick Plexiglas, yelling because of the barrier and the loud music. It never made much sense to me. It's not really the type of place you go to have a conversation. The two corner booths fit two people, sometimes three.

One club regular would come in around 3.30 a.m., get one of these corner booths, pull his pants down and proceed to suck his own cock for our viewing pleasure (and his as well, I presume). It was tremendous! He'd lie on his back (on the mini bench) and put his legs up and over his head. This brought his erect penis within mouth's reach. He couldn't deep throat himself, but it was a showstopper nonetheless. All the girls would gather around his window and ooh and aah, leaving the other men feeling left out and jacking off to our rear ends reflected in the mirrors.

Couples came into the club and would occupy these corner booths. Sadly, sometimes you could tell that the women weren't into it. Some of the men would pull at their clothing and try to get them semi-nude and we tried to pretend to be into it.

In addition to the live main room, the Lusty had a hallway of similar coin-operated booths showing adult videos and a single one-on-one booth with a dancer. The Private Pleasures booth was made up of two four-by-six rooms separated by a glass window. The dancer's side had lots of colored pillows and was situated such that when we were lying down, our pussies were at the same height as the men's cocks when they stood. The low ceiling, small space, cushy pillows, red light and curtains were why I always felt like Genie in her bottle when I was in the booth.

There was one particularly inventive regular who saw me a few times in the Private Pleasures room. He did the craziest shit. I suspect this particular chap may have been gay. I only say this because he didn't seem turned on or interested in me sexually. He just went through the motions. In fact, I'm not even sure if he ever came. But he had his routine.

For his first act, he'd put a hammer handle up his ass. No lube. Just out of his suitcase and up his ass.

Next, he'd put his own peen up his ass. I venture to say he'd been doing act number two for quite some time because his dick had an intense curve to it.

And finally, he'd use a small plastic water bottle sans label with the top cut off. He had rigged the bottle with a tiny light at the far end, which was connected to a battery pack in his magic briefcase. Mr Inventive would drop his trousers, back up to the glass and push the bottle up his bum (again without lube). This allowed (or forced) me to see nearly six inches up the man's arse! It was all pink and fleshy. 'Ooooh,' I'd say. What else could I do? It was my job to watch. Perhaps I should have clapped my hands. I would today. It was a simple case of 'look what I can do!'. I've never forgotten him or his visits and I suspect I never will.

The nastiest incident from that club happened one weekend night while I was in the 'genie bottle'. An unassuming, average-looking dude asked me for a show. 'Of course,' I said. I shut my curtain to the hallway and opened the one to his window. He locked the door and put cash in the machine. I did my usual. He took his shirt off, slid his pants down and did his usual. Then it got interesting. He reached around and took some poo out of his ass and used it as lubricant. He continued to get more from his seemingly never-ending personal poo lube hole and proceeded to smear it all over his body! I'm lying there naked, 'playing' with myself, making ooh-ing and mmm-ing sounds, thinking, 'Thank god for this thick Plexiglas!' He even put some in his mouth! Finally he came, put his clothes back on and left. You should have seen the look on poor Johnny the Jizz Mopper's face when he opened the door. I felt really bad for him. No way that room smelled good. But let's face it, that's a nasty job either way you slice it. Come to think of it, I didn't notice any baby wipes sticking out of Poo Dude's back pocket. I wonder if he went to get some fried rice smelling like that?

46

'DO YOU GIVE a good lap dance?' is one of the most annoying questions strippers get asked.

'No, I give the worst lap dance you've ever had,' with a wink and a smile is my response. What do they expect me to say? 'You're definitely going to want to take a nap after.' Wink, wink. Or better yet, 'I can guarantee that you will not come and that you will ask for a refund.' Look, I get it. They're asking if they'll enjoy the dance. Is it going to be money well spent? What I should say is, 'Hey, life's a gamble.'

I was asking a dude if he wanted a private lap dance and being my usual ridiculous self when he said, 'You are not a hooker.' It came out of left field. It caught me off guard, I paused and then I chuckled in amusement. I said something silly and sweet, and he said yes to the dance. And then he asked me if he could get a 'handy' in the VIP. I shit you not.

I used to have a weekly lunch rendezvous with a client at the LAX Hilton. We would meet at 1 p.m. on the dot every Tuesday. He insisted on having lunch with me before we humped, because he admitted that it turned him on to converse with me first, which I always found a tad comical. Believe me when I say that I am no Aaron Sorkin in the morning. Having to be awake, shaved and half-presentable by 1 p.m. still counts as the morning to me. After lunch, we'd walk across the marble floor to the elevators and up to our room, which he would reserve before I got there. The hotel offered half-day rates.

His heritage was exotic and he spoke with a slight accent. I can't remember where he was from even though he probably told me a million times. He had dark, soft skin, dark brown eyes, thinning hair and big lips. He also had a wife and two kids. He even showed me pictures of them once! Men are so weird. The whole business of hooking is weird. There's an abundance of nuisances you'd never think to expect. Even after all these years, I'm still confounded and thrown. Men never cease to amaze and amuse me.

We made an odd-looking couple. I tried my best not to look like a prostitute, but come on, we screamed sex trade. I thought about this every time we walked to the elevator. Not that I necessarily care about what people think, but I'd prefer not to get arrested.

Unfortunately, this arrangement was during a heavy drinking and partying period I was going through with Hattie and Frannie and therefore I was pretty wrecked for most of these 'dates'. It was a challenge keeping it together and not barfing in my soup while also trying to be engaging and interesting. I wonder if he ever noticed that I was pale or shaky. The sex bit was easier than the conversation segment, as it involved less brainpower. But fucking just after eating isn't ideal. Of course, neither is doing it hung-over or with a married forty-six-year-old you aren't attracted to.

We had a routine. Routines are common with johns. I'm a creature of habit, so a sex routine is fine with me. Plus, it helps in the not-thinking department. Unfortunately for me, this routine included him coming twice. I'd undress as he took a shower, which I loved because it gave me time to lay down and close my eyes. After his shower, he'd crawl into bed and go down on me for a bit. I'd fake an orgasm to make him stop. Then we'd swap positions and I'd lick his balls while he jacked off. He'd come like this and then wash off again. Then we'd go back to the bed for approximately three minutes of small talk, followed by round two. This was usually about the time when I'd really want to crawl out of my skin. Instead, I'd put on a brave face and slide the condom on and put a pillow under my butt. Approximately ten minutes of intercourse followed. Once the deed was done, I'd slink into the bathroom to pee and sink wash, then get dressed as he took another quick shower. We would walk down to the valet together, always turning my ticket in first. He would pay for the valet, give me tip money and hug me goodbye. I felt sheer elation when I drove away and returned home to crawl into my own bed.

47

CARGO PANTS CROSSED the line recently. I knew it was only a matter of time. He's been a walking time bomb for years. Like a million other people, I have a profile on Facebook. Cargo Pants asked if I was on it a year or so ago, and I lied. I thought it was a dead subject, but a couple of weeks ago, he found my profile. He sent me a private message, saying, 'I thought you didn't DO the social networking thing?' I was seriously annoyed. I also felt that my privacy had been violated. Dude, I obviously lied to you, so doesn't that say something? And to guilt-trip me on top of it? I didn't respond. Can't I have a fucking life of my own? No, not when you tell them your real name and not with the goddamn Internet.

After a day or so, he emailed me. Christ, Cargo Pants, do you have any self-respect? How do you not see what's happening? Now I have to put on a pair of kid gloves. I still wanted his money, but no way in hell did I want him to have access to my personal life. I delicately explained that I preferred to keep my work life and my outside life private and separate. There's no great way of saying, 'You are just a customer, not one of my real friends.' Yes, I care about you and am happy to see you when you come into the club, but if you didn't give me money, you wouldn't be in my life.

It's such a mixed bag. Although it's my job to make him feel good – and it really is just that, a job – I honestly want good things for him and it makes me feel good when he leaves the club with a smile on his face. In his email, he said it seemed, 'silly, acting like he knew about some stuff and not other stuff'. Then he added that he 'kind of understood'. I could tell he was hurt. He should never have written to me. He should have gotten the hint and not put me in the shitty position of explaining myself or turning him down.

The dust seemed to have settled. About a week later, he asked if I was okay financially. I always need money so I responded, 'Not really. Why?' He said that he wanted to help, or something to that effect. I said thanks, and that it meant a lot to me. He said

I could drop by his office and grab the cash, which would have been great and simple, but no, me being the big-hearted girl that I am, I had to say, 'How about dinner?' He should get something in return for his money, right? I was planning on working that night but figured a two-hour dinner and a guaranteed amount was better than spending six hours at the club with zero guarantee of making anything. If I were a smart girl, I would have grabbed the cash *and* gone to the club.

I met him at his office in Culver City. He suggested a Greek restaurant in Westwood, requiring us to travel in the same car unless I wanted to be an L.A. ass and have both of us drive to the same location. Fine, whatever. He drove – at a glacial pace. He was clearly going to squeeze every possible moment out of our time together.

We finally reached our destination, which was nothing special, and I ordered wine before we even sat down. Halfway into our dinner, he told me that he was waiting for me. As in, he was waiting for me to be in a relationship with him. He knew I had a man. Actually, Cash and I had broken up a while back, but I had never told Cargo Pants this. I took a deep breath. I had never hinted at him ever being my man or having a chance at being my man. I had never talked about us dating.

'Please don't do that,' I said. 'You know I have a boyfriend and that we're happy. You should meet someone and fall in love.' It fell on deaf ears. He didn't want to hear what I had to say. Our server poured more wine and the subject passed.

Minutes later, I was chatting about nothing. I don't know how I got on the subject, but I was talking about the park across the street from my apartment and the crazy people that hang out in it. The topic was of little consequence to me. It was just a stupid story I was telling to pass the time, but then Cargo Pants said, 'I can probably figure out where you live by that information.' I was stunned. Then irritated. And a wee bit alarmed. It's at moments like this that I fear I have a deeply miswired system. Why was I having dinner with someone who I worried may stalk me? I'd known this man for maybe six years, but just as he 'knew' me, I really didn't know him either. He could have been sizing me up to skin me and make himself a Sita suit.

Had I created a monster? I was only trying to pay my fucking bills. How long can a man be teased before he starts to get a little angry or pushed beyond reason? I wondered if he'd ever followed me home? I calmed myself and changed the subject again.

The drive back was excruciating. He took some 'scenic' back roads. I wanted to fucking kill him. When we got to his office parking lot, he gave me his famous full body groin-to-groin, strong hold hug. After a couple of minutes, I pried myself away, smiled, thanked him and hightailed it out of there.

Car payment: check. Dose of reality: check.

48

SPRAY TANNER IN a small dressing room is such horseshit. Do you know how much that crap stinks? It hangs in the air like Pigpen's dust cloud, choking me with its chemical taste. I swear it takes a full twenty minutes to dissipate. Why can't these girls do that shit at home or outside in the smoking area? Why are people so inconsiderate?

Apparently, there's a big boxing match *and* a basketball game on tonight. Wonderful. I'm going to have to wait it out and keep the faith, keep my spirits up and try not to drink too much. I don't have a lot of hooch tonight anyway. Unfortunately, the girls are driving me crazy. This is what happens when money isn't flowing: girls go bat shit. There's a ton of us here tonight, sitting around with our sparkly thumbs up our asses.

I just had a customer say, 'Spoil me, baby.' A ridiculous thing to say to a stripper. I am, I thought. Then he added, 'I want you to take advantage of me.' I rolled my eyes. Take advantage of you, huh? You mean I should charge you extra and skip the dance? No? Oh, you meant for me to use you sexually. I know it's a fantasy I'm selling, but I still wanted to scratch his eyeballs out. Then Numbnut tells me he would take care of me if I were his girl, and I wouldn't have to do this. He boasted about his accomplishments and financial status, but after our two sets, he didn't tip me a dime. Clearly, I missed my opportunity to take advantage of him.

In other news, Cargo Pants and I 'broke-up'. I can't tell you how much I 'love' breaking up with a customer. My own love life isn't enough to deal with, but now I've got to break-up with you? I had written him an email (which I had Hattie proofread first), explaining that I needed to restrict our contact to the club and that he had frightened me a little when he had said that he could probably figure out where I lived. I said that I wasn't trying to hurt his feelings, but I needed to protect myself. In the interest of keeping it light, I added that it would make me very happy to see his smiling face at the club; I just wouldn't be doing any drinks or dinners. I suppose I could have just pretended that I was busy and given him my work schedule like I always had, but I wanted him to know that he had made me uncomfortable. I couldn't let it slide. I had to stand up for myself.

He did not respond well to the email. I had suspected that he wouldn't. He said something about us just calling it quits and asked me to send him his DVD in the mail, which I had thought was a gift, not a loan. But whatever, of course, I would send it to him – with no return address and from a post office across town.

I was sorry to see his money go, but it was getting to be too much. This is supposed to be a relationship built on faux intimacy and a faux life. It should be all laughter and jean burn. I cancelled my work email. It was supposed to help me lure guys into the club, but it ended up being more irritating than lucrative. So, that's it; no more Cargo Pants.

It's 10 p.m. on a Thursday night and there's one despondent middle-aged couple, one Asian regular, four Mexicans (who've been here for two hours and haven't spent any money), and one lonely forty-something, whitish-looking guy, who sadly does not have the scent of money. But that isn't stopping every girl in here from champing at his bit. It's not the best financial climate for breaking up with a regular. But what are you gonna do?

I was on the phone yesterday with my long-distance customer (a Bay Area chap I met at Mitchell Brothers in the late nineties), and I found myself telling him about what had happened with Cargo Pants. I thought he would feel protective and sorry for me and would make a trip to the bank, but it's a fine line between the truth and too close to home. He didn't have much to say and didn't offer any money. Customers don't want to be reminded of what they are. They don't want reality; they want happy, giggly girls who talk about puppies and doughnuts.

49

RANDY IS ONE of my favorite managers at the Bare, not just because we get along, but because he has gone through so many different stages in the years I've known him. He's been at the Bare longer than I have, so it's been a while. He worked his way up the ladder and was once the general manager, but was then usurped by the current GM. In fact, poor Randy was demoted about a year ago and placed at the Valley Ball. They only recently started giving him some shifts back at the Bare.

Randy recently read *The Secret* and likes to work its premises into every conversation. Even if you're discussing the best fruit for a margarita, he'll work it in. Had he really never heard of self-visualization before the magical book? I have nothing against the power of positive thinking. I just don't necessarily need a hyped-up, pseudo-spiritual motivational speech while I'm standing naked in the dressing room covering my skin with shimmering, sugar-scented body spray. Plus, after all our years working together at the club, I can't help but notice that he hasn't won the lottery yet, and nothing has changed with his career. Except that now he walks around with this cult-y smile and a spiel for the girls on how to manifest their destiny and finances. Randy is a good guy, so I pardon his Kool-Aid behavior, but I find that I'm not standing next to him as often as I used to.

Coupled with this new and overly positive philosophy, he's also stopped drinking. Truthfully, I think I liked him better when he was buzzed and bitter. Now it's like working with Tony Robbins, only a tad more depressing. Sorry, Randy.

But God bless his heart, he always has a moneymaking scheme that's going to make him rich and get him out of the biz. I don't want him to fail. Quite the opposite, but after sixteen years, I've heard it all before, so it becomes rather moot because we're both still here. It's like mixing porn and religion. There's a time and a place, and while I'm high and half-naked isn't one of them.

I saw Twenty-Minute Man after work last night. He requested that I wear something sexy. Ugh. I loathe requests. And what's the point? You remove it within minutes anyway. I hate having to dress 'sexy' for customers. Their version of sexy is quite different from mine. They want run-of-the-mill: black lace with garter belts and mini tube-dresses, which is so dated and boring. But it's work and I was coming from the club, which made it easier, so I wore a mini skirt, thigh-high fishnets and a cute top. Just as I had expected, the clothes lasted for all of four seconds. I could wear a garbage bag as long as my mouth and pussy are involved.

After our twenty-two minutes, I got in my car and started the drive home, exhausted and ready for a shower. I made a right onto Rosecrans from Sepulveda and decided that driving in my Chucks was preferable to the high-heeled boots I was wearing, so I pulled over in an extra lane to the right of the six-lane street, which looked like a bus stop. These beach towns are barren of life at 2 a.m. on a weeknight. I wasn't obstructing a soul. As I was reaching for my boot zipper, I noticed a cop on the other side of the median heading toward me. Shit. As expected, he put on his lights and made a U-turn. I gave up on my shoe swap, turned my engine off, and fished out my ID and insurance info. I had been drinking earlier at work, but it was a while back, so I wasn't too concerned, only annoyed.

'Hello, ma'am,' he said. 'Where are you coming from?'

'Hi,' I said. 'A friend's house. I'm heading home.'

'Did you have anything to drink tonight?' he asked.

'Nope,' I said.

'Where's home?'

'Hollywood,' I said. 'I pulled over to switch out of my high-heeled boots to tennis shoes because they're better to drive in.'

Naturally he looked toward my legs. I followed his gaze and noticed that my mini skirt was barely covering my crotch and I was flashing the dude a lot of leg and inner thigh, which also included my fishnet thigh-highs with patent leather at the top. I checked for his reaction. He had a big smile. He took my information and said he'd be right back. I desperately wanted to change my footwear, but I know cops don't like it when people lean over or do anything while pulled over, so I left my half-unzipped boots alone.

He came back and handed me my things. 'So,' he said. 'Where's this party you were at and why are you leaving?' he asked in a flirty voice.

'Are we finished?'

Before he could finish telling me that we were, I rolled up the window and drove away. Lesson learned. Don't pull over with the engine running and parking lights on in small towns late at night. Switch clothes and shoes on side streets. But if you do get pulled over, it helps if you're wearing fishnets.

50

WHAT A NIGHT. I believed things were over with Cargo Pants, but nothing is ever over in this alternate universe. A week or so after I sent him the email I got a text from him asking if I was working this week and if so, could he come in? He promised not to make a scene and said he just wanted to see me one more time. I said yes. I hadn't been keeping solid boundaries with him anyway, so why start now? This is what happens when you're broke, and a bit broken.

He came in and I ended up making a grip of money. It was one of those magical nights when I only went on stage once and the rest of the night was a blur of private dances. You get to skip the stage at the Bare if you're dancing with a customer. Mitchell Brothers had a strict rotation list and we were expected to be on stage in that exact order. I'm famous for talking guys into a last-minute lap dance just to get out of going on stage. The money on stage isn't what it used to be, and I can't dance the way I used to because of my foot.

Cargo Pants walked in about an hour into my shift. I had just finished getting paid for a dance. Because I was buzzed and happy, I treated the situation as if nothing had happened. I'm good like that. But when I went in for a hug, it was clear that Cargo Pants wasn't good. He was wrought with trepidation and ill at ease. It was instantly uncomfortable. Ah crap, here we go. I told him to go find a table and that I'd be right there. I knew I would need a lot more alcohol before dealing with this.

Back from the dressing room and a little softer around the cerebrum, I sat down. He immediately started in on the issue. I was hoping to skip all that. I thought he'd come in and get dances and we'd be fine. Now I was worried that he wasn't planning on getting any dances, which would make sitting through this bullshit a complete waste of time and energy, not to mention that a dancer's emotional state is in direct correlation to her making money.

He talked; it was heavy. He had misinterpreted something I had said in my email. He described a scary incident he'd once had with a girl and her boyfriend. I had unwittingly set off some emotional bells for him by saying that I had told my boyfriend about the 'finding my house' comment, and he wasn't too happy. He took it as a threat. I had only said that in my email because I wanted him to know that I had told someone. I was simply trying to protect myself in case he decided to start cruising neighborhood parks in Hollywood. I was going to say 'friends' instead of 'boyfriend', but I thought it would embarrass him. I didn't want him to think I had been talking shit about him. There I go with the overthinking and worrying too much about other people's feelings. I reassured him that I hadn't been threatening to have my boyfriend beat him up. He relaxed a little. I put my hand on his knee – something I've done a hundred times – and he angrily swept it away. I don't know why, but his reaction caught me so off guard and was such a slap in the face that tears pooled in my eyes. Tears were rolling down my shiny cheeks. I could tell that he felt like an ass, as he should.

I couldn't have planned a better turn of events. I excused myself saying I would be back in a minute and locked myself in a bathroom stall. The tears were really coming!

I guess one of the hazards of having a fantasy relationship is that even the smallest gesture that veers off the happy road hits you hard. In a real relationship, curve balls are thrown at you all the time, but when there's a problem after six years of smooth sailing in fantasyland, it hits a bit harder. I'm guessing that's why I was crying, though it could have been the vodka.

I pulled it together and walked back to the table. Cargo Pants went into a monologue about how I was the only one who could deal with him and that he didn't have many friends. He also told me that he was crazy but refused to take medication. None of this made me feel any better about the possible stalking and the skin suit, but the dollar signs and stack of bills sitting in my house overruled reason. So I listened and smiled. Red flags were popping up everywhere, but I squashed them into oblivion. A little more time passed before he asked if I was ready for the VIP. Yes! I wanted to get my mind off this. I told him that I needed to go take a shot (or five) of vodka before we danced, the first time I have ever mentioned drinking at the club. He said he understood.

We went to dance, and it was as if nothing had happened. The same old program commenced. The shirts came off and we started the first song while we were standing, my back to him and my butt against his groin while I bent over. Then I turned around and hugged him as I put my knees on either side of his waist and held myself up using the horizontal bar, pushing my pelvis into his as I arched my back. Our dance is a well-oiled machine. Never mind the fact that I was crying ten minutes ago during our heated discussion; I'm super-stripper!

We did four sets and were sweaty and smiling by the end. Everything was back to normal. Funny how money and simulated sex can do that. He gave me a hundred-dollar tip. I told him that I had deleted my email account. He was bummed that he couldn't send me dumb jokes and kitty pictures. I told him that I would text when I was going into work. He knew the ball was in my court; he said okay. Good, that's the way it should be. After he left, I ran to the dressing room, reapplied my make-up, took a muscle relaxer and polished off the rest of my hooch. The remainder of the night was filled with back-to-back dances. I barely remember even asking. I wish it were always like that. Maybe I should cry more often.

51

IN A MANNER of speaking, the Hells Angels saved my life. I was seventeen and approximately five months clean and sober when I started dating one of the San Francisco skinheads. It wasn't my most awe-inspiring time. I was ripe with post-institution and childhood rage, which is really what the skinheads were: just a bunch of pissed-off youth with a side of racial hate. I only had the former.

My friend Portia from delinquent high school and I used to hang out at Buena Vista Park on Haight Street. A bunch of skinheads also spent time there. In fact, it was known as Skinhead Hill in the early eighties.

I don't remember exactly how I met Buzz, but it was either at that park, a show or a house party. Buzz was in his twenties: tall, strong and intense. He was also covered in tattoos, which included maggots on his head that looked like they were crawling in and out of his skull. He had lost a piece of his eyelid in a fight. He was a real charmer, certifiable with a crooked smile. He also had a huge cock.

A bunch of these skins lived in a flat on Baker Street. I had an apartment to myself in Marin, but spent most of my time with Buzz at the skin house because however stupid and horrid they were, they were a family. A brutal family that traveled in packs looking for trouble, but a family nonetheless. The violence made me uncomfortable, but the raw power of it also did something to me. I loved going to shows with the pack, knowing that if anyone dared fuck with me, all I'd have to do was point and they'd get jumped.

Buzz and I got into nasty arguments. He never hit me, but came close a couple of times. He was a scary motherfucker. No one wanted to be on the receiving end of his anger, including the other skinheads. When Buzz and I were alone and not fighting, he showed me a softer side of himself. Crazy as it sounds, underneath all the bullshit, he had a big heart. Buzz stayed at my apartment a few times, where, in secret, he'd listen to LL Cool J and other black artists that I had always liked.

Buzz had grown up in a predominantly black neighborhood and apparently the kids were ruthless and had beaten the shit out of him daily. He talked to me about it and explained that it's where his racism began. I, on the other hand, have never had a racist bone in my body. I'm the girl who decked a boy for calling a fellow classmate the n-word when I was eleven. Hanging out with the skins was simply an outlet for my rage against life. This is embarrassing to admit, but I had cassette tapes of racist country songs recorded by the KKK and I knew them by heart. I'd roll around town singing them! What can I say? I was seventeen and dealing with some major anger issues. I even marched with the skins in a white pride parade down Haight Street. It was on the news. It wasn't my proudest moment.

Buzz was in and out of jail for his various violent acts. I witnessed him kick a guy in the head once and the dude's eye popped out; it was horrible. While locked away, he threatened to kill me if I ever cheated on him or left him. Although I was the only one who stood up to him, I was also extremely scared of him, so I stuck around. I visited him in jail like a good girlfriend. I even took sexy pictures of myself, which, I found out later, he traded for cigarettes. The photos went to a man who was about to serve ten years in Quentin.

I kept going to NA meetings, including my home group. I wore Buzz's bomber jacket with its offensive bigoted and anti-Semitic patches as well as a San Francisco Drinking Team patch (I wish I had kept that one). My NA family never gave me a hard time about it. They just smiled and told me to keep coming back. Staying clean and sober was the most important thing to them, and I did that.

I knew I had to break it off with Buzz, but I didn't know how. I often prayed for the strength to leave him or for him to get locked up for good. But Buzz got out of jail and days later, we got into a colossal brawl on Baker Street. The fucker even jumped on the hood of my car and threatened to kick the windshield in. The boys were there, but I knew they couldn't help me. Then he jumped off my car, took four angry steps, put his big hands around my neck and started to squeeze. Being choked was a huge childhood trigger for me at the time, and I remember thinking very clearly that I was done. Something clicked, and I knew I couldn't do it anymore. He could try to kill me if he wanted, but I didn't care. I was leaving. It's wild that it took something from my childhood to overcome my fear, which is why I was so angry in the first place.

I squirmed out of his grip around my neck, looked him dead in the eyes and told him I was through. Then I got in my car and sped away. I was shaking, but I had done it. I went to a meeting immediately. I was terrified that Buzz would show up at my house, but he didn't and not long afterward, I got word that the Hell's Angels, whose headquarters were across the street from Buena Vista Park (aka Skinhead Hill), were fed up with the boys' antics and had kicked them out of the city. The skins weren't shit compared to the Hells Angels. I was so fucking relieved. I don't know where Buzz went (there were rumors that they all went to Seattle), but I knew he couldn't hurt me. I never would have guessed that my salvation would come at the hands of the San Francisco Hells Angels. I am supremely grateful to the universe for their intervention.

52

DO YOU KNOW how many things I've put on or around my pussy over the last eighteen years? It's my belief that strippers have the healthiest and most ironclad vaginas in the world. It may take time for the lady parts to adjust, but eventually they do and then they become immune. Rubbing on strangers. Climbing poles. Touching everything. Touching ourselves. Sweating in odd materials. Lube, toys, glitter, powder, tanning crap and perfume. Our pussies deal with some strange shit.

❧

A new girl just asked me if she smelled like a fucking yeast infection! She scratched her crotch as she did this. If I can smell your yeasty beaver from two feet away, it's a serious problem, sweetie. I could never in a million years imagine asking anyone, let alone a stranger, if they could smell my pungent and/or ill pussy.

But I laughed. I couldn't help it. It was so absurd. I stared into her vacant eyes, looking for intelligent life or a sense of humor. Neither appeared. I backed up a little and said that she should probably leave work and hit a Rite-Aid pronto if she was having lady biz troubles, especially if the issue had progressed to the point of a three-foot odor radius!

Dancers shouldn't come into work with yeast or bacterial infections, for several reasons. First, the club environment is the worst place for a yeasty vat. Second, who wants a girl touching her sick snatch and then touching everything else? And third – although I admit that this is a little funny – guys are going to leave the club with their crotches smelling like unwell pussy.

Get the fuck out of here and take care of your shit! Young girls these days don't know dick about their pussies. I witness these tweens spraying perfume directly on their pussies. That can't be good. I also see them drowning their beavers with that FDS shit, which is unnecessary and gross. Your pussy shouldn't smell like a baby or a rhododendron, it should smell like a clean vagina.

I'm going to kill the DJ! I don't like this guy, but he works day shifts so I don't usually have to deal with him. I guess he's covering a shift, or the night guy is running late. Either way, he called me on stage with only thirty seconds' notice. I ran to the DJ booth to pick my music. He said there was no time, and then blurted, 'I'll play rock that you dance to.'

I ran on stage. The motherfucker played '*That Smell*'. Are you fucking kidding me? I have never – nor would I ever – dance to that song. I know we aren't best buds, but come on, we're not enemies either. That's the last time I ever let him pick my music.

Later in the night, I may have overdone it with the mood-altering fun because my vision started blacking out during a VIP. There I was, straddling the bloke when suddenly the small cubicle started to dim and my vision narrowed. It was like looking down a long, dim hallway in a red-lit room with blurry edges and a stranger at the end. Lord knows what I looked like. My face was directly in front of his. When in doubt, smile. Smile and continue grinding. I rode it out, hoping I stayed conscious; it would be bad to pass out on a customer. God only knows what could happen. I could clunk his head hard with mine, and he could ask for a refund. But I did not lose consciousness. The vision returned, and I finished the dance. I got a good tip too.

I love how Randy thinks I'm one of the good girls. 'You never get fucked up,' he just said. I won't tell him that I almost passed out on a customer in the VIP eight minutes ago. He doesn't need to know.

53

A YEAR OR two ago, just as my limp was fading, I started photographing some of the dancers I work with. I had always loved photography but never thought of myself as an artist. Turns out, watching women dance on stage all these years and my neurosis have paid off! It's been an incredible outlet and alternative source of income. I recently befriended a young girl that I photographed for an alternative porn site. She was nineteen when I met her, and she's now a whopping twenty. I got her a job at the Bare. I don't usually help girls get a start in the business, but she had already done porn, so I figured what the fuck? The reason I don't like to assist in a girl's jumpstart into stripping is because, selfishly, I don't want to be responsible for them. That is, I don't want to have to vouch for them, let them borrow outfits, et cetera. Secondly, it's a dying industry. The whole point of stripping was to make a good living, not just learn pole tricks.

You would think that a young girl who's brand new to the industry would be somewhat demure and sponge-like, or even intimidated. Not this generation. On her first night, within the two hours it took her to put on her make-up (I generally take thirty minutes), she was already borrowing outfits and giving advice! The way I was raised in the industry – if you tried to get all cozy with the seasoned gals on your first night, they would have laughed and told you to shut your mouth and listen to how things worked. Or they would have told you to fuck off. This girl was acting like she owned the place! It was not like this when I started dancing. The vets schooled the new girls. This doesn't happen anymore, at least not that I've seen in the last few years. In my eighth or ninth year, I would talk to the new girls about how to behave, but now, I just do my own thing. I don't give a fuck how they act – within reason. I will certainly speak up if I see something grossly out of line.

I wonder, is it the fact that we've given up or are the young ones feeling more entitled in general these days? I've seen girls stripping straight out of high school. There's a girl at my club who was still *in* high school when she started! Maybe it's too easy. These kids aren't paying their menial employment dues. They aren't pumping gas or cleaning offices. They graduate from twelfth grade and segue directly to banking on their looks and sex appeal.

These tweens grew up in the late nineties and early 2000s watching Britney Spears and *Girls Gone Wild*. They're fully aware that there's power in being sexy. I knew this when I was in high school, but the difference is that there wasn't an easy way to make a living using my sex appeal in 1984. Times have changed.

54

I WASN'T ALWAYS a whore, stripper, exotic dancer or harlot. Actually, I guess I've already admitted that I've been that last one for a long time. But as far as work goes, I've done a wide variety of things. I cleaned offices when I was eleven. I've worked in restaurants. I sold vacuum cleaners in the late eighties. I taught first and second grade at Old Mill School in Mill Valley. For a few years before I moved out, I sold crystals and pewter figurines with my mom at craft shows and county fairs. My mom and I went up and down the West Coast pushing that bullshit. On my breaks, I would walk around and find other underage kids to hang with.

In later years (at the ripe age of fifteen), I'd drink booze with the guys who ran the rides and prize games at the county fairs. They were the real deal. Lifers. True carnies. We were interlopers from the craft and tchotchke area. Sometimes, my mom and I would rent a cheap hotel room and other times, we slept in the back of our crap crystal booth in a makeshift home and used the showers on the fairgrounds. Some of the fairs ran a month long. While working at my last Del Mar county fair (the one where I was fucking older guys to get Taylor off my mind), our crystal booth sat across from a Hot Dog on a Stick, and the manager, Colin, was one of the older guys. He was in his mid-twenties with dark, wavy hair, dark, olive skin and a great smile. Colin was one of the beneficiaries of my I-need-to-be-the-best sex days. I must've been bored and annoyed with my mom because I worked for a bit in his Hot Dog on a Stick booth. He would pour me vodka and orange juice in a large soda cup and I'd get wasted while dipping dogs.

During the fall and winter season, we'd work the harvest festivals and craft shows geared toward the holiday buying market. There was this awful song, '*Grandma Got Run Over by a Reindeer*', which went on to become a radio hit. But before it did, that band played the harvest circuit, and we had to listen to that crap song five times a day, at every harvest festival on the West Coast. By the time Christmas came, my mom and I were postal and ready to stick sharp objects in our ears.

At fourteen, I was the manager of a bakery in Larkspur. I lied about my age in order to get the job. When I was sixteen, as I've mentioned, I pumped gas for Chevron. My boss had a crush on me. He'd hook me up with Kahlua in my coffee. I went to delinquent high school from 8 a.m. to 12.30 p.m. and worked at Chevron from 2 p.m. to 10 p.m., five days a week. After I passed the proficiency exam, I stopped going to school and got a full-time job working at a store called Whole Earth in San Rafael.

My dad had left his landscaping business to become a music promoter. I worked my first concert at age eleven. It was a festival my father had created and produced each summer for a few years. The Band headlined at the first one. Unlike most of my life, that concert feels as if it happened yesterday. I ran around helping my dad and handed out water to the artists on stage. I definitely get my love of music from my father.

During the summer of 1987, my father lined up a job for me at Winterland Productions, which was owned by the legendary promoter Bill Graham. Named after the famous Winterland Ballroom in San Francisco, the company made and sold merchandise for music acts. My first show with Winterland was a David Bowie concert in San Jose. It was a large outdoor venue. We had a small crew, divided up into a few stands. We were paid minimum wage and split a commission of five percent of the total gross sales. It wasn't a bad gig for a sixteen-year-old. My check from that show was three hundred and nine dollars, the most money I had ever made in one day.

The guys at Winterland liked me. The music business is a male-dominated and ego-inflated industry, so it can be tough for a woman. You need to know how to roll with the punches and give back equal shit. I was by far the youngest person in the company, but I was honest and extremely hard working. I was hawking swag at a show at the Shoreline Amphitheater in Mountain View when Bill Graham himself came by and asked if I was old enough to be working for him. He was an intense dude and prone to yelling. Not wanting to get fired or yelled at, I said yes, and he grumbled and kept moving.

Back then we only dealt in cash, so during the first band, we'd count the money – we threw all the cash in a big cardboard box – and make a drop at the office while the bands played. I loved counting all that money. I often volunteered to make the drop. Walking through an audience of thirty thousand people with a duffel bag full of cash is empowering. At times, there would be fifty or sixty grand in the bag. The trick is to look like the last person on earth who would be holding that much cash, which, at sixteen, was easily achieved. It's funny how totally comfortable I felt. Maybe it was the proximity to the drug dealing and associated piles of cash when I was growing up.

After about six months, I became a captain. This meant that I was in charge of my booth for the night. I was responsible for the merchandise count and all the money that came in and went out. It was a pretty slap-dick system and things got lost in the shuffle. My boss and I would often stay until the wee hours, trying to figure out where discrepancies came from. He'd be snorting lines of cocaine, and I'd count, recount and calculate. We made a good team. I know some of my colleagues – all of whom were much older than me – were a tad annoyed that I was made a captain. Could you blame them? I was a fucking child! But I was good at what I did. Or maybe whatshisname just wanted to fuck me. Who knows?

After a while of selling swag for Winterland, I also started working as a stagehand for Bill Graham. It was more prestige but less money. I toggled between gigs for years. There weren't many female stagehands at the time, but I worked my ass off and earned the respect of my co-workers. I didn't play into their oversize, male egos, but I was smart enough not to challenge them much either. I treated the few other women, who were probably ten years or more my senior, with respect. In a predominately male profession, it's easy for women to get all macho with each other. I skipped all that bullshit; I just wanted to learn and do my best.

Of course, I ran into assholes from time to time. Tour managers who didn't know me. I was working a Rolling Stones show at the Oakland Coliseum, and as I was unloading a big rig, this British bloke walked up to me and said, 'Doll, why don't you let the big men do this?'

My co-workers and I looked at each other, and one of them said, 'She may look like a skinny young girl to you, but trust me, her dick is bigger than yours. She knows what she's doing.' We all laughed.

The Brit said, 'My apologies, carry on.'

I loved working onstage and behind the scenes.

There were the occasional shitty times, like Dead shows. In 1988, we were warned that people were dosing strangers with liquid acid in squirt guns. Why they wanted to waste their drugs on strangers is beyond me. Halfway into one of these shows at the Shoreline, when I was in the middle of peddling a million Dead buttons, patches and tie-dye shirts, this fucker sprays me with a water bottle. I totally lost my shit on him. I waited nervously for thirty minutes, but luckily it did not contain acid.

During this period of working for Winterland and Bill Graham, I had other random gigs to survive. I was a nanny. I worked various retail jobs, including at a gay-owned-and-run cowboy boot and country-western clothing store in the Castro where I was the only female.

Then I started dancing. It began innocently enough. I was sick of working a million jobs and barely getting by. I remember on my last day working for Bill Graham, I joked to all the guys that they'd finally be able to see me naked.

THERE'S A SPECIAL pressure put on dancers to quit the biz. It comes from varying places. It comes from lovers – as you might expect – but sometimes from friends as well. 'What are you working toward?' I've been asked. The idea most people have is that stripping is only a means to something else. This pressure comes from family members, even customers, and society in general. Although I think it's all a bit hypocritical due to everyone's obsession with strippers.

My self-induced pressure has been around for most of my stripping career. I say self-induced, but the pressure has always come from my boyfriends. Thankfully, this voice has lessened over the last few years, although it never fades away completely. The constant pressure to make others happy and comfortable by quitting has made me miserable and it doesn't get me any closer to ending my career as a dancer. In fact, the moment I decided to stop focusing on quitting, I felt a perceivable change in my body and soul.

Why can't I strip until I can't walk? I never thought this would be my life, but what if it is? It sure is shaping up that way. Would that be so bad? I'm good at my job, and I bring joy to others. I've given serious shots at other careers during my time as a dancer but nothing jelled. I worked at an interior design firm. I considered opening a shoe store. I have forty-two hours logged as a pilot in training. I've written business plans, invented things and even tried patenting one of them. In 2001, I studied at UCLA to become a sound engineer and worked as a runner at Sound City Recording Studios in Van Nuys. I was stripping on the weekends to pay the bills, but I never told my colleagues or my female boss. I wanted to be taken seriously, and I knew that if they heard I was a dancer, all the male runners, engineers, producers and artists would ask questions.

Although I loved studio life and everything that goes into recording music, the exhausting hours and singular lifestyle just weren't for me, and I ultimately decided to quit and look for a different path. It was a difficult decision because I thought I had finally found the thing that would get me out of dancing. I would have to start from scratch, once again.

These are just a few of the things I've done throughout my years as a dancer.

When I was a small child, often, as I walked home from school, I could feel myself rising up above the ground, as if my spirit was soaring above me. I felt as if I was meant to do something big and change the world somehow. Did we all feel this way? Am I just your average human being with crushed dreams of grandeur? I had such good intentions.

I went to India a few years ago in search of spiritual guidance. I remember thinking, 'So what? This guy meditated on top of a mountain for years.' That sounds pretty nice. Not a ton of fun, mind you, but it's certainly easier to maintain a peaceful and enlightened attitude on a mountain doing nothing than it is sitting in your car on any given day in Los Angeles. Or what about when telling a customer for the fifth time that no, he cannot touch between my legs, and that yes, I can feel him trying. I'm not a fucking doll. I have nerve endings. Everyone has their own path. Mine just has more glitter involved.

55

I WENT OUT with Hattie last night and met a boy. Although I guess he's technically a man since we were born in the same year. We had gone to the Cha Cha Lounge, one of our local bars. Hattie and I were doing the usual, drinking our faces off, when I spotted this guy on the other side of the bar who looked like he'd be perfect for Hattie. He was cute, nerdy and wearing glasses. I've never known someone to stick so fervently to a type as Hattie does. She had recently been singing the I'll-never-meet-anyone blues so I was out to prove her wrong. He was with a buddy and had clearly noticed us. I doubt anyone in the bar hadn't, though. Hattie is legally deaf in her right ear and isn't quiet when she's sober, so you can imagine how that goes down when she's had a few. There's no excuse for me. I just get loud sometimes.

I went to the bathroom and when I walked back, the cute guy with glasses had parked himself directly in my path. Nice move.

'Well, hello there,' I said.

'Hello, yourself,' he shot back.

'I like your style,' I told him.

'Kudos for taking initiative.'

'Thanks.'

'What's your name?' I asked.

'Daniel,' he told me.

I introduced them. 'Daniel, this is my friend, Hattie. Her hickies feel like pop rocks.'

He laughed.

'Hattie, meet Daniel.' Over the bar chatter I told her, 'You should give him a hickey.' I wasn't hiding my intention to hook them up and I was oblivious to the fact that he hadn't spoken to her while I was gone but had instead put himself in my path. Displaying good character and being a good sport, he let her give him a hickey.

'Doesn't it feel like pop rocks in your ear,' I said, drunkenly.

'Uh, sure.'

It didn't take me long to realize that he was interested in me and that he was intelligent and funny as shit. Hattie went about her business, talking to our bartender buddy. I got wrapped up in Daniel. A man hadn't made me laugh like that in a long time. Hattie eventually left, and I sat with Daniel and his best friend at the bar. The friend was cool, but I got the distinct vibe that he felt like I was intruding on their boy time. I ignored it. Eventually, he left, and Daniel and I made out at the bar. I'm normally a dark-corner-of-the-bar kind of gal (not front and center at the bar), but I had tunnel vision, and he kissed me like I've always wanted someone to.

We closed the bar and made a plan to go to his place (he lived the closest). I followed him from the Cha Cha. About halfway to his house, he pulled over and got out of his car. I rolled down my window, assuming he was going to give me parking instructions, but instead he leaned in and kissed me.

'I just wanted to do that. Keep following me,' he said.

Wow. This guy was the real deal. What a move! I was in. We got to his apartment, and I was pleasantly shocked by how beautifully decorated the place was. We shared similar tastes in art and blue walls. He put on a record (yes, an album), poured us a scotch, and we continued to make out and grind on the couch. I was so turned on. I could have kissed him for a year. But other parts of me also wanted attention, so we took it to the bedroom. He gave me the best head I've ever had! On the first meeting, no less. That's unheard of. We had sex and fooled around and laughed until almost dawn. I couldn't remember the last time I had laughed so hard. It takes a specific type of wit to really get me, and Daniel's was spot on. He was highly intelligent. He worked at a university and was also an established musician. He seemed like a nice mix of head and heart.

I had told him when we got to his house that I wouldn't be spending the night (I prefer to sleep alone in my own bed). He said that was nonsense. 'It's just who I am,' I explained. However, when the sleeping portion of the evening arrived, I was still too drunk to make the haul to Hollywood, so I stayed, but not for very long. As soon as the sun started to stream through his uncovered windows above our head and began searing my brain, I got up quietly. My head was killing me, but I needed to get to my big bed and my very dark bedroom, *stat*. I peed, splashed water on my face, put a dollop of toothpaste in my mouth and got dressed. I wrote down my number, said a quick goodbye and made the painful drive home.

I hope to see him again soon.

56

I GAVE JABBA the Hut a blowjob. I was on the hunt for a sugar daddy. Enter trusty Craigslist.org. I found a guy in the adult services section. We emailed a couple of times. He described his situation in detail and told me exactly the type of arrangement he was looking for. His wife, the 'love of his life', had passed away, and he didn't want to remarry, but he got lonely. He said that he'd had this arrangement with two other women in the past. According to him, they both went on to do great things.

His offer was twenty thousand a month, plus a new car, full medical and an expense account (apparently, I would be on his company's payroll). He also promised jewelry and travel. He described the diamond-band ring he bought all his 'ladies'. I was to wear this ring whenever I was in his company. He also wanted proof of an AIDS test. He would provide one as well, and I wasn't allowed to see any other men. He only needed to see me once or twice a month. If his offer was legit, I wouldn't need any other johns or clubs. I figured I could easily hide my personal enjoyment from him. It all sounded doable. He said he would meet me for one drink and if he liked me, he'd arrange a second 'interview' and book a hotel room.

I met him in the middle of the day at the bar of the Holiday Inn in Burbank. I'm generally, not a fan of the daytime meet-and-greet. It means I must make a tricky clothing decision. The goal is to look sexy without being inappropriately overdressed. I'm also not great at doing day make-up. I've perfected my stripper face, but it doesn't translate into the real world, certainly not at the Burbank Holiday Inn lounge during lunch hour.

I went to Macy's and charged a sundress on my account, which I planned to wear and then return. Macy's is a great place for medium-end hooker clothes. I also picked up some cute flats. In my experience, most johns tend to be short and nothing screams prostitute like a pretty woman towering over a stout, older, bald dude. My sincere apologies to any couples matching this description who are, in fact, in love.

So, there I was at 2 p.m., on a Wednesday, ordering a whiskey sour and looking for my sugar daddy. He had described himself only a little in our emails. Of course, I had sent him a picture. Most men won't even bother with a second email without an image. He had said that he was a regular at the hotel and knew everyone who worked there, so when a hefty white man came in and ordered 'the usual', I guessed it was him. I was anxious and ready to get it over with. This is why madams exist. Who wants to deal with this bullshit?

We said hello and took a seat at one of the old, round tables in the dark, depressing bar. We made idle chitchat. He was nice enough. I would guess he was in his fifties. He had thinning grey hair and pinkish skin and he weighed at least four hundred pounds. He made it clear again that this was the verbal interview portion and that I would need to pass it to meet him a second time. After that, he would decide. Whatever, dude. Let's just get through this, I thought.

He proceeded to tell me the same long story he'd already described in his email.

It's not as if I could say, 'Hey, man, I already know this shit. Do you think I'm pretty? Do you want to fuck me? Can't we just cut to the chase?' So instead, I sat there counting the minutes, wondering where I was going to grab dinner that night. I tried to be as charming as I could be in the middle of the day, but I'm not a day girl. I'm usually in sweats and a pigtail around this time, trying to stay away from the sunlight.

He thanked me for meeting him, and we went our separate ways. I couldn't really tell anything by his demeanor. I called Hattie on my way to the car and told her I didn't think I got the part. I lightly kicked myself for taking the time, showering, putting on make-up and driving to Burbank for free, but I had to keep the big picture in mind. I was surprised when a couple of days later, he emailed to say that I had passed the first interview and we set up our second one. This time, he told me to meet him at the Holiday Inn just off the 405. He added that he wanted to make sure he had 'chemistry' with the lady whom he chose to 'adopt'. Chemistry. Are you fucking kidding me? This guy is pasty and seriously obese. The only chemistry we're going to have is whatever it takes for me to get the job. I'm a hooker; chemistry is my profession.

We didn't discuss finances for the meeting, which made me itchy, but I kept my eyes on the prize. I also assumed, this not being his first rodeo, that he would know the drill and compensate me. Never assume anything in life. Men call me a hustler for my forthrightness. I call it being smart. But even I get caught up in protecting their feelings over my interests sometimes. I've run across a few men who respected my being upfront about the payment, but most get turned off. It's a delicate balance keeping them happy and making sure I'm taken care of, too. Personally, I like getting the financial part out of the way so the fun can commence.

I drove to the hotel, which was coincidentally next door to another hotel where I used to meet a past john. I'd had a cocktail before leaving the house to calm my nerves. I parked and found his room. We said our hellos and he turned the TV off. I tuned the radio to my go-to jazz station (I do this in every hotel/john situation – they don't play commercials and no one wants to fuck a stranger in silence).

I slipped out of my heels and peeled off my skirt. He was lying on the bed, propped up on a pillow – his gigantic body looking even bigger than before. It was a king bed but looked like a double. I climbed on top of his massive body and wondered how in the fuck I was going to physically do this. He was easily the largest man I've ever been with. No matter, I'm fearless! I can do almost anything I set my mind to. I kissed his pudgy lips. Ew. I put my boobs in his face. I tried to give him a makeshift lap dance as foreplay, but it was bizarre and nearly impossible. I wasn't even sure where his penis was. I removed his beige socks, then his boxer briefs. His cock was tiny. Of course, it was. There was no way I could have intercourse with him. I took my panties off, but it was just so he felt like he was getting the full experience. I kissed him again, and he fumbled around with my pussy with his pudgy left hand in a totally annoying manner. He was kind of pinching it between his fat fingers. I couldn't take it anymore, so I went south. I did it to get his uncoordinated and untalented fingers the fuck away from my bits, and to get this nightmare over with.

I grabbed the condom on the side table, wishing I had one of those finger condoms that nurses use to probe buttholes. I didn't even have to unroll it all the way to cover him. Whatever, I held it in place. I started to suck his baby penis. It was awful down there. He obviously showered, but he still had the smell of fat folds. I guess a person can only reach so much of their crevices when pure mass is in the way.

Thankfully, it didn't take long. He seemed slightly embarrassed, so I took that as my cue to climb off and trot to the bathroom. I grabbed a small towel and handed it to him, and then I leapt back inside and shut the door to wash out my mouth and take a few deep breaths.

I returned, all smiles and warm skin. He hadn't moved an inch, which was a small red flag. I lay on the bed half naked next to him, hugged his rolls of fat and kissed his cheek. After about three awkward minutes, I got off the bed and started to get dressed, slowly, waiting for him to make a move from the bed to his briefcase full of cash. Jabba didn't move a muscle. I began to panic. Did I really just give head to this monstrosity for free? When my heels were the only item left, I asked him casually about some sort of financial compensation for my time.

He hemmed and hawed, then finally rolled off the bed. He walked with elephantine steps over to his wallet and begrudgingly took out some bills for me. Thank Christ he had hundreds. What an asshole. Millionaire, my ass. He treated me as if I had committed some cardinal sin, that by asking for money I had ruined my chances for any future together. Bullshit. I was pissed. I left and never heard from Jabba again.

About a year later, a good friend of mine told me about a man she'd been communicating with from a sugar daddy website. They hadn't met in person yet, but she was excited to meet him. She described the exact situation Jabba had laid out for me. Without telling her the tale, I said she should forget him. He was a fake and a waste of time. Ah, the perils and pitfalls of prostitution.

57

IT'S 3.40 A.M. What's the point of getting high on speed if you don't clean your kitchen? I'm high right now, but it never makes me feel like cleaning. I clean when I'm hung-over, which makes absolutely no sense.

Here's what's on my mind tonight: relationships. In a new relationship, how much of your true self should you reveal? Should this person know me entirely and come to their own decision, or do I only show them what I think they want to see? I'm generally a pull-no-punches type, but not everyone can handle it. I suppose I should be myself and find out immediately if he or she can deal with it, but fuck, that seems so limiting. Plus, there are many different aspects to who I am. I don't want to be pigeonholed by one random, crazy thing I may say, or do. Lord knows I've had enough of that already. I could be the queen of pigeonhole town. But who wants that honor?

I've been seeing Daniel from the Cha Cha Lounge. He's great, and from what I can tell, he's a well-balanced adult. We've hung out two and a half times. I say a half because of our first late-night hook-up when we met. On our first official date, I word-vomited all over him, disclosing way too much information. Over cocktails, I tossed intimate stories out like grenades. I didn't mean to, but they just kept coming. 'I gave my first blowjob to a guy on a couch at a party when I was thirteen.' BOOM! 'I was a lesbian at fifteen; people used to think I was a boy, and I even had a mullet at one point.' POW! 'I was locked up in a mental institution at sixteen.' BOOM! 'I dated a skinhead when I was seventeen and marched in a white pride parade down Haight Street.' BANG! 'I was a member of Alcoholics Anonymous for twelve and a half years, but I'm not an alcoholic.' CRASH! 'Stripper since '92.' POW! 'I've had sex for money.' PING! 'I tried to end my life two years ago and have permanent nerve damage in my left foot.' CRACK! 'I just got out of a horribly unhealthy, four-year relationship, and I couldn't come with him because I didn't trust him.' SPLAT! 'I fooled around with LL Cool J's manager backstage while working at his show in '87.' POW! 'Oh, that hooker part, yeah, I still do that.' Motherfucking boom.

Sheeeiiiiit. What did I say about a boring life? That it sounds blissful? Thankfully, he handled it well, but obviously, it wasn't the greatest way to start. I was nervous and when that happens, I sometimes get a case of over-the-top Tourette's.

It's a battle. I like to say what I think when I think it. Finesse and timing is what I'm working on. Earlier tonight, while I was at work, I was all giddy and bored and filled with thoughts of Daniel. I wanted to send him a picture of myself from the dressing room, which, thanks to the invention of camera phones, turns into a photography studio on slow nights. Normally I would do this without a thought, but now I'm trying to be somewhat appropriate, especially after the unfortunate verbal bombings. Ugh, who the fuck told me to be appropriate? I don't do it well and the concern of it sends me into a mild mental frenzy. As if I didn't already consider people's feelings enough, now I have to be freaking appropriate! I'm screwed. I was second-guessing my cute-picture-sending idea.

Will he think I'm nuts? Or a dirty slut? Fucking him after only knowing him for two hours may have already put the ink on that one. I'm a proud slut, though. He should back out now if that sort of thing bothers him. What if he's offended? It seems absurd, but some men are put off by this kind of sexual display. Oh, for fuck's sake, what the shit is going on? Shouldn't he be thrilled? After all the people I've been with, all the lap dances and the sex shows, I'm anxious about sending a man a fuckin' G-rated picture of my sexy panties? How did I get here? My recent theory on why I haven't found 'the one' is that I've lacked the right kind of self-respect and filtering system, so I'm trying something different. But goddamn it, it's making me batty.

I want someone who enjoys me – all of me. The good. The bad. The experienced. The experimental. The haven't-done-it-yet. The over-thinker. And the sensitive. Everything. I have censored and compromised myself in one way or another in almost every relationship I've ever had. When do I just get to be myself? Who will love me for exactly the woman I am? I've met men, who prided themselves on being open-minded and experienced, who have winced at some of my life facts.

So here's what I did: I sent him a text that said, 'Tell me, is it in poor taste to send you a picture from the club?'

His response was, 'Maybe . . . depends . . . OK go ahead.'

Not what I was hoping for. 'I should have been more clear: a pic of me,' I wrote back.

'I still say OK,' he answered. Not wholly reassuring, but I resolved to stick with being myself.

I took an artsy, sexy, black and white picture of my panties and silver lace top. With it I said, 'You're on my mind, it's simple. Hope your night is going well.'

I waited with tiny knots in my belly. This guy doesn't know me, and I'm his first stripper, but what the fuck happened to fun? Why can't this be seen as simple flirtation? It's foreplay, people! An alluring way of saying hello. This is the twenty-first century, is it not? As if life weren't toilsome enough, I've got to stew over whether this man will be offended by a picture of my panties. It's exhausting.

Twenty minutes went by after my panty text. All I got in return was, 'Nice.' Okay, no more pictures.

❧──❀──☙

I love when men give me shit about my price for sex. 'How much would *you* charge to fuck a person you absolutely did not want to?' I should ask. I try to explain that money is relative, but it never works. When men are whining, having a tantrum or bargain hunting, common sense no longer applies. It's hard to find generous, clean and halfway normal guys to prostitute with. I totally get why girls have madams. Not street pimps. I'm speaking of a higher class of call girl here, a madam with a black book of wealthy clients, who sets everything up and weeds out the riffraff – vets the men. It would be worth giving up a percentage to have someone else sift through all the bullshit. I could have worked for the woman who took Heidi Fleiss's place a bunch of years back, but at the time I was making good money (and running my own impressive deals), so I told her thanks, but no thanks. It was a nice ego boost, however. She had come into Mitchell Brothers to recruit. I would welcome the help now, but I'm older and although there's a market for me, I'm not sure a high-end madam would see that. I suppose I could laser my sun damage and Botox myself a little, but getting a pimp isn't high on my to-do list.

I get the feeling my cat knows something is off. He's acting a little strange. Granted, I'm smoking crack, drinking booze out of the bottle, listening to music through headphones and ferociously typing at five thirty in the morning. I felt a headache coming on, so I took half a soma. They taste disgusting. I can't believe I choked down eighty of them once. I'm drinking whiskey now (vodka earlier), and the rest of the Jägermeister. I'm cooking up a fine hangover. But not if I get enough sleep. Sleep is the key. I also had a salad. The salad will save me.

Smoking out of a glass pipe reminds me of a C-list actor I fucked for a minute when I first separated from my husband. My girl Honey and I were hanging out a lot at the time. She is such an extraordinary woman. I know her from my Mitchell Brothers days. In fact, I'll never forget the first time I saw her on stage. I was upstairs standing next to the DJ, waiting to follow her – an impossible task.

She was on her second song. It was slow and sultry. Mike the DJ had the blue spotlight on her. She was buck naked, aside from heels and a thick rhinestone choker, which shimmered in the light. The blue glow was stunning against her caramel colored skin. I was in awe. I wasn't the only one. She commanded the audience. We were all under her spell.

Honey and I became friends not long after I was hired at the club. We both liked strong, feisty girls. Honey is Cuban, French and black. She's drop-dead gorgeous, witty, well-spoken and full of spice. She's the shit. One of the best qualities of our friendship is our ability to go anywhere together. We always said we could do uptown and downtown, meaning, we could easily feel at home at a ghetto party in Oakland, a pool hall full of sharks and gangsters, or ordering champagne at a swanky, five-star joint. And we certainly did. I would venture to say that of all the people I've known thus far, Honey is the one person I can truly be myself with, one hundred percent. Not only does she have zero judgment, she can also relate from personal experience. Our lives were parallel in such incredible ways, all the way back to our childhoods. We joke that she's the black version of me – with a much better vocabulary. My female friends today – no matter how much they love me and how close we are – will never be able to fully relate to my life. Honey does, one hustler to another. It's a bond you can't fuck with – or fake. It's quite a gift having a person like her in my life.

Honey had moved down from the Bay Area a few years before I did and also lived in Hollywood. Whenever she and I got together, it was pure debauchery. I never worried about anything when I was with Honey.

The Rainbow on Sunset Boulevard was one of our go-to spots. More than a few times, we hung out in the tiny wooden private tree house upstairs doing drugs and talking smack with random people. I even gave some dude a handjob in the kitchen bathroom to score some blow once. I loved the depravity, especially just coming off a decade of being so good. Another time, we snorted smack off a girl's fingernail in the bathroom. It was amazing.

One night, we went back to Honey's place. I was lying on her living room floor, melting into the carpet, while she played old-school R&B hit after hit. It was pure heaven.

Honey is intensely outgoing and meets people wherever she goes, so of course, she knew most of the tenants in her apartment complex. One of them was an actor who booked just enough work to afford being holed up in his apartment smoking drugs. My Cajun sister and I took the elevator up to his place. It was the first time I ever smoked cocaine. I was surprised to find that the high was mellower than snorting it, but that it kept you up longer.

Actor boy was cute, although clearly wrapped up in a serious addiction. His dealer (someone my girl also knew) delivered the rock to his door. The four of us got *fucked up* that night. It was a lot of fun. The actor took a liking to me and wanted to pass his lungfuls of hubba rock (eighties East Bay slang for crack cocaine) to me with a kiss. This move probably has a name, but I'm not that cool.

I hung out with Actor a few times after that first night. We'd hide out in his apartment smoking cocaine for a day or so, and then I'd go home to eat and sleep. Actor kept going. I was coming at it from a different angle. It was a novelty and a study in human behavior for me. I would watch him search the carpet for the fallout rocks he thought were there. I knew the fishing felt good, so I only intervened when I felt like fucking.

Actor was handsome and well-endowed. He couldn't always come due to all the rock, but he would stay hard for hours! That's cool and shit, but damn, a woman needs a break once in a while, especially a woman who's been freebasing for more than eight hours. The activity doesn't really aid in the slippery department, if you know what I mean. More than once I had to slow him down and suggest we take a time out. This often proved difficult when he was super high and getting his freak on. But I had to in order to save my poor pussy.

His routine soon bored me (and wore me the fuck out), so I skedaddled. I wonder if that dude is still alive.

Honey has since moved to the beach, and her life has chilled dramatically, but I will always look back fondly on those crazy times we had together.

The sun is coming up and the gates to the alien tranny park are opening. It's time to go to bed.

58

FLIP-FLOPS. REALLY? Who wears flip-flops to a strip club? Don't these guys realize that all the girls are wearing hospital-inducing heels? Flip-flops are a major pain in the ass. Now I have to add your toes to an already extensive list of things to think about during a lap dance. Nothing deflates a cock like pain – masochists excluded, of course.

There's an older white dude wearing glasses who's been getting dances. I should go over there and give it the old college try before he runs out of money.

It's an hour or so later and a good thing that I took a shot at the old guy. I mentioned the Sky Box to him (something I rarely do, which is dumb), and he said sure. Thank you, Jesus!

During the dance, I took off my boots, rockin' my cute argyle socks, then I climbed on top of him and started my ditty. He was a bit stiff but otherwise he had a sexy nature and from what I could feel through his Dockers, a decent cock. He said he wanted me to come, so I lay on my back with him by my side and I played with myself over my panties. I faked a good one for him. He was all excited, and in the interest of staying on my back, I continued to play with myself and gave him another small one, taking up another full song. Afterwards, I pulled his body to mine and rolled on my side. He spooned and dry humped me from behind, allowing me to close my eyes and relax my face. Half an hour can feel like an eternity. It's good to use up chunks of that time maneuvering into new positions.

The floater opened the curtain slightly, said our time was up and asked if we wanted to do another. Brilliant! My dude said yes. Fuckin' A. My dumb ass wouldn't have asked him for another. Exactly when did all my hustling skills go down the drain? Near the end of our second half hour, he asked if I'd go back to his hotel. I had explained earlier that I couldn't. He had seemed to understand. Now when I told him (sheepishly, of course) that I couldn't, he got pissy.

'That's not the answer I want to hear,' he said.

I tried to lighten the mood as we put our shoes on, hoping to get the tip that I had earned. We went downstairs to pay for the second Sky Box and as Allison was about to charge his card, I asked if he wanted to add the tip. He knew very well that the club took sixty percent of our money. He said, 'I think I've paid enough tonight.' Not that I could argue, but I was bummed nonetheless. I let it go and gave him a big, sugary hug.

Interestingly, when we were walking down the stairs, I felt envious eyes on me. I got the feeling that some of the dancers who don't know me, assumed I had been naughty. They figured you couldn't sell a five-hundred-dollar dance without doing extras. True, my hair was all fucked up and my make-up was barely there, but that's called acting.

I was feeling good. Making money will do that. After freshening up and taking a swig, I wanted to get at least one more dance in so I could pay the club and tip everyone. I was on the floor not three minutes when a guy approached me and asked for a dance. Like I've said before, monkey see, monkey do.

I took him to the VIP. I started the dance and went into my usual shtick. He interrupted my speech. 'How dirty can we be?' he asked. 'I'd like a blowjob.'

'Sorry, sweetie,' I said. 'This is a strip club. We don't do that.'

'Aw, come on, I know you can,' he said. Side note: his cock wasn't hard. After a beat he asked, 'Do you have any drugs?'

'Sorry, hun,' I said apologetically. I did, but no way was I telling him that. He got all gloomy even though I was half naked and straddling him.

'I can get whatever I want in the clubs in D.C.,' he whined. Bully for you. That argument means zilch and never works.

'California is pretty conservative,' I explained while rubbing my pussy – which was covered by a thin layer of sheer pink fabric – on his crotch.

'I've got money, lots of it. I'll give you five hundred for head,' he said.

It's not a horrible amount for a blowjob, but it was his attitude I didn't like. It's also something I've never done at the club.

'I got paid twenty grand to give a guy head,' I said, though I'm not sure why. 'This is bullshit.'

Either a blowjob was the only way to get this guy going or he had a micro peen because I just couldn't feel it. This may sound unbelievable, but no matter how nervous, guilty, drugged, or drunk a customer is, their dick is almost always hard.

He wouldn't let up. 'How 'bout a handjob?' he asked. 'You're really hot. I chose you 'cause you're the sexiest girl in the club.'

'Thanks!' I said, ignoring the rest. We had about a song left when he told me that I could just sit next to him. Fine by me.

'What's your passion in life?' I asked, mentally willing the song to end.

'My three-month-old daughter,' he said.

That was not what I was expecting. I gave him the appropriate, mushy, naked stripper response. Our time came to an end. He tipped me twenty, and as I got dressed, he asked me once again about the blowjob. I told him, once again, that I wouldn't do it and that I had a boyfriend. He replied, 'So what? I have a wife, I don't give a shit about your boyfriend.'

I laughed. 'Yeah, but I do.'

59

I'M DRINKING HIGH-END tequila and bottom-end vodka tonight. I haven't worked in a week, and I'm ready to get my party on.

I just finished a girl-girl show with my twenty-year-old protégé for a private party upstairs in the Sky Lounge. The stage (if you can call it that) up there is bizarre. It's small, maybe five by four, and it's the same level as the floor, surrounded by a low wall. I feel like an animal in a petting zoo when I dance there.

When I'm on my knees, the guys can pat my head or rest their drink on it, which could be a sexy head-to-crotch condition if it weren't for the uncomfortable wall. And if I weren't at work.

The Sky Lounge is bullshit anyway. It's upstairs in the narrow balcony that overlooks the club. The two Sky Boxes are to the left. On the right are three bikini dance chairs that we don't really use anymore and a walk space of approximately two feet. Go past those chairs and you're in the Sky Lounge, complete with a 'stage', a narrow bench couch and two small, round tables.

Our girl-girl show was half-baked, mostly due to lack of room but also because of the lack of financial motivation, her inexperience and my absence of stripper enthusiasm.

She was all giggles and flirtation. I was just aged and jaded.

I just got a cute text from Daniel. Besides the fact that he's keeping himself somewhat at bay (which I don't love and drives me crazy – I tend to go all-in pretty fast with someone I connect with), we've been having a really good time. He's been married twice. He doesn't want children (which he told me on that very first night in his bed after the Cha Cha). That's okay with me. I've never pictured myself having kids, and since I've been off the pill for about six or seven years and haven't gotten pregnant, I assume that means the universe has taken that option away.

Daniel is self-confident and not the jealous type. He's fine with the dancing, but not the outside work. He made this extremely clear when I disclosed the hooking to him a little over a month ago. He said it was a deal breaker if and when we decided to be monogamous, which seems to be the road we're on. He's fine with me getting drinks with Cargo Pants because I've never done anything with him. Making the decision to stop hooking is never easy on my pocketbook, but I'm falling for this guy and as always, love trumps.

I texted Twenty-Minute Man to tell him I wouldn't be available for a while. Not wanting to burn any bridges, I left it on a good note in case my situation changed. Who knows how this relationship will pan out? I learned that lesson a long time ago. Hopefully the club will be enough to survive on. I could cut back on the dinners and drinks with friends. Yeah, right. That's my reason for living! I'll have to give my Northern California regular (Daniel calls him WAMU, due to the fact that he deposits money into my Washington Mutual account) a little extra email and phone attention so he'll up his deposits. There's always a way to make money when you're lucky enough to have people in your life who love and support you. It also helps if they want to get in your pants.

I ate a Chinese chicken salad about twenty minutes ago and I just found one of the crispy curly things stuck to my white lace top. Which means that I've been asking men for dances with food stuck to my boobs! Way to keep it classy, Shannon.

Here's brilliant strip club tidbit number four hundred and two: the stage towel. We have a towel that sits by the stage on the carpeted stairs. Sometimes it hangs on the railing. Dancers use this towel to wipe the pole before they start their set. This is ridiculous, for several reasons. First, it looks bad, like we're septic or something. Second, that nasty towel has been wiping the used pole and sitting in various unclean areas for god knows how long. Do girls think the club actually washes that towel? I've never seen a washer or dryer in the building. And the worst part is that it's white so it glows from the black lights in all its stained and disgusting glory. It's a fucking menace! It's not small, either, like a washcloth. It's larger than a hand towel and therefore highly conspicuous. I understand that the girls are using this menace to wipe possible oil and pussy juice off the pole in order to climb it and show off their tricks, but if they think that they're also sanitizing the pole, they're sorely mistaken. I often kick the thing off stage. I don't want that radiant piece of shitty terrycloth on my stage. It's an eyesore, and it's staring at me as I write this.

60

I DECIDED TO take a road trip to Vegas. Daniel's band just left for a month-long tour. Knowing I'll miss the shit out of him, I decided to get out of town as well. My Sherriff's card (something everyone needs to work in Las Vegas) is about to expire and I don't see myself renewing it. I want to work at a new club this time, someplace smaller and divier. I don't want to work at one of the Vegas warehouses that pose as strip clubs. I've worked those, and they've never impressed me.

I drove here yesterday and made it in less than three hours. It was smooth sailing at an average of 95 mph, but as soon as I hit the Vegas city limits, it was bumper to bumper. It took me forty-five minutes to drive maybe twelve miles. I haven't been here in a few years and it's grown so much in that short time.

As I crawled into town through the parking lot that should have been the freeway (Vegas never used to have traffic), one of the first billboards I saw was advertising a nude beach at the Mandalay Bay Hotel. Just one of the many reasons it's becoming harder and harder for strippers to make real money these days.

It's Thursday. In the past, I would come on a Tuesday or Wednesday and get hired to work through Sunday night. But working more than two nights in Vegas at this point would send me to the madhouse. The last two times I worked in this town, I ended up in tears. Vegas is a tough gig and a tough sell.

There are five hundred girls on the floor (most of them pretty pissed that you're moonlighting in their town – although, let's be honest, most strippers in Vegas have come from somewhere else), men who are taking a break from being hit at the casinos or living out their *Hangover* fantasy, enough cigarette smoke to give you cancer within twenty-four hours, and more black light than anyone needs to be exposed to in one lifetime.

For this trip, I did some research and found a couple of clubs that sounded like they fit the scene I was looking for. The first place I went to was close to my dive motel. All made up and a little nervous, I walked up with a sexy smile and told the door guy I was a dancer and that I wanted to possibly work there, but he wouldn't let me check out the club without paying! I just wanted to walk in and see if it was even worth trying to get hired. This used to be standard practice. No big whoop. But the beefy dude at the door said that I'd have to pay the twenty-dollar fee – even if I was only going to stand inside for five minutes. He was a total ass about it, too. Greedy fucks. He told me to come back on Tuesday and enter the contest. He even had the gall to tell me to wear a schoolgirl outfit. Thanks for the gigantic tip, dude.

Fuck that noise. The guy at the second joint was nicer but he wouldn't let me in either. He said I should come back the next day around 2 p.m. and talk to a manager. When did Vegas get so corporate? At least this club had a bunch of Harleys parked outside. It seemed like it was my kind of joint, but shit, did I want to shave and put on full make-up and hair again tomorrow – at 2 p.m. no less – without the guarantee of work? Nope.

It's a couple of days later. Man, I need sleep. I didn't work, but I've been having fun drinking, doing drugs, taking self-portraits and writing instead. Dive motels make me so happy, although this bed sucks some serious ass. I feel so comfortable in filth. This place is a trip. There's no air conditioning, which is nuts, but it's spring, so it's not that hot. All of the entrance doors automatically lock at 4 p.m. To keep the undesirables out, I assume. Or in, I'm not sure. The hallways smell of bleach. I don't think I want to know why. The few people I've seen are down-in-the-dumps types. I think you can get weekly or monthly rates here. It's a medium-sized, two-story motel, but seems to be only about fifteen percent occupied. The fifteen percent consists of druggies, losers, boozers, hookers and me. I couldn't feel more at home. Was I ghetto born or ghetto made? My mom struggled financially, but I didn't grow up around this. I grew up out in the country, basically. But then again, when you live with a drug dealer, you see all types. And I spent my fair share of time walking through bad neighborhoods in the city. I like the so-called 'scum of the earth'. There's less pretense. People are straight shooters. I'm like that. I can dig that. I respect it.

I love Las Vegas, but I must admit it's awful. Which is also why I love it. There's so much construction on the strip now that it's unsightly. Not that Vegas has ever been beautiful, but the arrant greed isn't even trying to hide itself. And the people feeding that greed are quite the sight. I saw a young couple yesterday in the middle of the afternoon walking down the strip with those long-ass, plastic drink cups. They were literally three feet long! You know I don't frown on drinking at any hour, but the dude had the thing tied around his neck with a thick, neon ribbon. It was downright comical. And you know it's all sugar and ice with maybe an ounce of alcohol. But there he was, happy as a pig in shit.

I'm currently sitting at the Peppermill on the strip. I love the Peppermill. It's my Vegas tradition. I usually come here on my last day. I'm supposed to drive home, but I don't feel very good.

I certainly don't feel like driving more than two hundred miles. My back hurts, and I'm low on serotonin. Where's my goddamn chicken salad! Not that I can eat right now, but I know I should try. I may have overestimated my well-being.

61

I'M IN AUSTIN. Yes, ma'am. Texas. Daniel runs an educational summer camp in Austin every year, so I'm staying with him for a couple of weeks. On my second or third night in town, he and I went to a few strip clubs I'd heard about so I could decide where I wanted to work. He wasn't being that great about the whole thing, though. I thought we'd have fun, but while we sat in the second club, I was wishing I had left him behind. I didn't think he cared about what I did, but I guess knowing and seeing are two different things. He's not a strip club dude – I know that – but I figured, what's the harm? And after Vegas, I knew coming in as a couple would be a guaranteed way to scope the scene. I can usually tell if I'll make money at a club. I check the clientele, the dance prices, how bright the lights are on stage and see if girls are getting dances.

I settled on the Yellow Rose. This is my second night working. The first night, a couple of days ago, was decent money-wise, but I got a little too drunk. The club serves alcohol, and the men buy you drinks all night. I'm unaccustomed to this. At home, I work at all-nude clubs, and California law prohibits alcohol sales at nude clubs.

Although I had made some money, it wasn't a ton, and at the end of the night when I was to pay out, the friendly manager waived my forty-dollar house fee. That was unheard of! I didn't ask him to. He asked me how I did, and I sort of paused. He offered it up and made me promise to come back, which I did, and here I am.

It's Monday night and so far, the crowd is young and ghetto. I'm way too sober. I need the seasoned Texans to get in here and buy me drinks! I made the mistake of not bringing my own hooch tonight. My thinking was that I could save money and not get too wasted. Poor decision making, because now it looks like I'll have to buy myself a shot.

I don't want to sound like a stuck-up Californian because the girls have been nice to me so far, but they give the word 'trash' a whole new meaning. There's lots of baby-daddy discussion being thrown around. I feel like I'm in a daytime talk show. A girl in the dressing room was just talking about how she knows who each of her three babies' daddies are and how you won't see her on *The Jerry Springer Show*. I had to look around for hidden cameras. She was dead serious, too. This was a point of pride for her. She couldn't have been a day over twenty-four.

I like this place, but the lights are a little too bright for my taste (both in the club and on stage). I've been doing a pretty good job of skipping the stage. The club has three stages, so it's been a bit more difficult to achieve (no matter how cute, persuasive and cash-in-hand I am), but my trifecta has at least kept me off the large, uber-bright main stage. For some reason, that stage has a fan set into the floor near the front edge. That's a first. I suppose a girl could live out her Whitesnake hair-whipping fantasy, if she's even old enough to have seen that video. I guess I should face the masses. I'll take another soma first to aid in my fuzzy head goal.

Later, there's still no sauce, but I danced for a big, sweet Marine who begged – I'm talking true, whimpering begging – for me to leave the club and get drinks with him and his friends. He said he'd pay my house fee (obviously not a first-timer) and give me five hundred just to have drinks. He's shipping off to Iraq in two weeks and said he wanted to show up to meet his buddies with the 'prettiest girl in the bar'. I'll admit I was tempted and flattered. Although it would be above board, I have a sneaking suspicion that Daniel wouldn't be thrilled with the idea. Not to mention it would suck if I ran into him at the same bar. Austin's not that big. It pained me, but I told the Marine I couldn't do it. This turned out to be a good tactic for getting more dances, but he just wouldn't shut up about it. He wasn't listening to a word I was saying. Jesus, dude. Enjoy the moment. Would you like another?

When he finally said, he had to go, I was sort of relieved. I don't know how much more I could have taken. No matter how charming or generous a man is, it's not fun repeating yourself a hundred times. I need a drink!

❧❧❧

I've noticed that Texas men can get a bit testy if you're the tiniest bit forward about money. I just spent two hours with a man who fit this description. Great for my alcohol campaign, as well as my financial crusade, but trying to my patience. He was a decent guy, and he was smart and funny. But the second he felt like I was working him, he'd get grumpy. I had to talk him down from the proverbial ledge a couple of times. He acted all hurt and convinced that I was only with him for his money. Duh. 'Sweetie, you know I'm not like that, but I'm broke and this is a new system for me.' The second he gave me more money; I'd change the subject or put my boobs in his face. My tits are like Xanax.

Suddenly, I'm at summer camp and living in a dorm for the first time in my life.

This summer, Daniel and his staff are staying in the dorms on the UT Austin campus instead of in private rentals. That means that so is yours truly. We have two twin beds pushed together, a narrow desk area, a closet and two small dressers. The kitchen consists of a sink, a small countertop and a mini fridge. The bathroom is a windowless cave with only a toilet and a shower. Our dorm room is on the seventeenth floor and has a lovely view of super-flat Texas. Unluckily for me, our digs face east, which means that it's bright as hell in the morning. I've fashioned an eye cover out of a soft, argyle sock.

I'm only working part time at the Yellow Rose. The rest of my time is spent consuming Bloody Marys and whiskey sours, writing and socializing with Daniel's crew (aka more drinking).

The profound comical slice is that the dorm is filled with underage kids from various summer camps. This makes it especially interesting on my way to and from work.

When I start at a new club, I usually pre-do my make-up and dress sexier than I normally would. Until the club knows you're a moneymaker, it's best to look the part. This means riding the elevator with thirteen-year-old boys while wearing heels and glittery eyes. So, in an attempt to hide my working-girl face, I've been wearing sunglasses. It looks equally suspicious, but fuck it.

The kids have a curfew, so I don't usually run into anyone on my way back in at 3 a.m. when I'm tired, cracked out and reeking of booze and obnoxiously sweet body spray, but it's happened once or twice and was pretty humorous. I'm such a wonderful adult role model.

62

I FINALLY GOT my ass to a new club: the Seventh Veil on Sunset Boulevard. The Bare has been slow, so it was time to ante up and see what else was out there. This club has been around forever. It's in the song '*Girls, Girls, Girls*' by Mötley Crüe. So of course, they use it for every two-for-one. And although it's easy to get sick of, at least you know for a fact that we're doing a twofer as soon as those first two notes hit your eardrums. It could be worse. It could be '*Brick House*'.

This club is a gold mine! I always assumed it was a dump and never gave it much thought. Girls have clearly been keeping this place under wraps. Fine by me. I'll hop on that dog pile. I don't need a bunch of Bare Elegance girls descending on this place. Another plus about this club is that you're allowed to come and go during your shift, which is a first for me. Most clubs have the policy of once you're in the building, your ass is stuck. The Veil also doesn't ask for a schedule: girls just show up. How rad is that?

I kind of do this at the Bare, but they don't love it and always ask me to put in a schedule.

It's a nice-looking club. It's on the small side with a micro dressing room to match. Apparently, the new owners did some remodeling. No matter what year it is or how recent the upgrade was, strip clubs always look the same. There are always Roman statues (don't ask me why) and gobs of neon light. Inside, clubs have their variables but are basically the same. Red velvet, red lights, mirror balls, small round tables and the obligatory, booming, cheesy-sounding DJ. There's also a specific smell that all strip clubs have; it's a little like mold and perfume. The Veil has a big fish tank! Bizarro. The tank separates the small bar area and entry cash register from the lap dance area, which consists of five booths with benches to do single dances (nothing's private), and three chaise lounge chairs for twenty-minute, half-hour and hour-long dances. Personally, I think chaise lounges are bullshit to give lap dances on – these ones especially because they're so old and mushy. Smaller guys sink into them, making it almost impossible to effectively rub their crotch with any part of my body. I could try an elbow, but that would be weird.

The most novel element about this club is the dance prices and the system they have in place for paying for the dances. Hence the gold mine. Lap dances start at thirty bucks and go up to six hundred. The customers must pay for the dance in advance. A manager sits at the cash register and greets customers with a friendly hello and a sales pitch. All a girl has to do is get a guy to say yes to a single dance, and then the manager does the upsell for you. 'Hey, buddy, you should get the half-hour or the hour. Look at this beautiful girl. Don't you want her lying naked on top of you for half an hour?' There are two managers, and they both have thick Lebanese accents. They sound goofy (with the 'buddy buddy') and intimidating at the same time. The men almost always pay for more than they thought they would. It's brilliant! Their manhood is on the line. I've never worked at a club that did this. It's so simple and effective. I don't know why more clubs don't adopt this method. I told Randy at the Bare about it, and he just shrugged. I wanted to be like, 'Dude! Here's your "secret"!'

❧

Why do girls slam their heels on the stage? It drives me fucking crazy. Every time a stripper slams her heels together or down on the stage, my gut turns and my temperature rises just a little. It's jarring and not the least bit sexy. It's aggressive and weird.

A nice Indian couple just offered me a hundred bucks to go home with them, which is a ludicrous fee, but they were very sweet about it. Earlier in the night, the wife had bought her husband a forty-dollar dance from me. Some time had passed after the dance, and I was busy hanging with another customer, but I could tell they wanted to talk to me again. So, when I was done, I went over to them and the husband said, 'Would you like to make an easy hundred? Come home with us.'

'Aw, sorry, honey, I can't,' I said. No reason to be rude; they clearly don't know the score.

In other news, I moved out of Hollywood! The apartment had treated me well for many years, but it was time to say goodbye. It was time for a change. Time to get the fuck out of Hollywood and move closer to my friends and to Daniel. Unfortunately, change can be expensive. The rent at the new joint is a hike of six hundred bucks. Ouch. Hello Silver Lake, you overpriced so-and-so. But the new place is only a three-minute drive from Daniel and within walking distance of lots of things. It's great. I'd wanted to move to the east side for a while, but couldn't justify leaving my great deal of a place. I'm not in the same neighborhood as Daniel, but it's easy to get to him. It's close but not so close as to cause any trouble or unease if we don't work out. I'm a sucker for romance, but a firm believer in reality.

Things have been going really well with us. All that earlier bullshit has calmed down and we've gotten to a good place. He's fun and easy to be around. My friends love him. It's a nice, adult match. I love that he's creative. In fact, it looks like I'll be playing tambourine with his new band on their next live show, which is coming up. We've been practicing and it's a blast. It's a girlie gig, but I don't care. Music is important and personal for Daniel, and I'm flattered that he's invited me in. His best friend and co-creator has a girlfriend who will be jingling along with me. The four of us hang out frequently. I'm happy Daniel has such close friendships. Everyone needs people or a person they can confide in. He has a few of these in his life. This is another area in which we are similar. Our friends are our family. Daniel's biological family is small, and much like mine, they love one another but live separate lives. He doesn't have much in the way of family obligation, which is also fantastic, because neither do I.

I just gave an interesting lap dance. The guy was middle-aged and said yes to a dance after saying no to all the other ladies. A few minutes into it, he asks me to flex my muscles. I laughed and explained that I didn't believe in gyms. He didn't care. He thought I was fit, and he wanted to perv out on my muscles. So, I flexed. I'm a good little lab rat. I joked about being the oldest and laziest stripper while contorting into my laughable muscle contest poses and he spurts, 'I don't want to know how old you are!' Jesus.

Sorry, dude. Fuck me for being human. I'll just shut up and act like Popeye. Why didn't he choose one of the Barbie gym girls? We've got lots of those. Men are so weird.

63

YOU KNOW WHAT boggles my mind? The Veil opens at 7 p.m., but girls rarely come in until 9 p.m. or later, and yet the club lets men pay to get in, knowing full well there aren't any girls there yet. These unfortunate souls sit there listening to music and staring at an empty stage. I guess the extra-bizarre part is that men stay, even after it's clear that no heels are walking around. And the really screwed up thing is that any dancer who arrives early – which happened to be me tonight – the manager barks at. 'Shannon, beautiful, hurry! There are customers who've been waiting.'

Hey asshole, why did you let them in? Now I gotta rush to go on stage? Giving me exactly zero time to properly loosen up. Good thing I was drinking scotch (and eating carrots) on my way here. Since I'm new and have zero clout (I can't laugh at him and tell him no fucking way) I get undressed and redressed, during which I curse myself and promise myself never to get here that early again.

I just approached three guys. Two of them were sitting and one was standing behind his buddies, which was odd, as there were empty chairs around. I did my bit and the guy who was standing said, 'You wouldn't be happy with me. I will take my dick out.' Lovely.

His chum said, 'You're better than that' and pushed six ones into my hand. Better than what? I thought.

'Thanks, honey,' I said. 'But I promise you, I'm better in your lap,' I used a sugary-sweet, semi-sarcastic tone. No dice. He was holding. All the men were holding, so I walked away, knowing that they were staring at my ass.

❧

Fucking stoners. They never have anything they need. 'Does anyone have a wipe?' 'Does anyone have gum?' 'Body spray?' Yeah, honey, so does Rite-Aid.

I just got off stage. What a winner set. Two Euro types (one of them was wearing pleather silver pants!) were dancing around like it was a disco. A scantily clad white girl with two black men was passing out on one of their laps, but she still had her hands in the air during my song. The brother sans drunk girl was sporting cornrows and wearing dark sunglasses. He had a brand-new, one-dollar bill in one hand folded the long way (this meant he wanted me to shove it between my tits or pick it up with my crotch, neither of which would be happening) and a fistful of ones in the other. He was motioning with that crisp, folded bill for me to come over.

Also at the stage were two young guys I would guess were from Iceland or some other Nordic location. They looked a little panicky and didn't have any money out. Then, sitting at the far end of the stage was a large, black dude with a nice demeanor and a big smile. He had four ones on the stage for me before I even reached him and a stack sitting in front of him – clearly a veteran.

I was doing my jig and making my way back on the long rectangular stage to the nearly passed-out girl, who was sitting at full attention, waiting for me. I did my usual girl thing. Kneeling on the stage, I took her tiny hands in mine and put them on my boobs – always a crowd-pleaser – just another day at work. I wonder how many people have felt me up over the many years? Her cornrow companion was still holding onto that dollar for dear life, which cracked me up. With a big smile, I told him that he could put that one on the stage. The fucker wouldn't let it go. Literally. I tried to relieve him of the bill (I don't usually grab money from people, but it's a buck and I was having fun), but he wasn't giving it up. So, I took his sunglasses off his face, put them on mine and slinked away. I just love when a guy is sitting at the stage holding a single dollar bill as if it's a brick of gold.

I'm supposed to perform something extra for this dollar bill? You wanna see a monkey fly out of my coose? Just put the money on the stage. Don't try to stick it anywhere on or in my body. Don't put it in your mouth (yuck). Just lay it on the stage and smile.

Two and a half hours later, I've just spent a fuckload of time with a dude from Texas. He had Texas oil money to match his Texan accent. He was a white dude in his late forties, and he was funny, adventurous and clearly a man who knew what he wanted. At first he offered me money to leave with him – I turned him down – but instead of pouting and leaving, he dropped a bunch of cash on me. We had a blast. He travels for work, and Los Angeles is one of his regular spots. He said he'd come see me again on his next trip. I love getting wealthy and generous regulars.

64

A girl just asked me what 'libido' means. It's Halloween and I'm dressed like Barbarella. None of the girls get it. But it doesn't matter; they're not my demographic. I've got a Wonder Woman costume as a backup. Halloween is without a doubt my favorite holiday, so I can't believe I'm working, but the girls said it was incredible last year. It's better to work than go out and deal with cops and idiots. I'll still be dealing with the idiots, of course, but I'll be making money instead of spending it. Apparently, the Veil was open until 6 a.m. last year, and it was a Thursday night. I'm ready for a late one. Another win is that most of the police will be busy with paperwork and a crowded drunk tank by the time I drive home. God forbid I get arrested and end up in the tank with one of the dumbfucks I just danced for.

Cargo Pants told me that he looked up the Veil online, and someone had written a delightful blurb about his time with Shannon. Isn't that nice? Did you know that men do this? They do. There are tons of sites where men rate, complain and compliment strip clubs around the globe. Patrons spend a *lot* of time and thought on their critiques and criticisms. It's fantastic reading. You should check it out.

Apparently, I'm 'super nice and sexy and everyone should run down to the club and give me all their money'. No, I didn't ghostwrite it. That has never occurred to me, and even now that it has, I haven't bothered.

Sammy, my Lebanese manager, just walked through the club wearing a glow-in-the-dark sailor's hat. Perfect comic relief. He probably doesn't realize what a gay look that is. I found out recently that he's a cokehead, and I must admit that it made me feel better about him. I like deviants. For some reason, I trust them more. It's the goody-two-shoes that scare the shit out of me.

One of the dancers here insists on putting her crap on top of mine even though there's empty counter space. I don't get it. Then she's all bitchy to me about it. It's only later in the night that she's nice to me, probably after she's taken her mood-altering substance of choice.

There's been some good cock talk happening in the dressing room tonight. Strip club dressing rooms are like girls' night out on crack. Our minds and conversations are far dirtier than any men's locker room or most professional kitchens (chefs are an intense breed). It's one of my most treasured things about being a stripper. I'll miss the shit out of it when I'm done. It's like nothing else, cathouses excluded. We crack jokes, talk about sex, men and orgasms (having them *and* faking them). We share funny stories from the club, of which there is an endless supply. It can get weird in the dressing room, including the occasional hook-up among the girls. But by weird, I mean amazing. The level of amazingness varies depending on how much booze is being swilled and how the night is going. This is true for every strip club dressing room around the globe. The worst and best nights will yield the most incredible dressing room status. We get hyper to the extreme. The original *Girls Gone Wild*. Strippers are a magical group of people. I know we get a bad rep because people think there are constant catfights and backstabbing, but behind that curtain, we're mostly like the best all-girl sleepover you can imagine. There's a bond that forms among dancers that's similar to the bond among war vets. We're in the trenches together, battling wandering hands, insults and propositions.

We are each unique individuals, linked in this sisterhood. Television shows and films only scratch the surface of what we do and who we are. It's a misunderstood industry. For example, you might have an image of me after reading all this crazy and personal shit. You might think I'm a nut, but face-to-face, I'm quite normal. I'm serious; stop smirking. Strippers and sex workers operate on a different level of openness and pure, raw energy. We put our shit out there. What I'm saying is, it takes tenacity, je ne sais quoi and a bold personality to do what we do. It takes heart, a level of intelligence and the intestinal fortitude of the emotionally lobotomized to do it for as many years as I have.

The pretty, albeit annoying, black girl (the one who puts her shit on top of mine), just admitted that she likes being slapped in the face, spat on and having fingers thrust in her ass. I never would have guessed. Ten minutes before this confession, she was complaining about a new dancer hugging the pole with her bare ass cheeks. I'm not crazy about this either, but *are you serious*?

Look where we work. Our nude bodies roll around on stage (where we walk in heels that have been in the bathroom and in outdoor smoking areas). All night we give nude lap dances with our pussies, taint and assholes on men we don't know. Let's not forget that these men are (hopefully) getting dances from multiple girls. Use your imagination. It's not exactly a germaphobe's paradise. Life is a beautiful and provocative hot mess. I wouldn't want it any other way. Granted, I wash my hands a hundred times a day, but that's just common sense.

I was watching the movie *Boogie Nights* with Daniel the other night when I blurted out, 'I had sex with Nina Hartley.' He looked over at me with that I-hardly-thought-I-could-be-shocked-by-you-anymore glance. Then it turned into a look that said he didn't quite know who she was, at which point I, being the smartest girl in America, said, 'She's a porn star from the eighties.' His expression changed so that it looked like he had tasted something bad. It's not that he's judge-y or prudish (quite the opposite, actually). He probably just thinks I overshare, and I do.

Was he mentally booking me a blood test? Or perhaps he was reminiscing about the times he jacked it to eighties porn as a youngster. Who knows? I added, 'She was a feature at Mitchell Brothers and needed a dancer to do a girl-girl show on stage. She chose me.' I couldn't stop talking. 'It was stage sex, so it wasn't totally real.' Pause. 'Well, it was, but it wasn't.' Did I think I was winning cool points with all this info? Nothing against Nina Hartley (she's a pioneer), but she's not even my type. She was too tanned and too muscular. And she had a lisp! Lisps fall under my aversion to certain sounds, like someone talking while brushing their teeth. Horrible.

As the movie progressed, another scene reminded me of something my partner and I used to do at the Green Door: the double-headed dildo show. 'Rikki' (a beautiful blonde with a smoking body) and I often worked together in the Green Door. We had the whole blonde-brunette thing going and we perfected the art of getting into and out of different positions while keeping an eighteen-inch dildo inside of us. All of this while being sexy and not kicking the guys in the face. Already nude, we'd climb onto the padded table (surrounded on three sides by bench seating) and lie on our backs facing each other with our legs in the air. We'd lube up, and one of us would ease the veiny, rubber cock into our pussy. The other would follow suit. Our pumping rhythm started slow, each of us moaning with closed eyes. The rhythm was key. Eighteen inches of dildo can hurt your cervix if your partner pushes too hard. It takes finesse and a sense of timing.

We would rest our backs on the guys for support. Then I'd twist a leg over, lift slowly, and swivel, keeping the dildo inside both of us. Reverse cowgirl with my boobs bouncing in the dude's face. 'Aaahh, aahh, yeah baby.' That sort of thing. After a couple of minutes of that, Rikki would lift and twist onto her hands and knees for butt to butt. Men always loved the butt to butt.

If a birthday or bachelor party came in, we'd get the guy's name and yell it out, 'Oh, Brad, yes, Brad, just like that. Fuck me, Brad!' This always got laughs and hollers. I'd reach around and take the rubber phallus out of myself while keeping the other half inside Rikki as she rolled over onto her back. Then I'd give the dildo head, sucking my own juices and the ambrosial lube (I can't tell you how much lube I ingested over those nine years) while fucking her with the toy at the same time.

Our pièce de résistance (for the right price) was our ventriloquist fisting show. Yes, it's exactly what it sounds like. Strip clubs can be intimidating, so Rikki and I would often use humor and a fun, silly attitude to lighten the guys up. Using half a bottle of lube, she'd ease her tiny hand inside me and would pretend to be a ventriloquist with me as her dummy. This was always met with enthusiastic clapping and tip throwing. Good to go out with a bang.

I somehow had the wherewithal not to mention this story during my movie night with Daniel.

65

I HAVE A new regular at the Veil. He's in his fifties maybe, five-six or five-seven, at best, with long, thin, burnt-out, dyed-matte-black hair. He looks a little like Mick Mars or Eddie Munster. He's a political writer and always wears black jeans, a cool T-shirt and a bright, cherry-red blazer. He's been a long-time regular at the Veil and according to Sammy, had never gotten dances before meeting me. The girls told me he's been here looking for me every night since my last shift. 'Eddie Munster' is a real piece of work. He typically comes in past 2 a.m. The saving grace is that we usually go directly to the VIP when he arrives.

He's an okay guy, but not an easy dance. There's no phoning it in on my part. He's a serious ball of energy and oddly squirmy. He's also freakishly strong and likes to wrestle with me. I can hold my own, and sometimes it's fun because it's different, but the fucker has more energy than the Tasmanian Devil!

Unfortunately, he wanted to sit and talk when he came in tonight. Ugh. It was late and I wasn't in the mood. Can't I just put my tits in your face and call it a day? He told me that he has feelings for me. He said that he was married to an alcoholic who drank herself to death and that he had found her body just four months ago. Jesus. I just wanted to be silly and wrestle, but here he was, laying this heavy shit on me. I realize much of my job is to act as a therapist, but sometimes I just want to be the resident slut. He asked if I had a significant other but didn't pay attention to my response. He wants to be with me. I asked him for a dance, and he said he had a dilemma. I was beginning to have one, too. I told him I'd be right back. I needed to hit the locker, hard. He gave me the big bottom lip and sad eyes. I explained that I was working and needed to make money. He said he understood, but he didn't. After the bottle and bathroom, I asked a couple of other guys for dances instead of going straight back to him. Fuck him and his dilemma. Thankfully I got a half-hour nude. The guy I danced for was delightful. He was happy and tipped me well, then offered me money to have breakfast with him. I said no but was appreciative of his understanding of how the world works. On the way out of the VIP, I caught Eddie Munster's eye. He called me over. My shoulders slumped. I was exhausted and it was 3.40 a.m. But of course, I went over.

He still didn't want a dance and instead pulled out a large manila envelope and proceeded to apply for my love. It was one of the strangest things I've ever encountered in my many years as a sex worker. Inside the envelope were pictures of his dog, letters from politicians thanking him for his work and pictures of him in his early twenties. Apparently, he used to model, or so he said. The images were very seventies with feathered hair and all. It was abundantly clear that he wasn't going to spend any money. I wanted to cold-cock him. On top of all of that, he was holding me fucking tight. I could barely breathe. I finally got free of his death grip and said I needed to go. I walked to the dressing room contemplating a last effort around the floor but decided I didn't want him watching me. These guys drain me. I give too much of myself. I can't wait for the day when I'm completely self-sufficient financially. Obviously, no one is forcing me to do this. I fully recognize that I have no one else to blame when I'm driving away from work feeling like Bob Seger's song, '*Turn the Page*'.

❦

I hope Eddie Munster doesn't come in tonight. It's just too much. I don't feel well. I overdid everything last night. His emotions compounded with all the other regular work shit took a toll on me. I'm sitting at a bar down the street from the club right now. I needed a pre-work drink, a civilized cocktail, not the kind that I sneak from a Vitamin Water bottle. That will come soon enough. I've just got to get through this shift and then I'm off for a couple of days. I might have to get all tough-love on him if he shows up, which is never fun. You'd think it would feel good, but it doesn't. I don't understand why men must make it so complicated. You're paying for a good time, so just have a good time! Sheesh.

This drink is doing the trick. I can already feel the edges softening.

66

BORED AND BROKE equals a wasted Shannon. The guys I solicited for dances looked at me as if I had an arm coming out of my head. I swear Martin fetches the poorest, dumbest crowd ever. Is he advertising in McDonald's bathrooms? Great, a group of young guys just came in and sat as far away from the stage as possible.

Why does my Jewish regular smell like sulfur? He's a clean guy and always showers before he comes to see me. I can't figure it out. Do all Jews smell like this? Do I smell like sulfur?

I must be more inebriated than I thought because I just poked myself in the face and stumbled a little on my way to the dressing room. In my defense, the carpet needs to be replaced; there's a ripple in that spot.

I'm overheated, although it's a mystery why I'm sweating. I haven't done much (stage or lap dances) and I'm just sitting here writing.

The DJ is in a bad mood tonight. He was a bit of a bitch to me earlier, and he just dropped the microphone, causing an awful sound that made everyone put their hands over their ears. Then he snickered darkly and swore. DJs don't usually swear over the microphone. Strip club DJs deal with a lot of shit: strippers are nuts, owners are douchebags, the customers are needy – it's not surprising that the men who work at strip clubs also get affected by the business. In fact, I've witnessed a typical progression about men who work at strip clubs, regardless of the position they hold. At first they're innocent and amiable, responsible, excited to watch us on stage and only a tad flirty. There's very minimal touching – if any at all – and they say no when offered booze.

This can go on for up to a year. Then they start taking small shots of alcohol and hitting on the dancers. As time goes on, they get a little sleazier and heavy-handed with the touching, show less concern for their work duties, consume more alcohol and develop an attitude. Finally, they get bitter, burnt out and blasé about naked women.

In the wake of a recent lap dance, I feel like a living blow-up doll. A goofy seventy-something white dude conceded to a dance. We did a topless first and then a VIP. During the VIP, he kept readjusting his seventy-something penis, which wouldn't stay hard or in the position he wanted. I was doing my best given that there wasn't much to rub on. Then he had the nerve to say 'Go softer'. He was trying to come, I could tell. He was barely paying attention to me, just moving my hips with his hands on either side. He didn't need *me*. I could have been anything warm with tits and a little bit of weight. I wish I could have given him a piece of my mind.

Finally, I managed to say in an innocent and overly sugary tone, 'Sweetie, it's not really my job to get you off. It's just a lap dance.' And then, because I was bursting with angst, I added, 'I'm not getting paid enough for that.' I'm positive I felt his barely erect penis soften about eighteen percent. Not my problem. He didn't listen to a word I said.

He wanted me to go light and fast. That action rubs my pussy (through my shiny panties) in an annoying way. Now he had me irritated two ways. So, I stopped.

He said, 'I was just about there.' I sighed one of those monumental is-this-really-my-life sighs. I half-heartedly apologized. He wasn't happy. He can fuckin' blow me. I stood up and put my top on. He wanted to pay me at the booth instead of going to the bartender like he's supposed to. Sure, buddy, whatever. He counted out his twenties one at a time, all slow and shit. Then he begrudgingly added an extra twenty for my tip.

We walked out of the VIP, and he left the club. I went to the bar. I felt like Ginger in that scene in the movie *Casino* when she's all knackered and cashing out. I took my twenty-dollar tip and gave the bartender the rest. She said it was short. The motherfucker cheated me! I watched him count. I guess I'm more beat than I thought. What a jerk. Thanks, man. Getting one over on a hard-working stripper is something to be proud of. Cheat the government or the healthcare system but not the ass-grinding workers of America!

67

THE BODY SHOP (a Hollywood legend, not the soap and lotion chain store), finally reopened after a fire, and I went there tonight to see about getting hired. I've known girls from the Bare who've worked there over the years, sometimes even going after a night at the Bare because the Body Shop stays open until 4 a.m. or later. One of my friends told me that the money's been good at the Shop, and since they have the same no-schedule system as the Veil, I figured I'd give it a go. So, I went at 8 p.m. with my make-up and hair done. I was wearing the sluttiest street clothes I could find in my closet. I've noticed recently that clubs seem to judge you harshly on first impressions instead of waiting for you to get into your stripper gear. It never used to matter what you wore *to* the club, just what you wore *in* the club. It's stupid. What does it matter what I look like in my own clothes? That's not what I'll be working in.

I bit the bullet and dressed like a reality star. Nerves wracked, I got to the club early thinking that if they didn't let me work, I would drive down to the Bare. The manager came through the curtain and looked at me. He told me to come back the next day at noon. I didn't know they were open during the day! Bummer, but at least he didn't say the word 'contest'. I smiled and said I would, knowing full well that I would be going to sleep late that night and would never do all of this again that early in the morning. Another time.

I have a new semi-regular at the Bare. I call him Diaper Douchebag, because although he likes me and is mostly nice, he's a bit of a dick and also whiny, as if his shorts need to be changed – a stunning combo. He's a trip and a half. Last week he was sad because I wouldn't kiss him and texted me 'you suck' after he left. Now that I'm not hooking, I need every regular I can get, so I gave him my number to give him my schedule (I guess it's time to reinstate a work email). He's married, so I'm not worried about him bugging me too much. He wears these super stuffy suits and cufflinks with matching pocket squares. I wonder what he does for a living? He skirted the issue when I asked him. He reminds me of the guy in *American Psycho*, probably not the greatest candidate for a strip club regular. I sure can pick 'em!

A little while ago, we were sitting at one of the little cocktail tables on the floor. 'I was just joking around,' he said in reference to his 'you suck' text. He followed it up with, 'Why do you always wear the same thing?'

I chose to ignore this. 'Maybe your brand of humor just doesn't translate via text,' I suggested. Why did I give this guy my phone number? I immediately saw in his face that I'd hurt his feelings, so I smiled again and touched his arm. There, there. Let's go do some sets. He said he couldn't stay long and wasn't sure he wanted a dance. Jesus, so touchy. He ended up getting one VIP and whined the whole time.

I love when guys act all sanctimonious in the club, the whole I-don't-need-to-pay-for-it act. And then they come in their pants during the second song and say, 'That was weird.'

Was it, honey?

❦

I JUST DANCED for Peeping Tom. He had switched from his usual corduroy shorts to a pair made out of an extremely thin material. Now he's basically wearing boxers. I must applaud his ingenuity, although I'm happy it took him six years.

An hour and a few swigs later, I realize I'm such a dumbass. I just discussed world politics with a customer in the audience for half an hour, and then asked him if he wanted a lap dance. He said no. Of course, he said no! What the fuck was I thinking? Are politics sexy? Did I expect that a discussion on the Middle East and George W. Bush would get a guy's juices flowing? Clearly I'm losing the battle of the word vomits that used to be restricted to personal information. Before I could even squeeze in a 'by the way would you like a lap dance', he said, 'You went to school, didn't you?' I knew at that point I was a goner.

Shit. I still smell like Peeping Tom's cologne. It's so nerve-wracking. To the men who frequent strip clubs, please take my advice: although we appreciate you not smelling like a wet dog, we prefer that you not bathe in cologne either. It tends to leave us smelling like a man when the dance is over. I assume you don't want your local stripper smelling like a dude. Just a hint of cologne or a shower will do. I know we often leave you smelling like cupcakes or like you wrestled with a fairy, but that's the nature of the beast.

Being gassy at work is a real pain, especially when you're straddling a guy and he's pulling your butt cheeks apart. It takes some special muscle control to keep it together. I never pass gas in front of people. It's one of my crazy childhood phobias. We'll call it phlatuphobia. I can barely say the word 'fart', and even writing it down just now made me cringe. I don't know why I developed this intense phobia. We all learn not to fart in public, but I have a true toe-tingling fear of it. I even went to the emergency room once when I was eighteen because I was doubled over in pain from holding it in. Now, many years later, I allow myself to pass gas in bathrooms or when I'm alone, but even then it's under extremely controlled conditions. I might even flush the toilet while I'm still sitting on it to mask the sound. Yes, I'm crazy.

I don't care if someone else passes gas (although I don't think I would want to date a man who did it constantly). I don't really give a shit about smells or sounds from other people's bodies, just mine. It's the fear of being embarrassed or drawing attention to myself.

When I was a kid and we were still living in the drugged-up commune, one night when we were all eating dinner together at a big table, my older 'sister' said, 'What if everyone's name started with an "f"?' My younger 'sister' started laughing and got some looks from the adults. I didn't get the joke right away and when I did, I said, 'Oh! Farty.' As soon as the word escaped my mouth, Arty pelted me in the face from across the table with his corn on the cob. Since I wasn't allowed to cry, I had to pretend that the act of aggression didn't hurt or affect me. Clearly it wasn't the worst thing in the world, but it was just one of the many dysfunctional things that happened in my formative years that taught me not to behave like a kid.

68

I'M TRYING DESPERATELY to be positive, but I kind of want to blow my brains out. It's my fourth night in a row. I'm hung-over and there's a new girl doing things she shouldn't be doing: kissing the guys, letting them finger bang her and god knows what else. It sucks for lots of reasons – it's competition, for one – but mostly it sucks if you dance for a guy after she does. He'll think that what she does is normal behavior and either ask for it – and be bummed when you say no – or worse, he'll just jam his fingers were they shouldn't be. On top of this, I'm ready to kill Diaper Douchebag. He's such a time suck and a tease. When he's not here dangling cash, he's texting my eyes off. I never should have given him my phone number. He spent such serious dough the first time, I was weak. Or hopeful. Or something. I need water. I need a new brain. And a new will to be sparkly, sexy and psyched to be here.

I gave a topless dance to a white dude who'd clearly just eaten a huge Chinese meal. I'm still trying to get rid of the smell. Certain food smells stick to you. After our lap dance, I was sitting with him and his friends, shootin' the shit and a two-for-one was called. His homeboy said he'd like a dance. Great! He said he wanted a single topless, so I mentioned that his buddy had done a VIP and had really enjoyed himself. I added that the single topless was good but the private VIP was better. Wink, smile. He looked skeptical and confused, as if I were speaking Martian.

Time was running out. The DJ must've been on uppers because he was only giving us about thirty seconds to get a two-for-one. The dude sat back down, 'Never mind.' Are you fucking kidding me? Is it a fucking crime to explain the benefits of spending a little more dough? It's my damn job. I backtracked.

'I was just giving you options,' I said, putting my shoulder to my ear and bringing my boobs closer together. Bouncy, dumb Shannon. 'I promise we'll have fun no matter where we go.'

He was pouting hardcore. I didn't have the time to start from scratch with a new guy. Hey man, just give me the 'maybe later' on the VIP and let's go! I hate when guys do this. It's such a slap in the face and for absolutely no reason. How did my telling you about your other options suddenly make you *not* want a lap dance? I'm using all my finest used-car-salesman tricks. Am I begging? This is sad. Walk away, Shannon. Just walk away.

So, I do, but before I get to the dressing room, I turn on my heels and smile ('cause I'm a professional and a glutton for punishment), and the guy calls me back using the grand finger gesture.

'Let's do the topless. You gave me puppy eyes, and I felt bad,' he says. Did I?

We do the dance. I'm annoyed with the old, puffy chairs. I try to avoid these dances at all costs. It's tough to give an award-winning dance in these chairs. They're not designed for maximum pussy-cock connection. But I'm all smiles and cotton candy, with the slightest hint of Kung Pao chicken.

It ended up being a good night. Everyone was in a good mood and men were spending money. Two white boys from one of the local beach towns were partying and being downright ridiculous, in a good way. They were fun to watch. The short, cute brunette, wearing a crisp white man's shirt, stylish tie and a black vest, was dancing around and getting all jiggy with it. He kept trying to hump his friend. I thought maybe they were designer-loafer-hair-gel-closet-beach-town gays (I've met some in the club before), but when I spoke to them, they seemed pretty straight. They were tipping every girl on stage, and they were fun and nice. It was a refreshing change to see men having a good time at the club because it's been so morgue-ish lately.

I had a decent amount of money in my little purse, and when closing time approached, the two guys pulled me aside and asked if they could pay me to come to their house and party with them. Sure, why not! I was already high with a good buzz on and figured I might as well add to my evening's funds. I made it very clear that nothing sexual would happen. They assured me that they were on the same page.

I got directions to their place. I hate driving in the opposite direction to my house after a long night, but who can say no to five hundred bucks for doing nothing? I got dressed, paid out and made a last trip to the bathroom. The major bummer was that it was around four in the morning and Manhattan Beach is always crawling with bored cops. Fuck it, maybe I'd run into the same cop who had flirted with me.

The guys' condo was a block from the beach. This is about as opposite a lifestyle from mine as you can get. After some tricky parking, I walked to the front door. The tall one greeted me with a warm smile and handed me the cash. I suspect they'd done this before. He offered me scotch (nice) and blow (eh).

Music and a lot of chin wagging commenced. The one in the vest danced for us (for the next two hours), and it was hilarious. I was semi-comatose and fully amused. He was pulling out some serious dance moves. Neither of them asked for anything sexual or acted inappropriate in any way, although about an hour into it, Mr Vest started making some small advances. The tall one had a girlfriend of three years he was thinking of marrying, which we talked about at length. Drugs are funny. At one point, Mr Vest added a floor show to his performance. After his third attempt, I tried to be as nice as I could be, 'Sorry, sweetie, I'm taken,' I said. He gave me big, sad child eyes and pouty lips. Sorry buddy, even if I were single, you just guaranteed yourself no sex.

The sky started lightening and I have a rule about leaving a party before the sun is officially up. At least I try to. I said, 'You guys are awesome, but I really should get going.' As I started collecting myself, Mr Vest asked if I could drive him home. Ugh. He said it was close. I hate driving strangers home, and I was beyond burnt out, but they had been cool so I said okay.

I hugged the tall one goodbye and walked to my car with Mr Vest-A-Moves. He had said his apartment was only a few blocks away, but it was more like a few miles south! I was bushed but wired, clenching my jaw from their shitty coke and seeing spots from everything else. We finally reached his apartment complex, and he made one last-ditch effort. He was denied. I couldn't wait to get the fuck away from these beach towns and home safely to Silver Lake where there was a shower and a sleeping pill with my name on it.

69

THINGS HAVE BEEN going really well with Daniel. So, good in fact that we're moving in together. We spend almost every night at one of our respective homes, and although personal space is important to both of us, it seems crazy to spend a large amount of combined rent on separate housing. This is typical living in California. I wonder if couples would ever move in together if rent prices were dirt cheap. Finances aside, I think it will be nice to cohabitate with him. We both value our separate lives and alone time and our communication has been easy and free of drama as of late. I think it will work out nicely. We want a big house. We're looking at three-bedroom rentals. This way, we both get an office. A second bathroom would be nice, so my bathroom phobias won't land me in the hospital or the nuthouse. Daniel knows about my fear and is extremely sweet about it. He offers to play music or go outside for a smoke. I don't love that he smokes, but I don't try to change people. He's a smoker and I have poo phobias.

He's offered to pay a higher portion of the rent, which is incredibly generous. He has a good job and also earns money from his various musical projects. Money at the club has taken a dive, and he knows I'm making less money without the extracurricular activities. I've kicked myself a couple of times for leaving my reasonably priced apartment in Hollywood.

Daniel is a good man. He's my best friend. This is by far the healthiest relationship I've ever been in. We trust each other and have good boundaries. I never worry about Daniel going through my things and vice versa. I don't snoop. It's never been my style. If trust doesn't exist between two people, then the relationship doesn't have a chance. The other thing I truly love about Daniel is that he's a staunch realist. If it doesn't work, we'll just move out. No big deal. We've talked about it. Yes, moving blows, but we've both been down this road before. This ain't our first rodeo. We're taking a chance – with open eyes. Maturity is a beautiful thing.

70

VALENTINE'S DAY AT the Bare Elegance. Ugh, a girl just sprayed the most sickening perfume; it's burning my eyes. Aerosmith is playing. A new regular brought me a box of raspberry chocolates. I hate chocolate. Does he know that? Nope. I hate roses, too. I like pickles, whiskey, aged Amsterdam gouda and Casablanca lilies. But in here, I'm just a girl, and girls like chocolate. That's why they were eaten within minutes when I brought them into the dressing room.

Cargo Pants came in tonight. He brought me a Valentine's Day present: an iVibe. It's a pink vibrator that connects to an iPod. The volume changes the intensity. He told me about it a few days ago. I asked him how much it cost and said that I'd rather have the cash (so much for romance). I don't really need this device. I have my trusty back massager plugged in under my bed. He said he couldn't afford to get dances tonight but had really wanted to bring me the iVibe and would I like some tequila? Fine, why not.

I thought I could pull off my perfect mental state before his visit, but he was already in the club when I got here. How annoying. I had only had about four pulls of my Crown Royal, and the soma hadn't kicked in yet. I said hello and told him I'd be just a few minutes. I did the minimum for make-up and headed to the bathroom like a bat out of hell. Cargo Pants requires an upbeat Shannon, the I'm-really-interested-in-what-you're- saying, Shannon. This sometimes requires uppers.

Fuckin' iVibe, what am I going to do with this thing? Can I sell it on eBay? What are the chances that he'll be checking eBay and Craigslist to see if I sell it? I don't want to hurt his feelings. Maybe I'll just regift it.

Diaper Douchebag keeps texting me about my schedule but hasn't spent money during his last couple of visits – he just texted to say that he would be coming in tonight. Great, I can't wait to be degraded and hope he spends money. I asked him to please not wait until 1.29 a.m. to arrive. It's a weekday, it's slow, and we'll probably close early. Of course, he gave me guff and then asked if I was going to be fun. I hate that question. I replied that he was the one who should be sweet to me to make up for his behavior the last time. I added something about a C-note in the shape of a rose. He didn't address any of it. All he texted back was, 'How about a kiss?' Groan. I didn't respond. Really looking forward to this visit.

Oh lord. A Russian girl is dancing to '*Private Dancer*' by Tina Turner. That is, hands down, the *worst* song in history to play at a strip club. I fucking hate this song. It's so depressing. Do we really want to remind the men (or give them the impression) that we're ten-cent whores?

⚜

I just danced for a dude who was sporting a thick blond eighties hairband wig, plastic pants with an army fatigue pattern and a studded belt with a belt buckle that said 'FUCK'. He had snowballed this ensemble with a sheer black shirt with patent leather trim and a leather jacket. I saw him walk in and as life would have it, he chose me for his one lap dance. Emphasis on 'one'. He said that he was going to get just 'one' lap dance, and that he wanted me.

Snowball had a thick Boston accent. I'd place him at around forty-six years old, maybe a hair older. He informed me that he did porn and was in California looking for work. I almost spat my gum on him. Not to be mean, but he did not look like a porn stud. He told me about the films he'd made and asked if I had seen any of them. Sorry, Snowball. The truth is, I don't watch porn anymore. I've seen enough of it (both first-hand and otherwise) to last a lifetime.

A twofer came along and prince charming took me for a single nude dance. It was a little difficult to give him a proper dance due to the plastic pants. My legs were sticking to them. His breath reeked of stale cigarettes, but he had a sweet demeanor, so I did my best. I made him take off the belt. The oversize 'FUCK' buckle was in my way, and I feared injury to my muffin.

Our two songs ended and Snowball gave me five extra bucks. I hugged him and wished him much good luck, thinking that it would be a small miracle if he got work. Who knows? Maybe he has an elephantine cock … although if he does it was stifled by the plastic.

A couple of hours later and thank god, it's closing time. Men are so fucking strange. Diaper Douchebag came in. He spent a bunch of money and was even nice! Why all the rigmarole? I don't get it. He's a mystery in an expensive suit. Time to drive home to my other life.

71

IT'S SERIOUSLY DIFFICULT to curb the drinking at work when all I want is to get fucked up. I'm sure I'm already there, but as usual, I don't feel it. Cargo Pants brought tequila for us to share. We spent a bunch of time together on the floor before going to the VIP.

Frenchy is here; I haven't seen him in ages. He didn't tip me even one dollar while I was on stage. He was sitting at the bar close to the stage, watching my show. I kept waiting for the stand-up-and-throw-down, but it never came. You know I know you have money, and I've been in your fucking bed – doesn't that warrant a couple of bucks? To add insult to injury, no one was sitting at my stage. Granted it's slow, but is a pity tip from a guy who's been inside me too much to ask? Apparently, it is.

Shit, he just left. I'm a dumbbell for not asking for a dance when I said hello earlier. I meant to do something quick (like take a swig) and come back in forty seconds, but he was occupied when I returned.

I have a new regular. He wears a black puffy coat. Always. It's got to be hot in that thing. He's soft-spoken and pleasant, a little big around the middle, with a bitchin' afro. He always smells like laundry. He does two or three sets in the VIP and tips me three or four dollars. He moves and speaks slowly and apologizes for the small tip every time. He's too nice to aggravate me. Plus, he's in here all the time and that's a good thing.

He recently asked if I had a leather skirt or any leather outfits. I was thrown. He seemed like the last man on earth who would request that sort of thing. I changed into a pair of black patent leather boots and black pleather shorts for him before we did our dances and told him I had a leather skirt at home. It was a lie. I gave up on that look a long time ago. I make more money in white or Day-Glo. Why did I tell him I had a leather skirt? Now I have to buy a fucking leather skirt. Why didn't I tell him the truth and get money from him to buy one? That would have been the prudent thing to do. Come on, Shannon, get with it.

The result of this dumb oversight was that I had to make up excuses on his next couple of visits. 'I left it at home,' I said one night. 'A model from a photo shoot accidentally put it in with her stuff,' I told him the next time. Buying the skirt wasn't exactly a top priority, and truth be told, I try not to think about the club when I'm not here. So it was honestly something I kept forgetting to do. It didn't stop Puffy Coat from getting dances, but I sensed he was growing suspicious of my excuses. Then I saw a golden opportunity.

I told Cargo Pants the story, and he said he'd buy it for me as long as he could go with. Done! We met at 2 p.m. today to shop and grab lunch in Hollywood. I found a sexy, patent leather skirt within fifteen minutes. It was fifty bucks! No way would I have wanted to spend my own money on that. Cargo Pants thought it was a good deal. Of course, I had to try it on for him, but no biggie.

Afterward we had lunch: lemonade, white wine, a grilled cheese sandwich and an extra two hundred for my time. Win-win. Not only did I have my skirt for Puffy Coat, I also had a stroke of genius as I was getting ready for work: I texted Cargo Pants saying how sexy it would be to dance for him in the skirt he had just bought me. He responded saying that he was thinking the same thing! He did and we did. Now I'm just waiting for Puffy Coat to get here.

Quote of the night: 'There's a ten if you make me nut.' What I love about this statement is its absolute absurdity and the cojones it takes to say that to a stripper. Especially with a straight face. I was talking to a fellow dancer the other night about all the shit we hear and how if we took it seriously or let it upset us, we wouldn't last a week. Now, had he offered me five hundred, I would have gladly made him nut in his pants.

Thank god Cargo Pants came in earlier. There have been three bachelor parties tonight, all financially useless. They're here because they have to be. Friends of the bachelor rarely get dances themselves. Their wives know what's up and will be inspecting them when they get home. I used to love bachelor parties. They were gold for selling sex shows and drumming up business, but not so much anymore. My manager Shawn was yelling at one of the parties earlier to pay up, which is never a good sign.

❧

Ah, the 'spiritual guy'. Using up my time and kindness by telling me how wonderful I am and how connected we are. Yes, intensely connected. Mr Spiritual runs a successful contracting company. More squandered time goes by while he tells me about himself. Finally, a two-for-one is called and I ask him for a dance. He's reluctant. I explain how much fun we'll have and how it'll be unlike any other lap dance because of the 'law of attraction' we've got going on. I throw in a quick, 'We don't get paid to be here, and you'd be supporting an aspiring writer.' He said he could tell that I was the creative type and that he loved that about me.

He says the VIP is too rich for his blood. Groan. After some prattle about the universe and a little finagling, I get him to part with forty bucks for a topless. How successful can your contracting company be if you can't afford a hundred bucks, buddy?

On our way to the semi-hidden, topless dance chairs he tells me, 'I'm in your hands, it's been a really long time since my last lap dance.' Yeah, yeah. I know what part he's hoping will be in my hand. I show him to his chair and he sits. I close the curtain and start the dance. Mr Spiritual has his big paws all over me and is trying to touch between my legs even though I made it very clear that he couldn't. He's kissing my shoulder and trying to plant his lips on any part of my skin that he can. I want to punch him in his yoga balls, but I don't. I just smile and breathe, because that's the kind of spiritual stripper *I* am.

72

I'M DRINKING JÄGERMEISTER tonight. I felt a sore throat coming on, so I bought a small bottle on my way to work. I have found (even though it's gross) that Jäger is good for kicking that shit to the curb.

Six extremely young-looking boys with crew cuts just came in; they're probably in the service. I'll talk to them in a minute. There's a strange couple in here as well: an older white dude and a skinny, haggard-looking Asian chick. Call girl? She has that look. They don't seem very familiar with each other. Perhaps they're looking for a third? Or she's biding her time – the longer she's at the club, the less time she has to spend fucking this guy.

My tummy hurts. I've had too much salt and sugar. I just looked at the clock and it's only two minutes past the last time I checked! I wish I could take a nap in a VIP booth like in the old days, but Martin has a live feed of the club cameras – which are everywhere – to his computer at home. I'm not sure if this is legal, but whatever. Legal schmegal.

Oh boy, they let the Asian lady go on stage. She's getting super freaky with the beat. Fuck it, none of us want to go up there. I see a boy I want to ask for a dance. Be right back.

You gotta love the young ones who say they've never been to a strip club before. They act all shy, then ask if you can 'jerk them off' during the dance.

I also danced with a kind, level-headed Marine who had recently returned from his second tour in Iraq. He was smart and introspective. We spoke for a while after our VIP. He talked about how difficult it was to assimilate into society after seeing all that horrid shit. Didn't we learn this lesson from Vietnam? I guess not. He said that the short, post-leave therapy was bullshit and totally ineffective. I asked him what would be helpful. He said more time off between tours. Makes sense to me.

⌁✣⌁

IT'S ALWAYS INTERESTING when a customer asks me why my boyfriend doesn't help me financially. I think, but do not say, 'That's what you fucks are for!' Instead I say that he would like to but he doesn't have the money. If I wanted that kind of arrangement, I would have married a wealthy customer years ago.

'He's a lucky guy,' they say. Yes, he is . . . to a degree. He gets all of me, the real me. That includes the cranky, drunk, funny, horndog, picky and sweatpants-wearing me. These guys get the super-sexy, 'perfect' me.

Speaking of sweatpants, Daniel and I moved in together! We found a great house in the hills and our cats hate each other. I mean *hate* each other. It's been stressful as fuck, and it's affecting us as a couple. I'm at a total loss. We love our house, the neighborhood, and aside from a couple of decorating disagreements (Daniel is not one of those men who doesn't care about his surroundings), we're happy and enjoying living together. If only our damn cats felt the same way. His cat, Nadine, is an old, crotchety bitch and freaks out on Monkey, my big, gentle, furball of love, every time she sees him. Naturally he gets upset and defends himself. We've tried everything from calming cat treats to plug-ins, but nothing's working. Nadine is seventeen and not likely to change. She's old and unpredictable. She even bites Daniel! The fighting is non-stop. It's awful, and we've admitted that had we known or foreseen this, we would have waited until Nadine met her maker before moving in together. Of course, we knew there would be an adjustment period, but this is far beyond what we had imagined. It's been four months and it isn't getting better. The really fucked-up thing is that it's pitting Daniel and me against each other: each of us feeling the need to defend our pet. Nadine weighs less than dust yet makes the most unnerving sounds. I don't know what to do. People bring animals together all the time; why is this happening? I feel helpless. The house is big, so why can't they just stay the fuck away from each other? That would be grand, but of course, they both want to be near us, and we want to be near each other. It's a nightmare. Maybe we can get a lithium vaporizer – for Daniel and me.

❧

Here's the latest prize in my long-ass dancing career: hot flashes. I've always run a little warm, but this is getting ridiculous. For instance, all the girls tonight are complaining about being cold. Meanwhile, my chest is red, my earlobes are on fire, and my back is all sweaty, even though I haven't gone on stage for about a month! That's sexy, right? A pre-menopausal stripper. What eighteen-year-old doesn't want a dance from that?

I'll try to keep this information to myself and play the sweat off as something sexy, like I'm turned on rather than going through the beginning stages of the change of life. A cougar is one thing but clammy and barren is another. I suppose it could be the booze and the pills. At least I hope so.

So, you know how I was going to reel myself in on the sharing of private information? Well, I'm clearly not heeding my own advice because I told my last dance of the night about my roofie fantasy! What the fuck is wrong with me?

He asked me the age-old question, 'What's your sex fantasy?' I could have just made something up. I could have told him that I liked having sex on trampolines, in Denny's bathrooms, on top of moving trains, in a pickup truck on the 405 – anything! But no, that would have taken too much thought and brain synapses and I figured it would be easier to tell the truth. So, I tell this complete stranger, who's underneath my naked body and whom I am teasing the shit out of, that I have a roofie fantasy. I suppose I'll only have myself to blame if my head is found in a freezer someday.

73

I finally got my ass hired at the Body Shop. My first shift was about a week ago on a Wednesday night. I went with a girl I know from the Bare (who's a bit of a nutball) who's worked at the Body Shop for years and knows everyone. She was the one who suggested I give the club a try, and after my attempted drop-by, she said she was willing to go with me to make sure I got hired.

I met her at the club at 6 p.m., and there was not a soul in the place. It was a ghost town. The club was open, but zero girls, customers or managers were around. We put our bags upstairs in the dressing room. There are no lockers, which I find odd for a place I've heard so much sketchy shit about. A girl broke another girl's jaw once! This is the kind of place where I'd want to put my shit on lockdown. I guess it's the stuff that girls could lock up that the club doesn't want to deal with.

We head to the bar next door. The Body Shop lets you come and go as you please, even more so than the Veil. You can come in and leave in an hour if you want. It's full nude, so they don't serve booze, but the girls walk to the Trocadero next door where we get half off food and alcohol. Apparently, we get half off at all the restaurants and bars in the area.

It's while we're at the bar that I realize the Lakers are in the playoffs. No wonder the club is dead.

Three margaritas later, I'm starting to get antsy. I haven't been officially hired yet, and my bag is sitting in the dressing room, including my stash and a few hundred dollars' worth of make-up and outfits. My friend isn't concerned at all. She's talking to boys and getting us free drinks. At half price, I don't see the point, but she's just one of those girls.

She gets a call from a regular, and we leave to meet him outside the bar. He happens to be a guy I've danced for at the Bare a couple of times.

'Hi, Shannon,' he says.

'Hi . . .' I pause, trying unsuccessfully to remember his name. 'Honey.'

He's hungry and wants to go next door for sushi. We walk ten feet and get a table. We order more drinks even though I've already got a good buzz on. I'm nervous and feeling uneasy about the hiring process. They both keep telling me to relax. It's only 9.30 p.m. My friend doesn't usually start working at the club until 1 a.m. So why the fuck did we get here at 6 p.m.?

More shots are bought and downed, and we share some crazy mixed drink. I'm on my way to sloppy drunk. That's a great way to start a new job, right? My tension is wearing on my friend, so the three of us stumble to the club. She introduces me to the bouncer. He doesn't give a rat's ass. There are a couple of girls and a few men in the club now. We go upstairs and grab some things out of our bags. No one is near my bag, and it seems safe. We leave again. Her dude goes to get his car from the valet. It's a swanky BMW. It appears we're going to her apartment. She lives a few blocks away. He's got blow. I'm past caring at this point. She introduced me to the DJ and a manager before we left, so I guess I'm hired. She keeps assuring me that we won't be gone long. Eventually I need to make some money though.

Despite the fact that she's lived in this one-bedroom apartment for a few years, it looks as if she's just moved in. She's a major slob, and it doesn't smell amazing. It smells like little dogs live here, but I don't see evidence of any.

The dude lays out a comically fat, table-length line of jack, and we take turns from both ends. It's pretty fucking funny if you ask me, but I play along. I snort a nail-head size of speed in the bathroom. I do the blow out of boredom and because I need to sober up a bit. The classic cocaine nonsense commences. Who knows what the hell we're talking about? Two strippers and a philanthropic customer in an apartment on Sunset Boulevard snorting blow: could we be any more cliché?

The line is dwindling, and it's around midnight. I *have* to make some money. He gives her some dough, she offers me half, but I tell her to keep it. It's only a couple hundred bucks. He drives us back to the club. I can't remember if he came in or not.

I'm flying and need to redo my make-up. The dressing room is bustling with girls. The space I had chosen isn't a good one. With zero girls it seemed that I'd have room, but now, I have very little. Live and learn. An older Armenian-looking guy comes around the corner and asks who I am. I explain. He looks skeptical. My 'friend' has disappeared. He tells me to get dressed and come to the office. Ugh, fine.

I throw on some make-up and my boots and sneak swigs of my Crown in a plastic bottle before going to the office. There are eight guys in there. I don't know which one is in charge. They all turn and look at me. I smile and do a cute 360-degree turn. The man who told me to come in says, 'Okay, honey, go make some money,' in a thick accent. Phew. I'm in.

The DJ asks my name. They have a Shannon already so I choose Samantha. It doesn't really matter. I tell him that I don't like the stage much. He doesn't seem to mind. I add that I'll go up if he's in a jam, but otherwise to please not put me up there. He is nice and seems totally cool with that. Hurdle number two, check.

The club isn't very big. The lighting is insanely dark and there's way too much black light. In fact, certain corners of the room make you look downright insane when you smile. I'll try to stay away from those corners. God forbid I have glowing drugs in my nose! The club also has a chest-high gas fireplace in the southwest corner of the room. It's different, but at least it gives off a nice glow.

The stage is odd. There's a narrow staircase from the upstairs dressing room down to the main floor, and to the right of the foot of the stairs is an entry to the stage. There's a curtain and two stairs you step down to reach the stage. About five feet from the stairs, the stage – which is the strangest I've seen to date – splits in two directions. Both 'stages' are narrow serpentine lanes. The lane to the left is the 'main stage' and is longer than the one to the right, which they open on busy nights. There's a pole at each end of the stages, but not much space between the pole and the guys, so it limits the tricks you can do – that is, of course, unless you don't care about kicking the customers.

The Body Shop is cash only, so there are four ATMs against one of the walls. That's smart for them but sucky for us. We have better earning potential if the customer can charge a credit card. The dance area is in a separate room near the ATMs. There are eleven chairs for single (one song) topless dances. The chairs are plain, padded and made of metal and are surrounded by three-quarter mirrored walls about four and a half feet tall. It's tricky giving a good dance on these chairs. There's nothing to hold onto and the guys sit straight up. It's not ideal, but the mirrors are fun.

There are three private rooms. It costs four hundred for half an hour and six hundred for an hour, I think. The rooms are small and oddly shaped with mirrored walls and a slender chaise lounge chair. The curtains are sheer, and the light is bright. I wish they were on a dimmer, but that would be too civilized. One of the girls said that they were on a master switch somewhere. Of course, I asked about it right away.

I reckon girls are doing things in there that they aren't supposed to, but it's so bright and barely private, it's ballsy of them if you ask me. I've heard from a few guys already that they've been offered 'extras'. I never ask from whom. It's none of my business and I happen to know that sometimes girls lie about this to get the dance. Men lie too, thinking the lie will help their plight. Sorry buddy, the whole other-people-are-doing-it ploy has never worked on me.

That was last week. Tonight is my second shift at the Shop: so far, so good. I'm not cleaning up or anything, but it's only my second night, and I'm still getting the lay of the land. The bathroom is less than desirable for doing drugs, but I'll make do. Fellow dancers and lady patrons can see through the gaps in the stalls. But it's Sunset Boulevard so it's not as if anyone cares or is seeing anything new.

There's a twenty-five-dollar house fee, and the girls are responsible for collecting the money from the customers for the dances. I haven't worked like that since San Francisco. I'm way out of practice. Instead of getting the money up front, which is how I did it for the first half of my career, I'm taking the money after the dance. I can tell that this won't always work. The cash-only policy and the fact that most of the guys have been out drinking on Sunset Boulevard is a recipe for disaster. I've got to wrap my head around this system. The customer pays me for the dance, and I give the guy working the VIP area the club's cut. Not only am I responsible if he stiffs me, but I also must do the math. The guy collecting has gotten a little annoyed with me more than once. He better get used to it. I'm not here to use my brain, honey. My arithmetic is compromised once I've had even an ounce of alcohol. I miss the club doing the rigorous math for me, and I miss the system at the Veil, but for some unknown reason, they won't let me work there any longer.

It happened a few nights ago. I showed up for work and they turned me away. The manager said they had too many girls and that I should come back in two weeks. What bullshit. What's two weeks got to do with it? He wouldn't give me a reason. It was a Tuesday night, and I had worked the Sunday before and had done well. I tip everyone and get along with everyone. I was stumped and bummed. I know clubs do this – it's one of the reasons dancers are always trying out new clubs, either as job security or because they got booted. All these years as a stripper and it was only the second time I'd ever been 'fired'. I'll never know why. There is no way that I will go back in a week. If they don't want my money, fuck it, I'll take it somewhere else. The first time I was fired or let go, it was a similar situation – it was during the time when management at Mitchell Brothers was laying off twenty girls a month. I had just bought my first house. I was devastated and stressed beyond belief. Again, no reason or explanation. Thankfully, they let me come back after one month.

❧ ✦ ☙

I just danced for a fun couple. The DJ asked nicely if I would take the stage and I did. They were sitting at the end by the pole and tipped me well. Later, I was sitting with Cargo Pants (he visits me, no matter which club I'm at) in the audience and the woman approached me. I didn't realize it, but I guess they had been waiting for me. I said I'd be over in a minute, then told Cargo Pants it would probably only be a single song. He said to go for it and that he'd be waiting.

Her husband paid and watched me dance for her. Couples must pay double, and they ended up getting four nude dances. Me being me, I took her top off. It's a little daring for a new girl, but I figured it was best to test the waters quickly and much easier to play the I-didn't-know card. No one said anything about what to do or not to do. This club seems hands-off about the rules, which I like. The couple was from Ohio and had five kids. This was their first vacation by themselves in a long time, and god bless them, they were having fun. They gave me a generous tip and were all smiles when we finished. When I got back to Cargo Pants, he told me about the girls who'd approached him while I was with the couple. He had told each one that he was waiting for someone. One girl had said, 'Why don't you upgrade and dance with me?' I had to laugh. It was a good line. Okay, it's time to call it a night. It's almost 4 a.m. and I'm dog-tired.

74

THE BODY SHOP has one major flaw: there are too many managers. I don't even know which one is the official manager. I didn't ask the one who supposedly hired me what his name was. So when I was getting ready earlier tonight and a guy in a tracksuit asked, 'Who hired you?' I didn't have an answer. Mr Tracksuit had seen me in the dressing room last Friday night and had witnessed me working on the floor. Didn't the fact that I was working imply that someone had hired me? He told me to put on an outfit and come to the office. Again.

This was a first. I didn't rush like before. I took my time. When I got to the office, they were all watching a basketball game, so I stood in the doorway like a moron and waited for someone to notice me. No one did. Fuck this, I turned around and went to work. They don't pay me to be here. They take half! Don't they want my money? I made a decision: do not make eye contact with any of the Armenian men who look like they might work at the club – most of the men I've seen upstairs are Armenian and supposedly some of them are related. I can't deal with re-auditioning every time I come in. Fucking strip clubs, it's always something. You think it takes a certain type of girl to strip, but trust me, it takes a very specific breed of man to own a strip club. They tend to be on the sleazy side.

People often tell me that I should open a club, and I always say the same thing: hell no. Strippers are nuts. They're beautiful, creative and funny, yes, but they're also crazy. The customers are a handful. DJs are unpredictable. The clubs (dressing room, stage, chairs, et cetera) get beat to shit. There are unmentionable fluids everywhere. Then you've got the mob, local politicians and cops to pay off. It's an intense business. I come in for a few hours, make money, and then I walk out of the building and go about my life. Owners and managers live and breathe it, day in, day out.

❧

A COUPLE OF old Mitchell Brothers girls work here! An Asian girl just called out 'Rochelle'! That was my old stage name. Man, that's a blast from the past. Of course, I didn't remember her, but I was nice and played it off. She said I looked the same. I don't know about that, but sweet of her to say. Later, another girl from MB recognized me as well. She seemed even less familiar. It's good to know I'm among other career strippers. That's gotta say something about the club.

An odd thing just happened. The club is packed and a group of guys who were already chatting with a dancer called me over. I have a rule about not approaching customers while another dancer is talking to them. Most dancers adhere to this rule, but if men call you over, it's fair game.

The guys were sweet and gushy, grabbing me and telling me how pretty I was. I was perfectly drugged and sauced and happy. I introduced myself and said that one of them should dance with me and another should take my 'friend'. I didn't know this girl, but I'm a pro and that's how I roll. The boys asked if we really were friends. Does it matter? Who knows what I said, but the girl tuned in and asked what my name was. Over the tall cocktail tables and earsplitting music, I yelled, 'Samantha!' She crooked her head and suddenly she didn't seem so friendly. She took her arm from around her guy and came around to me. 'Did you say Samantha?' I was getting a bad feeling.

'Yes,' I said with trepidation, trying to figure out if I should have lied. But it was too late. Why does trouble always follow the call over? She told me that I had met her boyfriend a few days ago in the club and that we had talked about her. She was clearly on edge about me. I had no fucking clue what she was talking about. I told her as much.

She continued, 'He said that he told you to watch out for me.' That statement sort of jostled something in the wet noodle sloshing above my shoulders, but not enough for me to care. Why the fuck was her boyfriend in the club talking to other dancers about her? She didn't seem convinced or satisfied. What did she want from me? I tried to explain that I'm a boozer and my memory is for shit. I wasn't helping the situation. She looked pissed but I didn't care. I turned back to the guy still holding me and asked if he wanted a dance. Luckily, he said yes and I got the hell outta there. I need to be careful. The girls here are way more prone to drama than the girls at the Bare.

I just found out that the first man to 'hire' me has an identical twin brother who also works at (or owns) the club. No wonder I was confused.

It smells something fierce in here and I'm not talking about the dressing room. The club smells like a goddamn male brothel! I've never seen so many metrosexual tools in one place. They're all wearing what I like to call Melrose shirts: men's collared button-up shirts with embroidered and bedazzled skulls and flowers and shit. I've seen a lot of this type of clothing down on Melrose Avenue, both inside the shops and on the sidewalk. These guys use way too much hair product and are soaked in cologne. They wear big watches and fancy jeans, often with more bedazzling on the back pockets.

They're not my kind of men to date, but I do well with these types at work. The only real downside is that after a lap dance, I reek of their cologne.

I have only two shifts left before I leave for Austin. I'm seriously excited. I'm taking a month off from work. No Yellow Rose this summer. I can't really afford it, but I'm doing it anyway. I need a break and I'm excited to hang out with Daniel. He's been gone for a month and I miss him. Things were a little strained before he left – our combative cats have put a major damper on the romance. But I'm hoping we can enjoy each other's company in Austin and get some of the magic back.

A girl just told me that several people have died in the Body Shop over the sixty years it's been open. I find this surprising because I've never felt any bad energy here. I have, however, heard someone snorting in the bathroom stall next to me. I just assumed it was a girl snorting drugs, but after the ninth or tenth time, I checked for heels. None. Ghost partier.

The bartender, who only serves juice and soda, is such a curmudgeon. He swears like a sailor and is constantly agitated. He scares his waitresses and has made a couple of them cry. He's probably been here since the sixties. I find him rather amusing, as long as he's not yelling at me. There's something about cranky people that I find comforting.

I spent an hour at the Trocadero with a fellow dancer, and then the Texan came in. Good timing; I was happy, buzzed and relaxed. He got two hour-long VIP dances and tipped me generously. He's a great addition to my work life. I made one more round after he left. The last man I spoke to said, 'You know what I'm going to do for you? I'm gonna give you my number and invite you to a party in the hills.' Great, it's my 'lucky' night. Time to go home.

75

I'VE COME TO realize that dancing is a release for me. I've been in Austin with Daniel for about two weeks. It's nice taking a break from dancing, but I'm starting to feel a little crazy and bitchy. We're staying in a rental with his camp co-worker. No dorm room for us this year. The first week was great. Daniel and I hadn't seen each other since he had left Los Angeles, so just being around him was magical. Everything is basically still good, but I feel different, less sexy, unsure of who I am and restless. On top of that, I haven't had roommates in more than fifteen years. It's an adjustment, and I fear that I'm not dealing with it all that well. The co-worker's girlfriend is visiting from New York, and they've been going off to have sex for the last two nights. We haven't. We used to fuck almost every night back at home (and before co-habitation), but we haven't in three days. I should probably just force Daniel to fool around. It would do us both a world of good, but the opportunity never presents itself. If I were working at the club like I did last summer, I'd be coming home late, smelling like candy, horny and vivacious from my 'perfect state'. Or my sensual and deviant needs would have been met with all the flirting and contact, and I would be relaxed and sated. Also, we didn't have roomies last year, so there's that.

The co-worker and his girl both have roommates back in Brooklyn, so they're used to this living situation. I thought having prison sex would be fun, but it's getting going that's tough. At home, Daniel and I drink and lay around, just the two of us. It's easy to get in the mood when you're rubbing up against each other on the couch. But this, this is all wonky. I'm wearing friend-appropriate house clothes and we're just shootin' the shit. It's not a sensual environment. I need sex and connection!

This time off has driven home the reality that when I eventually quit the business, I'll have to find a new way to exercise my deviant nature and feel foxy. I dress up pretty when we go out, but it's not the same as shiny gold booty shorts, sheer tops and cake-frosting perfume.

76

I'M HOME FROM Austin and back in the saddle at the Bare. Drink specials: this is what it's come to. If I'm sitting with a customer and a waitress asks if he'd like to buy me a soda, I'm now required to say yes. We get a whopping two bucks a drink at the end of the night. What crap, this only guarantees that I won't be sitting with anyone for too long. Drinks are a time suck, and unless the customer is paying for the company, or the drink follows him spending a grip of money, it's not worth it. I haven't worked here in a little while so I figured I'd give it a shot and break up the routine; what a mistake. It's dead and the vibe is sad. But it's early, so I shouldn't throw in the towel just yet.

Plenty of things bug me about the Shop, too. There's no such thing as the perfect club. For example, it's too bright in the Bare and too dark in certain corners of the Shop. The booths are better at the Bare, but the Shop has more financial options. I wish I could take all the positives and make one club that's just right.

Martin sold the Bare to a guy named Patrick. I'm not sure how old he is or where he came from, but I do know that he's over-tanned and roided out. He has bleached hair and walks with these strange little baby steps, like he's got a pole up his ass. He holds his shoulders a tad too wide and puffs his chest out. It's a trip. Does he get carpet shock from not lifting his feet? I would classify him as a member of the metrosexual-beach-closet gays. He wears bedazzled jeans and Ed Hardy tees. I heard he's dating one of the new dancers, so I guess he's not actually gay, but the jury is still out. Even my male co-worker commented on it. It might be cool to have a gay boss – 'might' being the operative word. We had an ultra-gay make-up artist at the Bare for a couple of weeks and he drove me crazy.

There have been a few changes since Patrick took over. We have to pay a stage fee for the first time. They've lowered the dance prices and placed an ad on Craigslist for more dancers, which has resulted in a bazillion girls trying to get hired. Most of them look like first-timers. It used to be that you had to get your dancing chops at shittier clubs before getting into the good clubs. Now it's the opposite. They're weeding out the professionals for young, dumb, inexperienced girls. The new owner hasn't brought in any new customers using new advertising or creative marketing. Instead he's going the cheapest route, hiring a fuck-ton of new girls who have to pay a stage fee. I love how the industry is always coming up with new ways to get their cheddar through the dancers and not the clientele. I feel like I'm the punter. If I'm paying out the ass, where's my lap dance? Yay, more girls just walked in! I feel like chopping up one of the chairs and snorting it. Fuck. It has to get better. I hope it gets better. I only need a few good men.

Another one of Patrick's changes is that he's encouraging girls to walk around the club naked or topless, soliciting men for dances. As I left tonight, I saw a brand-new girl gyrating all over a dude on the floor, completely naked! Why would he pay for a dance when he's getting an eyeful of her junk for free? It doesn't make sense unless her next show is of the five-fingered kind.

The other night, Patrick came into the dressing room to announce that girls who weren't getting with the topless or naked-on-the-floor program were hurting the other girls. Nice try, Pat. I wonder if anyone fell for that. I doubt it. It's called a strip tease for a reason. We're in the business of selling the cow.

Patrick was just in the dressing room again. He asked us to gather around, and he introduced himself as the new owner. Then he asked us what we thought the tipping policy was. No one wanted to speak up. Finally, an older girl did.

'We tip the bartender, DJ and floater,' she said.

Patrick responded, 'Actually, we're changing things. The only person you have to tip now is the manager.'

Allison, the bartender, had told me earlier that Patrick had fired a bunch of employees and lowered everyone's hourly pay. Awesome. Now he's telling us not to tip them but to give money to the guy who's on a salary. Nice. I know the deal: just smile at the man and then do whatever I please. There's no way in hell I'm going to stop tipping my friends who've factored that money into their livelihood. Patrick said some more non-essential shit before finally ending his spiel. Then he shooed us out to the floor. Yes, master.

I despise my life sometimes. I'm tired. I'm clearly inebriated, but I don't feel it. I wish I had a tranquilizer gun so I could shoot

myself in the thigh. Lobotomize me, please! I hate weekend
nights now; I used to love them. I'm sitting on the toilet in the
women's bathroom, writing in my composition book, trying to
wish myself into a different situation.

77

FOR THOSE OF you who still think that stripping is uber-
glamorous, I just got vomited on in the eyeball. I'm at the
Body Shop. I had walked up to a group of young guys and
introduced myself. The guy closest to me put his arm around
me and asked if I would give him a lap dance. I was psyched.
Not only did I *not* have to car-sales him, but right after I said
yes, he said he wanted a thirty-minute VIP. God, I love when
that happens.

We walked to the back and claimed the last open VIP room,
our mirrored oasis with the narrow chaise lounge. I asked if he
had keys or a cell phone in his pockets, and if so, to place them
on the little glass table by the chaise. I usually make some cute
comment about not wanting to accidentally call their mom with
my thigh. I took off my heels and started the lap dance. He
apologized for being a little drunk. I told him it was no problem
and that so was I.

I was doing my thing and he was enjoying it. I was lying
on top of his stretched-out body, moving my hips slowly and
leaning in close to his face in an intimate manner, and bam!
Without any warning, he projectile vomited directly into my
right eye. Thin alcohol puke. He was mortified and as my eye

was stinging from vomit, I told him it was okay and that I'd be right back. I ran naked to the ladies' room. Fresh vomit in the eye is not amazing.

After flushing my eye with several gallons of water and smearing my make-up in the process, I returned to the scene of the crime. He seemed a bit more sober. It was then that I noticed he had emptied out his belly while I was in the bathroom because there was now a puddle on the chaise lounge where his back had been. Why he didn't hurl on the floor is a mystery. Needless to say, the dance was over. He was visibly horrified and asked if I would accompany him to the ATM so that he could tip me. I said of course. Poor kid. His emotional state only made me feel more protective. What was I going to do, make him feel worse than he already did? Sadly, I think most girls would have. He's the guy who has to live with the memory of puking into the face of a naked stripper. I kept telling him it was all right. I mean it wasn't, but it had happened, so there was nothing to be done about it. I guess in a way it was sort of lucky that I was so close and that it only went into my eye and not all over me. I suppose the word 'lucky' is debatable here. Poor guy, I bet he cringes every time he remembers.

A couple of hours later, I realize that this is the night of bodily fluids. Have I mentioned that really drunk dancers sometimes pee in the small trashcans in the dressing room? How fucking foul and absurd is that? There's a bathroom not twenty feet away, sweetheart. This very thing happened tonight, and the managers are ticked off. Who fucking does that? Actually, I think I know who the culprit is. I witnessed her do this once – *in* the bathroom! The line was apparently too long, so she pulled her panties down and squatted over the trashcan. I haven't worked here long, and I know she's nuts, so I didn't say anything. I don't want a broken jaw over some girl's inability to piss in the correct spot. But I feel bad for the janitor. Trash bags often have holes, and these thin ones are not meant to handle piss. You know our nice janitor is going to get urine all over him. It's such a cunty move.

❧

I just danced for a pretty cool guy. And he had money to boot! He owns real estate in Los Angeles, San Francisco and New York, which is pretty much the American dream. He travels constantly, mostly to high-end, international, soul-searching retreats. It takes big money to reach enlightenment these days. At one point during our two hours together, he told me he had written an article for the *New Yorker*. He was cavalier, but I could tell he was fishing for a reaction. I couldn't fault him; an article in the *New Yorker* is impressive. I gave him the proper response. But then he said that his article had been about strip clubs. Oh boy, here we go. He hadn't been to a strip club before writing the article, so he went to a whopping three to research his piece. He now considered himself an expert on life as a stripper. Give me a fuckin' break. That was his writing stint, and now he's in the movie business because he figured it would be fun. Being privileged must be a hoot.

78

THERE'S AN INSANE new girl at the Bare. I met her last night. She ordered a sandwich and fries and after eating only half of it, left the plate sitting on a table near the stage and the ATM. It sat there for a very long time, so eventually, I introduced myself.

'Hi, I'm Shannon, what's your name, sweetie?' I asked.

She told me and I instantly forgot. I was focused on that plate of half-eaten food that was collecting dust.

'I just wanted to let you know that we bus our own dishes,' I said with a big, friendly smile.

'Bus?' she asked, confused.

Oh boy. 'Yeah, we throw out our food and return the plate to the kitchen.' I said this a little slower and gave her another big smile.

'Oh! I'm not finished eating my sandwich,' she said. 'I paid the bathroom attendant five bucks to watch my food.'

My big smile faded and I furrowed my brows.

'I can't eat it all at once,' she said, 'so I'm gonna eat it all night.'

'Uh. Okay,' I said. The words 'all night' bounced around in my head. A two-for-one was called, so the conversation ended there.

That nasty, half-eaten sandwich and fries sat on the floor for hours. Classy. That was last night.

Tonight I chatted her up as soon as I got to work. 'I didn't think of it until I was driving home,' I said. 'But you should ask the chef to put your food in a to-go container with your name on it next time.' I added that she should keep the container on the service counter and not on a table reserved for customers. She was grateful, I think. Sometimes I wonder if I'm the only one who gives a shit.

Later, I overheard one of my friends telling the same nutroll why it's bad and unsanitary to have open sores on stage. Christ. She's a peach, this one. Near the end of the night, a super-juiced-up dude went on stage for a chair dance because he was getting a divorce. His friends paid for three girls. Into the first song, I heard hollering and loud whipping, so I stepped out of the dressing room to see the show. The dude was bent over the short stool and the girls had taken off his shirt and his belt and were using it as a whip. He was going to have welts for days! I felt bad for the guy. I don't think men understand what happens when women get them on the stage in front of a crowd. Yes, you'll get tits and ass in your face, but you're also likely to end up with blood rushing to your face rather than to your dick.

Then the crazy new girl ran onto the stage, shoved her tits in his face, and punched him in the balls! Things were getting weird. His time was up. The audience clapped and whistled as he stepped off the stage. I ducked back into the dressing room for vodka and a sanity check. The girls were telling the whipping girl that perhaps she had gone a little too far, so she rolled out to him and apologized. He thanked her and said it was awesome! The fucker probably didn't feel a thing.

79

IT'S SUNDAY NIGHT at the Bare. 7.52 p.m. Not much is happening yet. Patrick has been coming in on weekend nights and stressing everybody out. He's trying to be cool to us, but his presence isn't making him more money. Strippers need to be loose and happy, not anxious. Of course, it's his prerogative if he wants to check out what he just spent a fortune on, but he isn't thrilling anyone – hence my working on a Sunday night. I needed a tension-free shift. Sunday nights are notoriously chill at every club I've ever known. I'm hoping a couple of my semi-regulars make it in. Sundays are good for them because they get more of my time, since it's relaxed. Money has been shitty at the clubs – it's freaking me out. I miss the extra money I made from hooking.

I'm sitting near the back watching a girl dance on stage, and she's the epitome of why strippers don't need to be perfectly gorgeous in order to make money. She's young, short, a little dumpy, has small boobs, and her mousy hair is cut above her shoulders. She's wearing barely any make-up, and – wait for it – she's cleaning up! This is a common myth about being a stripper: that your body must be perfect. I've seen dancers of all shapes, sizes and varying levels of beauty. Yes, a good body is generally required, but what I've found is that men respond to our confidence and comfort with sexuality.

I've been watching this girl over the past week and I suspect she may be doing extras in the back, but I can't say for sure. She recently told me that she carries hand sanitizer around with her, for both her and the guys she dances for. She squirts it on their hands before she starts the dance. This is definitely suspect, but I guess she could just be paranoid about guys touching her skin with dirty hands. It's a valid concern, for sure, but it seems a bit excessive. As I've said, there's no way a true germaphobe could ever be in this line of work. She's nice, though, and I dig her taste in music.

I don't begrudge her. Shit, if I were smarter, I'd offer extras too, but I'm a creature of habit, and I've gotten used to being a clean dancer. Plus, when I gave handjobs back at Mitchell Brothers, it was in total privacy. Our lap dances here are only semi-private and there are cameras. I'm way too paranoid.

Shit, I forgot that the kitchen is closed on Sundays. I'm hungry and I don't even have an energy bar. I guess it's just more vodka and gum. Speaking of vodka, a customer just asked me my real age and when I told him, he said, 'Wow, you look incredible. Do you dip yourself in formaldehyde?'

I responded, 'Only the kind you buy at the liquor store. And not giving birth has helped.' Sleep is one of my favorite pastimes and you lose way more of it when you have children.

Cargo Pants and I broke up, for real this time. It was about a month ago. I've been busy and, to be honest, I didn't want to think about it, let alone write about it. I'd often wondered how it would happen, but it happened sort of randomly. He had been seeing me less and less but was texting and emailing more often, which was exactly the opposite of what I wanted.

I had responded to one of his dumb kitty-picture emails by saying, 'Hey you! Wanna get together for a drink this Thursday night?'

He responded with, 'I really wish you'd stop wasting your time with me. I can't be what you want.'

What? Are you kidding me? After everything we've been through? This came out of left field. Fuck it, I took the opening.

'Okay, let's stop communicating. If you give me a mailing address, I'll send you your *Dr. Who* DVDs. I wish you the very best in life. We had an amazing run. You will be in my thoughts, and I will miss our times together.'

Of course, he responded eight minutes later. 'I still have a book of yours. How can I get it to you? I don't want to end it, but I can't give you as much money as I have in the past. If there was anything else to us on your end, I'd be fine, but I don't figure you're getting anything out of it other than being embarrassed when random people think we're together.'

I suppose it was delusional to think that after all these years we could have a clean break. What the fuck was he even talking about? A second email came twenty minutes later. 'I get the feeling even after all these years that you still think I'm gonna jump on you and slit your throat. If you were to ask me what bugs me about our thing, that's it. No idea what I could've done about it because you blew me off every time I tried to talk about it. Really don't want to end it, but I wish there was something I could do to demonstrate you can trust me more than your average serial killer. I'm not asking for more than you want to let me have – really, I'm not. For reasons I don't understand, you stopped talking to me about your work ages ago. I've missed that a lot.'

I wanted to punch him through the computer screen. I don't want to discuss serious issues with customers. That's what boyfriends are for. Aren't they paying me for a good time? I just want light and easy. I want wham, bam, thank you ma'am.

I wrote, 'I don't want any back and forth. If you'd like your DVDs back, give me an address. I tried to end this nicely. Please, give me an address, and let's not communicate any further.'

I know I sounded cold, but there's no great way to end the dancer-customer relationship, and I just wanted to rip the goddamn Band-Aid off! Even now as I type this, my stomach is twisting into knots. This is exactly why some girls don't have regulars.

He responded, 'Sorry', and included his address.

I don't have any ill will toward Cargo Pants. I just couldn't continue. It wasn't worth it anymore. I'll tell you something, though. Although it was a bit scary to lose what I thought of as my security blanket, I've been making more money since our break-up and I already have two new and better regulars. They both came into my life within ten days of the split. The universe was giving me a high five. One of them, whom I call Windmill because he builds wind farms, is in his early fifties, smart and has a kind heart. The first night we met, he gave me money to hang out while he drank coffee, killing time before his flight. The second time I saw him was a couple of weeks later. He took me for a late lunch at the Proud Bird, an old-school restaurant near LAX, and then met me at the club afterward. It turns out that, like me, he has some experience with off-the-market drugs. He was fascinated when I told him about the missile base.

Although I'll admit there have been times, like tonight, when I've wanted to text Cargo Pants and ask him to visit me at the club, not hearing from him has been wonderful. But I miss our dances, and the money, of course. I was rarely bothered by our time together in the VIP. In fact, I mostly enjoyed it. I don't know why I let the customers into my outside life. I should have kept it separate like I used to. I will refrain from texting him. It wouldn't be right or fair to either of us. I hate this aspect of my job.

Asian Teddy Bear and I had a fine separation. He moved to the Bay Area and except for a couple of nice emails, it was over. No drama. No 'talks'. Easy. I've had other regulars in the past explain that they couldn't see me anymore, that they needed to move on with their lives, and I'd hug them and wish them happiness. It was trouble-free. It doesn't need to be complicated. But some guys get attached, and considering the strange nature of the relationship, I guess having it end smoothly is a lot to hope for.

Case in point, I am currently breaking up with WAMU via text. It's been the same financial decline and increase in personal contact as with Cargo Pants. He's been texting and emailing me but hasn't made any extra trips to the bank. I haven't been responding, hoping he would get the subtle hint. I don't want to hurt his feelings, but I wouldn't mind if our relationship just faded away. He always wants to chat on the phone, which I loathe. The conversation inevitably involves him telling me how horny he is. I know he wants phone sex, and this may be difficult to believe, but I'm not interested in phone sex, unless it's with someone I actually want to have sex with. I'm good at faking interest in a person face-to-face, but not so much over the phone. It doesn't help that he wants to have these conversations during the day while he's at work and while I'm dead sober. He lives in Marin, so we don't see each other very often. His financial help and support over the years has been astonishing. I'm not ungrateful. I know times have been tough on him financially, and I haven't asked for money in a long time. He's not stupid though. He knows the score – or at least I thought he did – we trade money for attention.

As I sat at the bar with my gin and tonic, he texted me: 'Haven't heard from you in a while. Hoping you're OK?'

'Hi. Sorry I haven't responded,' I replied. 'I am good. Honestly, our relationship isn't working for me any longer. I will always have a place in my heart for you and am grateful to have known you and for everything you have done. Please take care.'

'Are you referring to me and you?' he wrote back. 'Yes,' I answered.

'Crying a bit,' he said. 'But respect you. But will never understand this.'

'I'm sorry, you know I would never intentionally hurt you,' I responded. 'I really wish you all the best!'

'Feel used,' he wrote. 'Friends just don't stop being friends unless one hurts the other. You must have a reason, and I'll remember you fondly despite this. Never felt I intruded on you – felt I was supportive of you professionally and personally as anyone could be – this is disturbing.'

I haven't responded to that last one. I won't. I'm being short with him, I realize, but I'm fucking sick of this. It's like having six boyfriends! I'm an idiot. I need to be plain and say: 'You're giving me money in exchange for my attention. It's simple. Do you enjoy me being in your life? Good. *That's* what you're paying for! You stop paying, I stop with the attention.' But I can't be this straight with them. It's not what they want to hear. Maybe I'm treating them too gently; I don't know. Some girls are downright mean to their customers, and they get brand-new BMWs! I'm too nice. This balance drives me mad. And it's exhausting.

I guess I could have been more up front. I used to be explicitly clear with customers when I was making really good money at the club and I didn't need them. Once the tables were turned, I lost my boundaries and started capitulating to their needs. I would have liked to tell him that I was ending it because I hate talking on the phone and I don't want to hear about him jacking off. His last three deposits of less than two hundred dollars each just aren't worth it for me. I know I must sound like a total brat, but this is why men pay women like me. No one else wants to hear about their sex addiction. Especially their wives (WAMU's married), most of whom don't even know it exists. WAMU's wife doesn't have a clue as to how often he jacks off, how much porn he watches, or how many whores he pays.

I should have lied. I should have made something up about my boyfriend giving me an ultimatum or told him that I was getting married. That would have been the intelligent thing to do. But I'm on my third cocktail and I'm just plain tired of being nice. There should be people you can pay to do this, to break it off for you. 'Shannon will no longer be in contact. Have a nice life.'

I'll change my phone number when I'm done with all of this. That's a fact.

80

WHAT A GREAT night! It felt like the old days. I was already having a financially successful night when a group of young, cute guys called me over. I'd noticed them earlier due to their strong bodies and thick suspenders, which I find endearing. I soon found out they were ironworkers. They were a friendly bunch. The buddy of the one who had called me over took a liking to me; I took him to the VIP. He was at most twenty-six and clearly inebriated. That was good, because I was past drunkish. Plus, I was on my new kick, Adderall! Meth has been making me too spacey, unmotivated and introspective, which is a bad combination for work. Adderall is my new work jam. I take a quarter and I'm set for the night.

My ironworker was adorable. He barely wanted anything in terms of a dance, but he kept shushing me, which was hilarious. He kept pulling me close so that he could whisper in my ear. But it's better than losing layers of skin and being groped!

'I want to support you. You should get dressed and leave with me tonight. Quit. You have a good heart, I can tell,' he said. 'You don't need to do this anymore. I make really good money. Let me take care of you.' As he said this, he pulled me even closer.

We almost knocked foreheads. The ultra-close whispering continued. 'I'm not talking about sex. You don't have to do anything. Just enjoy life. You don't need to do this.'

'Sounds like a dream,' I said.

Our third song was over, and he said he wanted a Sky Box. Nice! More of the same. Every time I giggled, he pulled me in super-duper close and whispered his alcohol-induced captain-save-a-ho declarations. I have to admit, I was intrigued. He definitely had money. Not I-sold-my-Toyota-Corolla-to-impress-you cash, but honest-to-goodness, hard-working, blue-collar cash. And he was good looking! He was Irish boy with ink, but alas, I have Daniel. Plus, I'm not taking this guy too seriously. However, life has been less than ideal in our house on the hill. We've lost ourselves and our spark. We've barely been having sex, and when we do, it's uninspired. Between the cats and Daniel's depression, it's a tough battle. Like myself, Daniel is on an antidepressant, but unlike me, his depression is of the textbook variety. I wouldn't even categorize myself as a depressive; I just try to kill myself sometimes. I'm actually a pretty upbeat person. The low dose of Wellbutrin I take mostly helps with my composure, temper and ability to think before I act. But Daniel has a more classically melancholic personality. I was aware of it but hadn't truly witnessed it until recent months. I've been trying to keep our relationship spirits going, but have just about given up. Our sex life took a major hit with the move in, and it's never fully recovered. I wouldn't even entertain the thought of being saved by a customer if I was blissed out in love and my sexual needs were being met.

A whole mess of songs later, he seemed even more intoxicated. That's a neat trick. We'd been dancing for well over forty-five minutes. How could the lad be more buzzed than before? A transfer of blood flow from his brain to his dick? As I was thinking this, the floater came up to tell us that our time was up.

'Would you like to stay?' I asked him.

'I'd rather give you the dough. You are fuckin' awesome,' he said.

Thank you, Jesus! 'You sure?' I asked. 'That would be amazing!'

'Yes, I'm sure.'

I started to get dressed. I loved this kid! He got his bankroll out and peeled off the amount for the Sky Box, then an extra few hundred. I kissed his cheek and almost broke his ribs when I hugged him. We walked down the stairs and I told him I'd be back in a second to hang out with him. He stumbled to his pack of friends. I went to the dressing room feeling renewed and grateful. I felt as if I was walking on air. Money and a good lap dance have a funny way of doing that. Even a girl in the dressing room told me I looked happy.

I took a swig and checked my face. When I went back to the floor, my ironworker was gone. It was probably for the best. He was done dance-wise. He knows where I work. He can always put his cape back on and come see me.

81

IT'S TUESDAY NIGHT. There are only six girls and three customers in the club. Shawn, the manager, seems cranky. He used to be a party guy, but since Patrick bought the place, he's been pretty straight-laced and not much fun. Some girls don't like Shawn, but he and I have always had a bond. He's been in this biz for about the same amount of time as I have, so we can relate to each other. He's a smart guy, but now that he's all business, he's taken on the role of cheerleader. He knows times are bad. We know times are bad.

Instead of drinking with us like he used to, now he's all, 'Go get that one, girl! You can do it!' At least his delivery is upbeat. He seems to realize that straight pressure doesn't yield results.

Case in point: ten minutes ago, an old, homeless-looking dude came in and sat at the bar. Within two minutes, the bouncer was talking to him. It seemed by his body language that there was a problem. Did he not pay on the way in? Did he just pee on our stool? The bouncer walked away and the old guy stayed the bar. I guessed everything was fine. Bored, I asked Shawn about it. He said, 'He looks homeless, but he's not. He has some teeth missing and doesn't speak English, but he's wearing new shoes. You should go talk to him.'

I laughed, but Shawn was dead serious. He wasn't trying to be funny. I laughed again. Okay, I gotta see these 'new shoes'. I was picturing shiny Italian leather. Nope. His shoes were no-nothing, cream-colored loafers. Shawn was watching me, so I sidled up to Loafers to say hello. Not only did he not speak a lick of English and have horrible breath, but he also didn't seem to understand the mechanics of what was happening here. I couldn't even tell what his native tongue was. 'Well, let me know when you're ready!' I said, smiling. Then I walked away, not caring that he probably didn't understand me. Sorry, Shawn, no sale.

A fellow dancer just sat down next to me. We talked about why men with real money don't come into the club anymore. I have an idea: it's loud as hell. The music is monotonous and sort of ghetto. Girls badger the guys – because we're broke and getting pressure from management – and a good portion of them can barely hold their alcohol, let alone carry on an intriguing exchange. The DJs harass the customers by saying shit like, 'This is a no homo promo'. Aside from masochists, who wants to pay to be belittled and berated? Not to mention the escort market has quadrupled, and some of the girls are charging less for sex than we are for a clean lap dance. Are wealthy men done with cheeseball strip clubs? For the most part, I would say, yes.

The new DJ just walked around the room tormenting the guys about not getting any dances. Nice upscale move, dude. That would sure make me want to spend some dough and return to the club. No wonder my regulars don't like coming here anymore. I've seen this time and time again where owners feel the crunch of the economy and make all the wrong decisions, ultimately bringing the club down. They start letting guys in for free (which only attracts customers without money), giving away free dances and hiring cheap-looking and dirty girls (who do things during dances that they shouldn't). I'm not saying that strippers aren't making money, or that men don't still come in and spend it, but the days of three-thousand-dollar nights are long gone.

If I owned a club, I would do the opposite. I would raise the door fee and be very selective in my hiring. I'd stop putting advertisements inside buses and try to make the club an exclusive destination again, as it once was. The truth is that despite our economy taking a hit, people are still making and spending a lot of money. Does management ever listen to our suggestions? Nope. What do us silly girls know? Oh, I don't know, just everything about getting people to part with their money, that's all.

IT'S HARD TO believe Cargo Pants isn't in my life anymore. However, my birthday was last week and I got an email with a hundred-dollar Amazon gift certificate from him. I needed another external hard drive, so the timing was perfect. I sent him an email with a simple 'Thank you' and spent the money. He said via email that he had set it up a year ago and had forgotten about it. He added that he assured me he wasn't trying to be weird. I didn't respond. I know a trap when I see one.

Then today I got a text from him, 'I have a joke, and you're the only person I can tell it to.' It was clearly a ruse to open a channel. If he were a little smarter, he would have said, 'I have some money burning a hole in my pocket. May I come in to see you?' I didn't respond, which was difficult. I've known him for so long, but I just can't do it anymore. He'll have to find someone else to share his dirty jokes with.

82

I JUST LEFT work after being on the floor for only fifteen minutes. I was in a crap mood all day and thought I could turn it around, but no such luck. I got on the floor at 6.52 p.m. I've been waiting until 7 p.m. these days to avoid going on stage before the shift change.

I figured it was close enough. But of course, the day DJ (I don't like him much) called me up to the big stage the second he saw me. It was the last thing on earth I needed, but Patrick was there so I didn't have much of a choice. Unfortunately, I had zero time to prepare or change outfits. I was wearing a black lace one-piece, and had I had time, I would have told him to use red lights, but no, he put blue lights on me, and I have all these bruises that look worse under blue lights. I like blue lights when I'm wearing Day-Glo, but not on black clothing and not without covering my bruises with make-up. I felt like something the cat had dragged in.

Apparently, I acted like it because I got one dollar – a single dollar from a raggedy dude wearing a Santa hat with blinking lights. The man I had briefly chatted up before I was called on stage just sat there looking at me. Nothing. No smile, no pity money, nada. Way to make a girl feel good. My second song finally ended, after what felt like two decades, and I humbly scooped up my dollar and my pride and walked through the back curtain to the dressing room, just as my eyes welled up with tears – so much for turning my mood around. But right at that moment, a customer I haven't seen in a while texted me, asking if I wanted to get drinks for a few hundred. Yes, I fucking did!

I figured I'd use the salt water in my eyes to my advantage and leave before I'd really even started. In my nine years at the Bare, I've only left like this maybe a handful of times. Luckily Shawn – now a general manager – loves me and knew I was having a bad day and that I've been going through a rough time, so he said he had no problem with me leaving. He wasn't thrilled, but he trusts that I know when I can make money and when I can't. There was very little chance I was going to make money in my emotional state, so I left with bells on.

I've moved out on my own again, living apart from Daniel. We liked living together, but it killed our sex life. I used to wear vintage slips when we drank, talked, fucked and listened to music. That turned into sweats and T-shirts in our shared home. I realized after about six months that home is the one place where I don't want to be sexy unless it's after a night out or part of a sleepover date. I hadn't anticipated this. Also, the cats never figured out their bullshit. They fought for the entire time we lived together.

We've been extremely civilized about the move. I knew we had both been thinking about it. That's the great thing about our relationship: fights are rare and we're generally on the same page. The move-out conversation took place over Mongolian food and took about eleven minutes. However, post moving out, things have been a little weird. We're still a couple, but we're waiting to decide whether we want to stay the course or separate.

I love Daniel. I even still like him and enjoy his company, but I lost my oomph for him and that's when I realized that I was the one who initiated all the sex and contact between us. I started paying attention, and sure enough, once I stopped making intimate gestures, the contact stopped completely. That meant our entire sex life was on me! With my high sex drive and forward attitude, this worked for the first three years, but since he's been mopey and less appealing, the system has broken down. I've been feeling guilty about not wanting to be intimate with him. I know what it means when intimacy is lacking. It's not a good sign. One week would go by, then two weeks or even three, without sex. We would talk about the situation but nothing would change. He mentioned being intimidated by me. He never used to be. He had balls and bluster when we first met, but he's been depressed and depleted of testosterone for a while now. Anyone battling depression and self-confidence issues is going to have a tough time coming on to their partner. But it's not fair that I carry the burden. It's been going on for a while now and I've been trying, but if he doesn't get happy and find his dick again, he'll lose me.

We'll see what happens. Hopefully, a little space will bring our swagger back. That aside, I'm feeling quite lucky right now. I'm at a cute bar in Redondo Beach.

Or is it Hermosa? I'm drinking and eating small plates of yummy food while I wait to make easy money. I could have been at the sad-ass club, stressing about whether the owner thinks I'm fat. My regular said he'd be here a little after 10 p.m., and I'm enjoying this time to myself. I'll hunker down after he shows up;

he's not a big drinker. Honestly, the way I was feeling earlier, I imagine I would have ended up driving home in a boozier state had I stayed at the club.

'Beemer', my regular, and I met a few months ago at the Bare. He was at the club entertaining clients and we hit it off. He got a Sky Box right away and we had a great time. I gave him my email info, and he's been to the club a few times. He's a good guy and easy to be around.

The other unfortunate thing about Daniel is that he rarely compliments me or tells me that I'm beautiful. It wasn't a deal breaker. I fell for him regardless. I had just come out of my final breakup with Cash and was hoping the next person I dated would be more open with his admiration, but I put it on the shelf again. But shit, is it too much to ask to hear a heartfelt 'you're beautiful' from the person you're intimate with? I don't need a fucking jumbotron, just something genuine. The few times I brought it up, his response was, 'You don't tell me,' which was infuriating.

Early in the relationship, he gave me the same shit as Cash. 'You hear how incredible you are all the time. I don't want to be one of the herd.'

'Yes,' I'd say, 'but I don't give a rat fuck about what the masses have to say about me. Only a few, which includes you.' But it didn't matter. He doesn't understand. After four years of this crap from Cash, I thought I was done. When did it become a sin for a woman to receive compliments? No. That's not it. It's these supposedly confident men handing me lines of bullshit. Even after I tell them what I want, they want to be 'different'. They don't want to 'be like every other guy'. So, I'm punished because strangers compliment me? Yeah, that's fair. It's not as if I brag about what the guys say. I don't use my job as a weapon.

If anything, after all these years and the painful crap with the men in my life, I downplay that shit. Please, find another way to stand out.

I don't know. I'm not sure I'm meant to spend my life with one person. If my history is any indication, then I'm probably not. I'm okay with that. I'd rather be happy and single than the other way around.

I just realized I'm sitting in a normal bar in normal clothes and in full, ho-bag make-up, including blood-shot eyes and fake lashes. I stick out for sure; people are more conservative down here. A couple of cute local boys just chatted me up. They told me that the Bare Elegance is known as 'bravo echo'. How fantastic is that? I can't believe I've never heard that before! They said the name originated from the local cops – it's how they reference the club when they talk over the air. I love it!

It's close to the time of needing to turn it 'on' and get paid. Too bad I'm sleepy and would rather teleport myself into nothingness.

83

IT'S OFFICIAL: DANIEL and I broke up. It's been about a month and a half since I moved out. I was hoping we'd get back to a good place, but we never did. It only put a wider gap between us. I think we saw each other about three times after I moved out, and New Year's Eve was one of them. He made very little effort. I suppose neither did I, but I was sick of feeling like I was the only one trying.

We made plans to go out to dinner – which I had to initiate. I went to the cheese store in the afternoon and got some of our favorites and a bottle of wine. I told him about the cheese and said I'd be there a little early so we could snack on that before dinner. We hadn't seen each other in a couple of weeks. I sort of knew what was going to go down and I didn't want it to happen at one of our cherished restaurants.

I got to the house. He was still living in our house on the hill. He'd been looking for a place since I had moved out, but hadn't found the right rental yet. We were both looking at the same time and had the same budget, the same needs and wanted to stay near our hood, so we looked at a bunch of the same properties. Since we were still together, it was all very copacetic. In fact, he had looked at my place before I did, but he stood down, knowing that it was perfect for me and that he could afford a bit more.

I parked in my usual spot and walked down the stairs into the house. We hugged, kissed and caught up as I opened the cheese and he opened the wine. We moved it over to the expensive couch we had designed together. Approximately twenty-six minutes into our what-have-you-been-up-to's I said, 'We need to talk about us.'

'I know,' he said.

'This isn't working.'

'I agree.'

'What do you want to do?'

'I don't really know, but I have a feeling that you do.'

'Yeah, well, I love you,' I told him, 'but this current circumstance isn't making me happy.'

'Me either.'

'So that's it?'

'Looks like it.'

'Did you know this was going to happen tonight?'

'I did when you called to say you had bought wine and cheese to have before dinner.'

I laughed. He did as well. It felt good. These conversations are never fun, but this is the ideal way to do it.

'Should we still go out to dinner?' I asked.

'I don't really see the reason to,' he said.

'Okay then. I'll be off.'

We hugged and I walked out of the house on the hill for the last time.

Daniel's a great guy. It was a tough decision, but our relationship just wasn't satisfying anymore. We weren't planning to get married or have children; we were very clear on both. So, what's the point in being a monogamous couple if we aren't happy? There are plenty of good men out there, and truth be told, I feel like being single. I'm done with editing myself, both in action and online. Daniel pulled what Hattie calls the 'combo move'; he de-friended and blocked me within twenty-four hours of the break-up conversation. He also un-liked my artist pages. I didn't expect him to do that. It seems childish. I guess he's giving me the freedom to be myself, but it feels petty. I was hoping it wouldn't be weird. I don't need to be buddy-buddy, but because there's no ill will, I don't see why we can't be human. I won't un-like his band pages. Granted it's less intimate than my writing, but still. I support him and want him to do well in life. We loved each other, right? In fact, lack of love was not our issue. I thought the break-up was a mutual decision. Why can't we be civil and in each other's lives? Or at the very least, not be cold. Now I'm dreading the inevitable run-in. We drink and eat at the same places.

I had an epiphany a couple of days before I went set see him. I knew I had to make a decision. There was no way I would stay in a relationship with someone I wasn't seeing or hardly speaking to. It had to get better or end, and the month or so apart indicated which direction it was going in. My epiphany was that I've chosen love over money for twenty years and look where I am: forty-one years old and still busting my ass at the strip club. I wouldn't change a thing or my decisions, but this time I wanted to choose me! I want to make money. I want to make the most out of my career and then get the hell out. Not that Daniel was holding me back on that last one, but relationships take work and energy. It wasn't even about Daniel anymore; it was about me. I will always find love.

Love is easy. I've had love my whole life. It's money and success that have eluded me. I want creative and financial success. This is not an earth-shattering sentiment, but it was a big moment for me. Realizing that I didn't have to apologize for choosing money over a relationship was big. And let's face it, how much longer are men going to pay me for my company?

This feels good. Yes, I will miss him. Yes, he made me laugh. Yes, we had a good thing, but things change. Yes, I sound like Deepak Chopra. Everyone deserves to be happy. Happiness is key. So, that's it. Single again.

84

A NEW GIRL tried to start a fight with me in the bathroom. I don't often get into fights with my co-workers. In my lengthy career, I think I've had a total of four incidents. The first confrontation I got into was with one of the older girls at Mitchell Brothers. I don't know what I did to her, but for some reason she decided that she didn't like me, and this woman was no joke. She reminded me of the girls in my grade school I used to look up to, the ones who wore roach clips with feathers in their hair.

The O'Farrell Theatre had a zero-tolerance policy with regard to fights among dancers and usually fired both parties no matter the circumstance, so I was eager to squash it.

The older girls mostly worked the day shift, and I would see her in the crossover. She and her pack of old-school girls would give me shitty looks and major attitude. They also talked shit about me in the dressing room. It was ridiculous. We were grown-ass women. I hate unresolved issues with people, and I hate having to watch my back. So, one day I sucked up the courage and went into their separated smoking-cum-dressing room to face the silliness head on.

I stood in the doorway of their cougar lair. 'Hey, can we talk?' I asked her. All the girls looked a bit stunned. It was rare for a new girl to approach old girls back then or to address a bad situation, but I'm not known to cower, and there was no way I could continue to work like that. I wasn't bullied in school and I certainly wasn't going to be bullied at a strip club. Mitchell Brothers wasn't as high-drama as the Shop, but put a bunch of strong-minded, ballsy, drunk, high girls together and trouble sometimes finds a way.

'Look, I don't know what I did to piss you off,' I said, 'but I can't stand this shit. I'm a chill person. I don't know you, but if there's a real problem, I'd prefer you tell me, so we can figure it out.'

They all just stared at me. 'Nah, we're cool,' she said. And that was it. After that, the old girls started treating me with respect and even gave me some tips on how to make more money.

The second time I had a snag with a dancer was at the Market Street Cinema. It wasn't a classic fight; it was a classic looting. Market Street Cinema was ghetto as fuck, and the girls hated anyone who worked at Mitchell Brothers, which was a notoriously difficult place to get hired and known as the highest earning club in the country at the time. I wasn't stupid. I never mentioned that I also worked at Mitchell Brothers, but that didn't stop a girl from cutting my padlocked duffel bag with a knife and stealing my money and designer jeans. It did stop me from ever keeping my money anywhere else but on my person, though. It was silly of me to think that my bag was safe because it was five feet from the DJ and the zipper was locked. A good ol' fashioned slashing was not on my radar. Bitch had to take my damn jeans too? What the shit was I supposed to wear home? I was incensed, not only to have my hard-earned cash stolen but because of the total disregard for the rules and respect. I went down the long-ass staircase to the basement dressing room and yelled, 'Whoever fuckin' stole my shit, I hope you OD on the smack you're going to buy with my money!' Yes, it was dramatic and yes, it was a tad cruel, but when I see red, I see red.

My best friend, Andrew, came down to the club near the end of the shift to hang out – I had stayed longer than intended because I needed to make up the dough I had lost. I left at 2 a.m. with his flannel shirt tied around my waist.

Back to the foolishness tonight: a girl patron and I were in line in the bathroom. The large stall has been out of order, so we were waiting for the smaller one.

A customer was waiting for me on the floor, and the DJ had just announced that a two-for-one was coming up. We had said we'd use the next dance special to go to the VIP. I needed to get back out there before it started, but I hate dancing when I have to pee, so skipping the bathroom wasn't an option. I noticed two sets of feet in the microscopic stall. Ugh, I had no time for this. So I said, 'Hey chicas, if you're not peeing – and I don't care what you're doing – you can use the larger stall.' This may not be verbatim, but you get the gist. I said it in a light, friendly manner and tried to convey that I wasn't judging. I was simply saying that it would be more convenient for everyone if they moved to the larger stall. It didn't look like either pair of heels could be sitting on the toilet, which is why I said anything in the first place. The Adderall may have assisted with my bravado.

The girls spilled out of the stall and I got some serious stink eye. Girl number one, whom I'd never seen before, barked, 'Who said that?' Smelling trouble, the female patron darted into the stall as soon as girl number two came out. 'I did,' I said.

She walked right up to me. 'You? Do you work here?' She flipped the bottom of my cute T-shirt up. 'You're not seriously working here, are you,' she said, as she looked me up and down.

I knew what she was implying. I smirked at her. Girl number two walked up to the second sink. 'I was peeing,' she said. I'd seen her a few times. We'd even spoken. She's nice and she used to date Patrick. I have no beef with her. I have no beef with anyone. I'm wearing a T-shirt with a kitty face and a rose, for fuck's sake.

I ignored the feisty ho in front of me and spoke to the nice one, 'Hey, girl. I was simply saying that the larger stall would fit two girls better. You and I are cool.' I wanted to say, 'I don't give a deep fuck what you guys were or were not doing. Maybe you were reading Faulkner to each other. I don't give a shit. I just want to pee and make some fucking money!'

The nice one wasn't saying much, which is better than an argument. I think she knows I'm an okay gal. But her friend was on fire, looking to push my buttons. Sorry sister, I'm not getting fired over a piss-ant like you, so I didn't address any of her degrading questions. I just looked her in the eyes and kept grinning. It took some restraint not to say, 'Yeah, I get it. I'm an old ass ho, but I've got forty dances already. How much money have *you* made?'

Meanwhile, the poor non-dancer came out of the stall and, likely with visions of daytime talk show hair-pulling flashing in her mind, decided to skip washing her hands and ran out the door. I took the stall and, as I was peeing, I heard giggling and whispering and then the lights went out, plunging me into total darkness. I laughed. Is this the fifth grade? After about ten seconds, the lights came back on. It wasn't too hard to figure out who had turned them off or who had turned them back on. The dancer I knew is far more mature than her counterpart. But I hold no grudges. It's too idiotic to be taken seriously. The flipping of my T-shirt and the blackout will go down as two of the top ten most absurd things a stripper has done to me.

I went out to my dude. As I danced for him, I told him the tale. We laughed about it, and he made me promise to point her out to him.

During our second dance, I got a text from Beemer. It was the perfect timing to get me out of this night. Windmill and the Choker had come in earlier. No more regulars were scheduled and the air was getting thick with stress and bullshit. I left an hour early and didn't even ask for permission.

Shawn wanted a schedule for the following week. I told him I would be traveling a bunch and that I'd let him know. He said, 'I wish I had your life.'

'Me too,' I said.

85

HOLY MOTHER OF god. The Texan and I are in Vegas. He was so excited to hear that I was boyfriend-free that he immediately bought me a plane ticket to meet him in Vegas for a night. He texted me his room number as I landed, and when I arrived at the hotel, there were Post-It notes with messages for me everywhere: on the elevator ceiling, down the long hallway, and all over the room. They said things like 'Hello!' and cute instructions about where to put my stuff. Next to that area was a note with an order to go to the bar in the suite. There was a note by a bottle of Crown and a glass telling me to drink, then to shower. It was cute and playful. After I showered and got ready, we met for dinner with his friends, a nice, local couple. I liked them right off the bat. They were good people.

In the middle of our sushi dinner, Shelly announced that they had mushrooms at the house. 'Let's eat 'em!' I said.

No one needed arm-twisting. We finished our meal and drinks, drove to a cigar store and loaded up on random things, including a T-shirt for me that said 'Iron Mexican' in the Iron Maiden font. At their house, we made drinks and shot the shit. Shelly went upstairs and came back with this huge bag of mushrooms. I had a plan for myself. Knowing mushrooms and wanting to only get to the giggly stage, I said, 'Break off just half of a stem for me, please.' My plan was wise and doable. If only I had stuck to it.

Music was played. Drinks were sucked back: diet Dr Pepper and Crown for The Texan, Crown neat for me. Time was passing, but nothing was happening on the mushroom front. I kept thinking that maybe they had some weak-ass mushrooms. I may have voiced this at some juncture because The Texan kept slicing up stems and caps for him and me to share. And me, being a fool and knowing better, kept eating them. I don't know what it is about mushrooms, but my well-meaning plans go out the window and I seem to misplace the information I gained the other times I've eaten them once they're in my system.

An hour and a half later, I'm high as fuck. Shelly put on the soundtrack to *The Wall*. *The* fucking *Wall*, my most emotional album! About four songs in, I was on the ground crying. It was probably the worst album she could have played. Fuck it, it felt good to cry. I hadn't listened to that album in so long. It was cathartic, but the poor Texan didn't know what to do with me. I wanted to be left alone. I'm extremely antisocial when I get to that level. And of course, as time wore on, the higher I got. The Texan was partially to blame, so I didn't feel too bad about being antisocial, but I wasn't too pleased with the fact that I was getting further and further away from my plan. So, I started watching the clock. This is how I've always dealt with being overly high. It helps me keep a handle on reality. When it feels like an hour has passed, I look at the clock and realize that nope, only two minutes have gone by.

The Texan tried at one point to get me to have sex with him in front of our guests in the living room. Hilarious, buddy, not going to happen. It's not that kind of party. I kept asking him to leave me alone. I wanted space to trip, but he kept 'checking in' on me, although it felt more like he was creeping around corners.

'Go back to the living room! I'm good,' I told him. 'Please. I just need to be alone.' At some point, they had all moved to the living room and I had commandeered the kitchen.

This went on for a while. On his fourth creepy check-in, I yelled at him, 'You are the worst drug buddy!' I wasn't being very nice, but all's fair in paid-for-sex and mushrooms night. A little later, the house fell silent. The Texan came into the kitchen for the hundredth time.

'We gotta go,' he said.

'Huh?'

'We need to leave.'

'Can you drive? I don't think you can drive. If you're as high as I am, and we ate the same amount, you cannot drive,' I said.

'I'll be fine. Let's go.'

It took me a minute to find the car keys in my purse. I had this sinking feeling that we were leaving a crime scene. Did he murder the nice couple? We slipped out and got into the rented Escalade. The next six miles were the longest of my life. We were surrounded by cops at one point and I was freaked the fuck out. I could tell he was too, but that he was trying not to show it because I certainly wasn't holding back.

'Holy shit. We're going to die. Please just get us to the hotel!' I yelled. Who knew I wanted to be alive so much? 'But don't speed. Don't get pulled over,' I added.

Jail is pretty much the last place on earth where you'd want to be on hallucinogens. Plus, his wife would find out. That would be such a disaster.

By some miracle – and what felt like two years later – he got us to the hotel in one piece. I opened the door and toppled out of the truck Ab Fab style, clutching my Iron Mexican T-shirt. I was so grateful we weren't in jail. After a bunch of deep breaths, I looked down at the T-shirt and broke down into a serious laughing fit. Oh, sure, *now* the laughter comes. I couldn't stop. The Texan had to pick me up off the ground.

Walking through the hotel, I had to keep twelve paces behind him, lest we ran into any of his colleagues. I was a hot mess. The Texan took a separate elevator, and I wasn't sure which floor we were on. Vegas and its goddamn monolithic hotels! By the grace of god, I found our suite. The following three to five hours consisted of a lot of idiosyncratic, hyper-dimensional sex with a couple of suicidal moments thrown in for good measure. My pussy was raw from the condoms and his shitty lube. The fucker uses Vaseline! Who has used Vaseline as lube since the fifties? When the sky started to lighten, I forced a couple of Tylenol PMs down our throats. Fucking mushrooms. Never again. At least not that many.

86

THE TEXAN HAS been boasting about all the girls in his life: cocktail waitresses who 'want to fuck him', strippers fighting over him. Pretty much every woman he meets apparently wants him. They're showboating stories. I couldn't give a shit of course, but if it means he's talking and I don't have to, then whatever.

I drink and give him the occasional, 'Oh shit, really?' and 'That sounds fun.' I think he's slowed down on the action since we've been intimate, and his ego isn't quite comfortable with it. He might even be trying to make me jealous. How ridiculous. He says to girls, 'You like it. You know it,' when he's being a little too rough with them. I laugh, but he doesn't understand why I'm laughing. He's so cocky and delusional. If he wants to please women so badly, why doesn't he actually pay attention? He's also convinced himself that all of his girls come four to eleven times; he's told me so. It's absurd. Of course, we're faking. I don't even know these girls, and *I* know they're faking. If they're getting paid, then they just want it over with; trust me. And if he needs to think we're coming our faces off to get his, then he gets the performance. Maybe a couple of these ladies are having real ones thrown in for shits and grins. *Maybe.*

The real problem with the Texan is that he puts off coming until we've had at least four to eleven 'orgasms' so he can brag about it to each of us separately and to his buddies. As if I give a fuck how many times Candy 'came' last Tuesday. It wears me (and my pussy) out. It's a lot of fucking. And a lot of faking. It's exhausting. He also watches a ton of porn, often while this fuck-fest is happening. He'll say, 'Oooh, she's so into it. She loves it in the ass.'

I'm thinking, 'No she doesn't. She's dry as the desert and can't wait for the director to call for the dude to spuge so she can get her check and go to the nearest Taco Bell.' Not that women don't like sex or anal, but it's work, and that changes the game.

It's clear that he picks up a lot of his sex moves from watching porn. I can always tell when guys do this. If you've never had sex or really suck at it, then fine, pick up some basics, but it's more important to be attuned to your partner's body. Because let's face it, porn is made mostly for men. It's what men *want* women to want. I like porn, and I'm certainly no Pollyanna in the sack, but there's a whole mess of shit I see that doesn't do it for me sexually. I hate my pussy being slapped, for example. Ouch. My pussy is fucking sensitive. That action will likely get you slugged. Porn shouldn't shape a man's sex life.

I was going to direct and produce adult movies a bunch of years ago. I would have made awesome porn: no story line, no non-sex dialogue, a lot of close shots of insertion and head (not of the dude's face, unless it's Clive Owen). And I'd keep the camera on the money shot for a longer period of time. I hate when a good shot is doing the trick, and I'm about to come and the cameraman pivots to the dude's face. Also, does a porno flick really need to last three hours? I'm no dude, but when I masturbate, I want to get in, get off and get out. I guess the companies boast about the length of their movies to charge more, and I know guys who can beat off for-fucking-ever, but it seems excessive. The Texan is one of these marathon men, often until he's got a raw cock.

Sometimes I wonder which one of us is putting on the biggest show. The Texan is also playing a character: the fifty-something-year-old sex stud. He has nothing to prove to me. I couldn't care less. In fact, I wish he'd knock it off. But this is the charade we perform. I just wish it involved less 'coming' on my part.

87

I'M IN REDONDO (or Hermosa), waiting, writing and drinking at the bar down the street from Beemer's house. I haven't been working at the club much these days. I think my last shift was on a Friday about three weeks ago when that new girl tried to pick a fight with me.

I went to Hawaii to see Windmill (who was there for work), and after being home for only about nine hours, I flew to Chicago to see The Texan. I was dead tired and emotionally spent, which is not a good way to start a work trip. I will never book myself back-to-back work trips again. I had a tough time keeping my grip, so I got super fucked up in order not to kill him, and so I could have some fun. But that's what I get paid for.

Windmill got us separate rooms at this cute hotel across the street from the beach in Maui. I was there in companion capacity only. The trip was nice (who doesn't love Hawaii?), but there were a few things that irked me. Windmill is a wonderful man with a big heart, but he watches me. I don't mean he looks at me while I'm eating dinner. I mean he watches every move I make. It's nerve-wracking to have someone leer at you. I know he's developing strong feelings for me, but I've never had someone watch me like this. It makes me want to pull my hair out. So, I got drunk.

On the second day, he thanked me for wearing shorts. Thanked me! I instantly wanted to change back into jeans. I had worn shorts knowing that he would like to see my legs, but the act of thanking me made me mad. I can't explain it. It felt creepy, not complimentary. It would have been different if he had simply said, 'You look nice.' I've been downplaying my body, trying not to turn him on. Women like being appreciated and noticed, but we don't like being ogled. I don't mind it at the club; I'm used to it there. But it's unwelcome at lunch. And lastly, he calls me 'madam'. I hate being called ma'am, and this is even worse. He's from the South, but come on, I'm not ninety years old. I know it's just a word, but when a person is bugging you, then the way they breathe can be a problem. I'm sure things will get more comfortable as we get to know each other. Perhaps I'll tell him sweetly not to call me madam. Or maybe I'll get used to it with time. But the watching my every move will never be okay with me. It makes me ill at ease.

Hung-over and mentally beat from Hawaii, I met The Texan at the airport. He had brought a bottle of whiskey and a bullet of blow. I was instructed to have both as he drove us to the hotel. Blow is bullshit. But when instructed, and when one requires a certain frame of mind, preferences go out the window. The hotel he stays at is cool. The room was rad: high ceilings, two beds (thank fuck), a gorgeous chandelier and exposed brick.

I set my bag down and peed. He had things to unload from the car, which gave me a few minutes to acclimate and get ready for what was to come. He unpacked several bottles of various libations and water.

He grabbed me and kissed me way too hard as he jammed my hand on his crotch and told me that his dick was already hard. I knew I was going to have to perform a lot sooner than I would have liked. As he got ice, I hit the bottle of whiskey and snorted a tiny bit of meth in the bathroom (I had travelled with a little in my bra).

When he got back, he stripped down and drank. We banged it out, drank and did drugs for the next couple of hours. My pussy was raw. She's not used to that kind of action. I said that I wanted to go out and see the town. It was my way of asking for a motherfucking break. I've been to Chicago, but I don't think I told him that. I figured it was better to ruffle his egotistical feathers by letting him think it was my first time.

So, I attempted to get dressed up. Putting make-up on when you're smashed and high on uppers with bloodshot eyes is laughable, but I attempted to make myself look like a woman worth paying. He hadn't come yet. He said he wanted to wait for later. I, of course, had to satisfy his faux-orgasm quota first. Earn my acting awards. We went to a couple of bars and then to a strip club, but by the time we got there, we were thoroughly wrecked, and I barely remember what happened. We fucked for several more hours when we got back to the hotel, and then I took some sleeping pills and retired to my separate bed. Luckily he went to work early in the morning, so I could enjoy my hangover in peace.

While I have fun with The Texan, he's intense and the closer we get, the more I lose my work self. My non-work self doesn't want to have sex with him. Do you see the problem? I did come on the second night despite myself. I was not in the mood to fuck. I was hung-over and bone-tired. In fact, over dinner, I almost told him to give me less money so that I could have the night off. But that's a no-win. I needed the money and no john wants to be reminded that you're only there because of the money.

Even the smart ones, like The Texan, who knows I'm there for financial gain. But he's so immersed in the fantasy, he also believes I'm with him because it's so much fun. It helps that I'm a damn good actress. So I drank to shake Sita and dive into Shannon. It worked, and the night ended up being exactly what it needed to be – what I was getting paid for.

I often wonder how much brain hoopla a john needs to go through in order to convince himself that we're totally slutting over his dick? I suppose it helps that we pretend that we are. Right, right, right. All of this is still preferable to begging guys for dances at the club, and it feels good to have a bit of real money again. It's not like my baller days, but it's infinitely better than the club. I've always said money doesn't buy you happiness, but it sure is freedom. It feels good to be free.

I'm flying to New Hampshire at the crack of dawn this Wednesday to see him again. This time, I'll get plenty of rest beforehand.

88

I'VE GOT A brand-new man. We met at my friend's midnight show. He's her neighbor. He walked in, and there was an immediate attraction. It was instant, like a bolt of lightning. That kind of spark doesn't happen to me very often. Who is this? I thought. We were introduced. His name is Cole. I swear I felt a shock when he shook my hand. I was excited. But it was squashed quickly when my girlfriend mentioned that he was married with a baby on the way. Too bad.

After a couple of drinks, my friend Dave left to set up, and Erin went to the bathroom when Mr Married informed me that he was separated. Oh, *really*? Clearly my friends were in the dark about this development. Even then, I kept him on my off-limits list, but was intrigued nonetheless. It was clear that he had also felt the spark.

There was something about him; I couldn't stop watching him. I told Erin what he'd said the first chance I could.

'Oh! Very interesting,' she said. 'You should hump him, he's cute.'

'I dunno. That's a heated situation,' I said.

We all grabbed a table after the show, and he and I were flirting, but we all went our separate ways. The following morning, I went out of town.

A week or so later, he friends me on social media, then messages me. 'Good hang at Dave's thing. Your photography is beautiful,' he said.

'Hey there,' I answered. 'It was really good to meet you, too. Let me know if you want to grab a drink sometime.'

'Would love to.'

'Cool. Maybe next week,' I suggested.

Six days later, Cole messaged me again, 'Let's drink!'

'Hey there! Yes!' I said.

'When for F's sake?' he asked.

'Cute. Maybe this weekend.'

The next day, I said, 'Hey yous. I'll be driving through the Valley tonight around 10 p.m. I might meet Dave and Erin for a drink. You should join.' Shame is not my middle name. He said yes. The three of them were already at the bar when I arrived. Erin ordered me a gin and tonic with two limes.

I didn't feel like myself. It was a foreign situation. I wasn't even sure if this guy liked me, so I played it weird and distant. After five or so drinks, my weirdness faded and the four of us were having a good time. Cole has a quick wit and was cracking me up.

One of the female bartenders was clearly flirting with him. I should have been flirting too, but the whole situation was so bizarre. I was more relaxed than when I had arrived, but I still felt awkward with regard to Cole. I also wasn't sure if anyone at the bar knew about his situation – this being his regular spot – and if anyone did, I didn't want them to know what a shameless hussy I was hoping to be. But after more cocktails and two shots of tequila, I found my sense of self-preservation taking a backseat to my other animal instincts. Also, he was holding my hand under the bar, an obvious sign. Game on!

We left the bar and made out in the alley. He was pressing me against the wall. Our spark was Fourth-of-July-in-the-barrio style. Off the charts! Breathtaking kisses, but unfortunately, he was pretty tanked. There was no way could he drive; he could barely stand. He even fell off his bar stool at one point! We all laughed about it, but perhaps it should have made a larger impression, a red flag.

'I'll drive you home, honey,' I said.

'Okay. I don't live far,' he said.

'Where's your car?'

'You're sitting on it,' I told him.

I cleared out the front seat, and he spilled in. I'm no Valley rat, but I knew Sepulveda was to the left. Drunkard kept insisting it was to the right. Okay, cowboy. He held my right hand in his left and my dashboard with the other. I drove slowly. I didn't want him puking in my car.

'Tell me if you need me to pull over,' I said.

'Take a right at Church Street,' he told me.

'Okay.'

'Take a right here.'

'This isn't Church Street,' I said.

'Take a right.'

'Okay.' I did as I was told.

'Park wherever.'

I slowed to a crawl. 'Do you live on a one-way street?' I asked. I didn't think we were in the correct spot.

'No.'

'Well, I'm looking at a dead-end sign. Are you sure you live here?'

'Yes,' he said.

Okay. I parked the car, and he stumbled out. He came around from the backside of my car and fell so hard I was surprised he didn't break his head open. He's at least six foot three. That's a lot of space between his head and the asphalt. Not the sexy hookup I was hoping for. He got up and over corrected to the left, running into the neighbor's gate. Then he meandered across the street. I followed. He opened a side gate, and we walked beside a garage to a backhouse. He opened the front door. Did he even use a key? I entered. He walked over to the bed and flopped face down diagonally.

I looked around. It was a cute studio. Didn't look like it had been lived in for long. There was a desk behind me to the right. I checked for mail. A few credit cards were strewn about. Yes. His name. Good.

'Come over here,' he said.

I set my purse down and joined him. It probably wasn't the smartest move on my part, but I wasn't sober either.

We started to kiss. After only minutes, he backed up a few inches, and I could tell he was gonna hurl.

'Lean over the side of the bed,' I told him.

He did and proceeded to empty his stomach onto the floor. All righty. Time to go home. I jumped up and went to the fridge. Should I get him water? A towel? As I pondered this, he started up again and farted at the same time. Nope. The best thing I could do for him would be to leave and hope he wouldn't remember much of it.

He was still lying on his stomach when I left. I was sure he wouldn't pull a Jimi Hendrix. I fled the scene. Where the fuck was I? Time to get back to the east side.

The following morning, a text from him was waiting for me. 'Embarrassed', it read. I told him not to worry, that it's happened to the best of us.

The next night was a Friday, and I was getting ready to go to the club for the first time in more than a month. I was nervous. The Choker was coming in which was good, but sadly, another good regular had told me he could no longer see me. He wanted to marry me and knew it would never happen. At least he was civilized about it. No drama. It's a fine line between making them want you but also maintaining enough distance that they don't lose sight of the reality of the relationship. He will be missed. He was sweet and easy and spent good money.

I don't recall exactly how the plan came about. Cole must have texted me during my shift, but I left work early. I met him at the Chimneysweep. I didn't even bother to put my bra on. My outfit wasn't what I would have worn had I known I was going to see him, but fuck it. My panties were cute and I smelled like sex on a beach.

He was way more sober than he had been the night before. It had only been a night since I'd seen him, but it felt like a week. I was already buzzed from the club, so I was fine with a one and done. I wanted to finish what we had never got to start the night before.

'You're so different tonight,' he said.

'I know. I wasn't sure how you felt about me,' I told him.

'Silly girl,' he said. It's hot being called a girl by a tall man who's younger than me.

'Let's get out of here.'

'Okie dokie!'

I followed him home. The beginning is fuzzy, but the bulk of the next five and a half hours is pretty clear in my mind. Holy fuckballs, so much fucking fun! We had sex, laughed and we wrestled. I could make out with him for years! He went down on me for a long time too. I got close a couple of times but couldn't come. He's good at giving head, but I was on too much shit. He didn't seem to mind.

'You taste so incredible.' He was sexy and complimentary. The sky was getting lighter.

'Is it getting light outside?' I asked.

'Yep.'

'Shit.' I could see that he had poor window coverage and with the angle and window placement, I would get burnt by the sun. On top of this, he slept on a double bed and there was still a faint lingering hint of puke in the air.

'You can stay,' he said, as he spooned me tightly. He felt good. I'll give him that. I stayed a while longer. I liked the way he touched me and pulled me in close.

'I gotta get going,' I said.

I got up and started to get dressed. I was about to tie my shoelaces when he got on his knees on the bed, naked and with a stiff cock. 'You shouldn't leave now,' he said.

'You wanna fuck me one more time?' I asked with a devilish grin.

'Yes,' he said.

I took off all my bottom things and climbed on top of him. I rode him slowly while kissing him and holding the back of his neck.

'You are trouble,' he said just before he came.

I went to the bathroom to pee and wash my area. Now it was time to go home. 'We'll be in touch,' I said.

'You're such a dude.'

I laughed.

'But I know you're not that hard,' he said.

'I never said that I was.'

'Sweet girl.'

I drove home with a huge smile on my face.

89

I GOT HAMMERED last night and divulged my hooker status to two of my male friends. I'm sick of hiding the real me; it's not my style. Before I moved to Los Angeles, my life was an open book. But when I started a life here, I made friends with non-sex workers for the first time in years, and I decided to tone it down. I did this for several reasons. One was that I was older and didn't feel the need to tell people everything, and two, I didn't want to attract that type of attention from the men in our group. Hattie, Sally and Frannie all knew I danced, but it was a while before we told any of our male buddies. I was working at the recording studio when I met them all and was only dancing part time, so it was easy to leave it out. They were also some of the first truly platonic male friends I'd ever had. I've had male friends before, of course, but I can't think of many I didn't also sleep with at one time or another.

The information about my dancing was mildly amusing to them when they finally heard it a couple of years into the friendship, but I think the revelation about my hooking may have thrown them a bit. It's not every day you find out that one of your close friends of eight years is a prostitute.

❦

Cole and I have been hanging out a lot over the past few weeks. The magnetism is off the charts. It's been phenomenal, plus he makes me laugh like crazy. If only he wasn't newly separated from his wife and they weren't about to have their first child. And if only I hadn't just ended something in order to be single. I can't believe I'm falling for this man. He's nothing I need right now, but I'm drawn to him in an undeniable way. And vice versa.

It's the passion I was missing with Daniel, but also the clusterfuck of feelings and considerations that I was trying to avoid. A major reason for my leaving Daniel was to be on my own – to be free from worrying about how my actions and lifestyle would affect my partner. But I'm already in deep. I knew I was a goner the second Cole walked into the bar that night. I couldn't help it if I tried; it's chemical. Unfortunately, this undeniable pull is causing me to act like a crazy person. I'm not my best self. This less-than-perfect behavior is happening because I'm conflicted:

I don't want to feel this way about him, but of course, I'm all in because I've never denied feelings like this. The rub is that I want to be myself and live my unconventional life unapologetically, yet I care too much about what he thinks of me. It's not a good recipe for normal behavior. And sadly, it tends to rear its ugly head while we're fucking. One minute I'm playing it casual, enjoying myself, and the next I'm crying because I can't achieve an orgasm. And not only crying, I've also lashed out at him during the act. It's insane. It's not his fault when I can't come – it's my damn head. But when we're in sync, it's epic. We had sex seven times within twenty-four hours yesterday, with only three hours of sleep in between! We've been having morning sex, too. Me! Morning sex! I usually hate morning sex, but it's really, really good with him. This connection is fucking nuts. It's reminiscent of the chef, but dare I say it, even better. The problem – aside from the personal battle – is that this is not your ordinary courtship. It's a precarious state of affairs, given his situation and my line of work. Neither is helping in the trust-building department. This, in turn, isn't helping in my orgasm department. I can't figure out where I stand with him. He's keeping himself guarded – understandable given the circumstances – but I know he's feeling this magic as much as I am. At least, I hope he is.

I can't believe this is happening. I was single for like five minutes! Ridiculous. And why this guy? Married with a baby on the way? Are you fucking kidding me? I don't want to have sex with anyone else, excluding my customers. Actually, I don't want to have sex with them either, but it's unavoidable.

Perhaps it's just a line, but every person I've ever been intimate with has told me that being with me feels different from anything they've ever felt before. Cole said this too. Some guys have asked me if I've ever felt this way, and I usually lie or skirt the answer.

No one wants to hear that yes; I've felt it a hundred times and so has everyone I've ever slept with. I don't know what it is. My openness? Magic vagina? I'm extremely present in the sack, but shouldn't we all be? I can't say why, but with Cole, it feels different to me, too. We breathe each other in. I've never loved someone's breath like this. Hattie and Erin have been making fun of what Hattie has started to call our 'tantric' breathing.

I'm screwed on so many levels. Cole knows about the hooking. I didn't want to tell him. It's such a tough subject to broach, especially when new feelings are involved. But I've been traveling a lot more, and in my quest to be myself, I didn't want to lie. Actually, I did lie about a trip to Denver, because I wasn't sure I wanted to deal with it yet. Not that I was planning on keeping it from him, I just didn't see the need to get into all of it this early on, but he's crafty and seems to read my mind. So I fessed up. He asked a lot of questions, questions I wasn't ready to discuss. But I was feeling the need to make him happy, so I did, and I fumbled it. I lied about small things. I felt out of control. It didn't feel good. I was at odds with myself.

Daniel never asked questions, even when I first told him. Actually, he didn't really ask questions about the club either, which made things a lot easier. But Cole is not like Daniel. Cole wants to know everything, which I'm not sure is a good thing. He's not thrilled that I'm a hooker, of course, but I've made it clear that I'm not quitting anytime soon. With his baby drama, he's got no leg to stand on in that argument, but there's no denying that it's different. I'll be screwing other men – he'll be changing shitty diapers. I feel for the guy.

He's definitely taking some flak for leaving his wife, and I think he feels a little guilty about how great it feels to be with me. They rarely had sex. He wasn't even close to being satisfied in that department. He also didn't really want a child, but she did, so in an effort to make her happy – and be a good husband – they tried. It was once she got pregnant that he realized he needed to be honest about how unhappy he was in the relationship. Obviously, this epiphany would have been better timed before she got pregnant, but I've always lived by the philosophy that things happen for a reason. Or at the very least, they happen and all you can do is make the best decisions you can at the time. I also believe that it's better to have two happy, separated parents than to grow up in a miserable household. Granted, I'm not five months pregnant. She probably has a different opinion on the matter.

Who knows? Maybe I'll lose interest before my usual two to four years. It would certainly be easier if I did, but I don't see it happening anytime soon. The sex is better than it was with Daniel, which was incredible for the first couple of years. But this? This is off the charts. I can't get enough of him. I've always loved kissing, and Daniel was a great kisser, but I don't remember ever loving someone's breath so much. Life is so crazy.

This is not what I set out to do. I wanted independence and freedom. Freedom from judgement and self-editing due to another person's reaction to my profession. Freedom to finally and peacefully allow myself to choose money over love. An independent life in which what I do for a living doesn't hurt anyone. Honestly, I'm praying that I get Cole out of my system sooner rather than later. I don't want to have the 'please stop hooking' talk. Especially with the way things are going at the club – a downward spiral of shit – no way do I want to drop the extra money again after just making this major decision for myself. But here's the real kicker, the part that scares me the most: I didn't like being with Beemer the other night. Not in the normal way I don't like being with him; it felt more like I'm falling for someone, and I don't want to be intimate with anyone else. Not good.

The irony is I told Cole on our second or third rendezvous that I was the perfect girl for him to sleep with because I wouldn't get attached. It could be casual, and I wouldn't get in between him and his estranged wife. I meant it when I said it. But his kisses, the way he makes me feel – I'm royally fucked. I haven't said the L word yet. I sort of whispered it the other night while we were in the throes, but I don't think he heard me. I need to reel that shit in. He's in a tough situation. He doesn't need me laying on an 'I love you'. I don't know what I'm doing. Nothing about this affair is casual. Two months ago, I was all woman hear me roar, and now I'm falling for a guy who makes me want to trade my condoms in for a mini-van. It's in opposition to my recent life-altering mission statement I struck in the dirt with such conviction. Of which I mean to keep. I've never attempted to hook while simultaneously being in love. I'll give it my best shot and see where it takes me.

I swear, the minutes I feel like I have a handle on things, life throws me a six-foot-three banana peel with magic kisses.

Epilogue

THAT DIDN'T GO quite as I had planned. In fact, it ended up being one of the toughest years of my life. I stuck to my guns though. I did not quit the biz. However, it proved more difficult than I ever could have imagined. It took a toll. Plus, it coincided with an extremely arduous and emotionally draining period with The Texan. The perfect storm. By New Year's, I had made a new mission statement: no more love until I can retire from prostitution.